The New Context for International Relations

Global Ecopolitics

Duxbury Press Series in International Studies

Arpad von Lazar, *General Editor*
Fletcher School of Law and Diplomacy, Tufts University

The New Context for International Relations: Global Ecopolitics
Dennis Pirages, *University of Maryland*

Individuals and World Politics
Robert Isaak, *Columbia University*

FORTHCOMING

Comparative Public Policy
Charles Andrain, *San Diego State University*

The New Context for International Relations

Global Ecopolitics

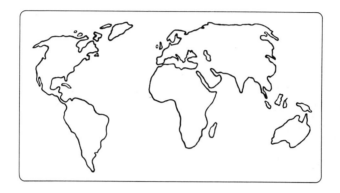

Dennis Pirages,   University of Maryland

Duxbury Press   **North Scituate, Massachusetts**

Duxbury Press
A Division of Wadsworth Publishing Company, Inc.

Interior design for *The New Context for International Relations: Global Ecopolitics* was provided by Amato Prudente.
The cover was designed by Joseph Landry.

Photograph Credits

Ch. 1—Burk Uzzle, Magnum
Ch. 2—Grant Heilman
Ch. 3—Eastfoto
Ch. 4—Constantine Manos, Magnum
Ch. 5—Grant Heilman
Ch. 6—Grant Heilman
Ch. 7—Rene Burri, Magnum
Ch. 8—Bob Henriques, Magnum

Library of Congress Cataloging in Publication Data

Pirages, Dennis.
   The new context for international relations.

   Includes index.
   1. International economic relations.   2.   Environmental policy.   3.   International relations.   I.   Ti-
tle.
HF1411.P536   382.1   78–6521

ISBN 0–87872–165–7

Printed in the United States of America
         2   3   4   5   6   7   8   9 — 82   81   80   79

Contents

Foreword

There is a spectre haunting the world of politics, economics, and public affairs. It knows no boundaries; it ignores the old rules of international intercourse, pays no respect to the weighty traditions of the past, and barely acknowledges the ruling tenets of an international order and the norms and values that helped shape it. It cares not to emulate the past because it cannot control the future. It is the awesome ghost of a waning century, the ghost of scarcity.

The concern with access to and control of strategic resources, population size and growth rates, the conflicts and convergence of economic systems, trade relations, and growth patterns has always been integral to students of international relations. While the actors tended to change from time to time, together with their relative significance and prestige in the international arena, many of the "hard core" essentials of power and influence remained the same. The population, size, economic wealth and organizational strength, political cohesion and maturity, soundness of the societal fiber, political culture and astuteness of a political will and skill all contributed to the composite posture a nation was able to manipulate to her best advantage on the international scene. And such were the dynamics of relations among nations.

Now, in the last quarter of the twentieth century, we have clamoring new actors on the international scene, new rules of the game, new priorities, a new set of rewards and punishments, *and* a new perception of what and who ought to determine what is valued in international economics and politics. So far so good and, as the complacent would sigh, ". . . nothing new since Metternich. . . ." But what matters is that all of a sudden it has dawned on man that decisions made in order to control and manipulate the course of events in international relations have acquired certain disturbing qualities of *finiteness*. If the honeymoon of cheap energy is over for the industrialized world, the quicky marriage of wealth and oil might be equally shortlived for the new Croesuses dictating life/death and unemployment rates. New equations enter with the ever increasing force of finality, and the world of politics and economics as we have learned to recognize it merely

79-338

manages to fight back with rearguard holding actions. While international and national bureaucracies watch and worry about their institutional survival, the time bombs of population, resources, energy, debt financing, unemployment, and social policy quietly tick away, ever more forcefully helped along by the ghost of scarcity.

Dennis Pirages' work, *The New Context for International Relations: Global Ecopolitics*, dissects and analyzes the factors, new and old, that contribute to the changes that highlight the pattern of international relations of our troubled times. It is a thoughtful treatise, empirically sound and analytically skilled. But above all it is a policy-oriented work, attacking the conflict issues that inexorably link economics and politics on the international level. In this sense, Professor Pirages' book is a welcome addition to the Duxbury Press Series in International Studies. In reading it I felt compelled to extend my welcome to the first substantive volume on international relations designed to bid farewell to our waning century.

Arpad von Lazar
The Fletcher School of Law and Diplomacy
Tufts University

Preface

The next fifty years are likely to be the most revolutionary in the history of relations among nations. The presently industrialized countries have collectively experienced more than three centuries of rapid economic growth and expansion. In the past, abundant fuels, land, water and other natural resources have been available to sustain high levels of both consumption and growth. But the petroleum crisis, food shortages, and economic chaos of the mid–1970s called attention to the fact that human numbers and technological growth on a global scale are now seriously taxing environmental and social systems.

For many reasons that are detailed in this book, this extended period of rapid economic growth and expansion is now coming to a close. The colonial empires that helped to sustain rapid growth in industrial countries have been dissolved. The subjugation of less developed peoples by those technologically more sophisticated is now considered to be wrong. Many natural resources that were once considered to be abundant in relation to human demands are now in short supply. In the "postindustrial" world of limited opportunities that is now emerging many of the expansionist industrial norms, values, and modes of international behavior are increasingly being called into question because they no longer seem appropriate in a more complex world of perceived scarcity.

This transformation of perspective in international relations is part of a more general social "paradigm shift" that is now taking place world-wide. The new context for international relations that is emerging as we approach the turn of the century can best be described as "ecopolitics;" that is, the new international politics centers around economic, ecological, energy, environmental, and ethical issues. This book examines these new ecopolitical concerns and related issues such as access to natural resources, new types of economic leverage in international affairs, adequacy of future world food supplies, questions of social justice and human rights, new economic development problems for less developed countries, and the equitable and efficient distribution of world resources.

This book is intended to serve both as a theoretical contribution to knowledge about the ecological, economic, and technological forces that shape the new context for international relations and as a readable text or supplement for college courses in international relations, environmental studies, and related areas.

ACKNOWLEDGMENTS

This book, like any other, is a result of intellectual contacts with and dedication from colleagues, graduate students, and staff. Among the many members of the intellectual team that helped shape the book, I would especially like to thank Paul Ehrlich, Robert North, Willis Harman, Herman Daly, John Holdren, Stephan Schneider, Cheryl Christensen, Davis Brobrow, Arpad Von Lazar, and Robert Kudrle for their valuable insights at many different points in its development. I would also like to thank Burns Weston, Michael Washburn, and the Institute for World Order for both intellectual and financial support while the book was being written. I would like to thank the reviewers who contributed their insights to this book: James F. Morrison, University of Florida; James Murray, University of Iowa; Frederick C. Turner, University of Connecticut, Storrs; and Robert West, Tufts. Finally, I owe a great debt to William Greene, Leesa Weiss, Marjorie Cox, Lamar Robert, Lily Fountain, and Lewell Gunter for their research assistance and specialized help with the manuscript.

1

The Origins of Ecopolitics

THE IMPENDING REVOLUTION

The last quarter of the twentieth century marks the beginning of a fundamental shift in human history as the world's rapidly growing human population encounters environmental limits to growth on a global scale. Since ancient times, the world's population has been dutifully following a biological imperative and the biblical admonition to increase and multiply. In the year 8000 B.C., there were only about 5 million people on the earth, a much smaller population than that of contemporary New York. For the next ten thousand years, population increased slowly. This slow pace of growth resulted in a world population of about 500 million in A.D. 1650. Thus, world population doubled only six or seven times during this entire ten-thousand-year period. Then, something happened to trigger enormous population growth. World population doubled from 500 million to 1 billion in only two hundred years, between 1650 and 1850, and then it doubled again in the eighty-year-period between 1850 and 1930. At present, there are more than 4 billion human beings, and this number is expected to double once again in only thirty-six years.[1]

When humanity greets the year 2000, then, there will be more than 6 billion human beings to jointly celebrate (or lament) the occasion. And each one of them will be a much greater burden on the earth's natural resources than they are at present if current economic development plans are followed. This explosion of population and consumption is unparalleled in human history, and the burden that it places and will place on human institutions and natural resources is staggering.

This impending revolution will not be the first time that human beings have changed their impact on the environment. Two previous revolutions in human history also dramatically altered the nature of the human environment. The first, the Agricultural Revolution, began around the year 8000 B.C. It was driven by the domestication of plants and animals, which, in turn, provided better diets, more energy, and a more secure source of food for human beings than existed in the preceding hunting and gathering societies. The growth of agriculture was closely paralleled by a slow expansion of a more secure and sedentary human population, which no longer depended on the hunt for food.

The second great revolution, the Industrial Revolution, began to gather momentum in the fifteenth and sixteenth centuries and culminated in the rapid advance of technology characteristic of the twentieth century. The Industrial Revolution enhanced human productivity by harnessing energy derived from fossil fuels to do tasks previously performed by human beings and beasts of burden. It produced increasing abundance through the large-scale exploitation of many nonrenewable natural resources, and this abundance has, in turn, helped cause the contemporary population and consumption explosion.

There are many indications that the coming decades mark the beginning of a third great revolutionary period in human history. Unlike the previous revolutions, which were growth-oriented and given impetus by new technologies and greater abundance, there is as yet no positive guiding vision of economic abundance to facilitate the impending transformation. The nature of the transformation is now unclear but, from the present perspective, it appears that the rapid growth of population and per capita consumption, and the related institutions dependent upon growth, cannot much longer endure within the closed ecological system represented by planet Earth. The curves of population growth and increased consumption, which slope sharply upward, cannot continue to go up further since eventually there would be standing room only on the planet's surface.[2]

The causes and the consequences of this third great revolution and its impact on international relations are the subjects of the chapters that follow. Just as the Agricultural Revolution made possible highly organized warfare and empires, and just as the Industrial Revolution made possible an international system, colonialism, and two world wars, the third great revolution is once again transforming the nature of society as well as the nature of international relations.

The impending revolution has already given birth to a new set of perceptions and new rules of behavior in international relations. These new perceptions and rules can be summed up by the term "global ecopolitics." Global ecopolitics involves the use of environmental issues, control over natural resources, scarcity arguments, and related concerns of social justice to overturn the international political hierarchy and related system of rules established during the period of industrial expansion. Along with this partial erosion of the old international power hierarchy, the focus of international political conflict has now shifted from an East-West to a North-South direction. The consensus that has bound existing international alliances together in the industrial world is also changing as alliance concerns shift from military matters to economic issues and the problem of maintaining cheap access to the commodities that are the essential building blocks of industrial societies. Finally, even the language of international relations has begun to change, and terms such as "exponential growth," "resource depletion," "energy gap," and "never to be developed countries" are replacing terms that were more common to analysts of past decades.

Recent international conferences on population, environment, water, and food have been dealing with the moral aspects of current ecopolitical issues. These include life and death questions of whether nations should be permitted to maintain high rates of population growth, whether foreign assistance should be offered to nations having no birth control policies, whether food should be sold only to those who can buy it, and whether moral obligations exist to provide food to the starving. The right of some industrialized countries to increase consumption at the expense of global environmental integrity also has been challenged. Control over natural resources and their use as an economic and political weapon has become a critical bargaining chip in the nascent ecopolitics. And the usefulness of the old energy- and resource-intensive model of industrial development to contemporary less developed countries is being questioned by less developed countries, as are the advantages of trading with the highly industrialized nations.

The Changing World View

In his work on scientific revolutions, Thomas Kuhn has used the word "paradigm" to describe the model of reality that is internalized when people become socialized as members of scientific communities. Research in these scientific communities is based on shared paradigms —a collective understanding of facts, rules of scientific inquiry, and shared standards. Paradigms endure in the sciences because when they are initially established they have enough intellectual power to attract some adherents from competing models of reality, and they also raise interesting scientific problems yet to be solved by scientists working within the paradigm.[3]

Scientific paradigms have occasionally changed throughout the history of science. Perhaps the best example of a paradigm shift, or complete change in perception of reality, is the Copernican revolution in astronomy. Prior to the Copernican revolution, astronomers invested a great deal of time and effort in shoring up the Ptolemaic paradigm, which placed the earth at the center of the universe. As astronomy became a more precise science, many measurements could be fit into the Ptolemaic model only with great difficulty. These "anomalies" began to mount up, and they led to extremely complex explanations of planetary behavior. Eventually, the anomalies became so obvious that a new view of the solar system, one that placed the sun at the center, provided the model for a scientific revolution in astronomy—a revolution that also affected humanity's view of its place in the universe.

A paradigm, then, guides scientists in choosing research topics, in searching for data, and in interpreting results. It is like a pair of glasses that clarifies a fuzzy world of empirical data for the researcher. It also defines the "is" and "ought" of a profession, the problems that are worthy of solution, and suggests methods by which they can be solved. A paradigm also insulates a scientific community from problems and anomalies that may be important but are not amenable to solution within the framework provided by it.[4] Paradigms remain dominant within the social system of science for long periods because disciplinary reward structures encourage conformity to the established scientific norms. In other words, a good scientist accepts the "givens" of his profession, doesn't rock the boat, and is rewarded with cash, power, and scientific prestige.

On a much larger scale, shared paradigms not only guide scientific research but help members of all societies define social, economic, and political reality. The collection of norms, beliefs, values, habits, and survival rules that provides a frame of reference for members of a society is called a dominant social paradigm (DSP). A dominant social paradigm, then, is the predominant world view, model, or frame of reference through which individuals or, collectively, a society gives meaning to the world in which persons live. A DSP defines the nature of both the physical and social world, indicates problems in need of solutions, and outlines the range of acceptable solutions to these problems. It also defines the "is" and the "ought" in society, or rules of social survival and social ethics.[5] Throughout most of history, ethical codes or rules of survival have been embedded in organized religions, which helped to pass social paradigms from generation to generation.

A DSP represents a mental image of reality that forms social expectations. Thus, social paradigms are essential for social stability. Dominant social paradigms are passed from generation to generation through socialization and education processes. In normal times they change only very slowly in response to experience with the real world; a world that historically has changed very slowly. But during periods of major social upheaval, characterized by mounting social anomalies caused by discontinuities between what people perceive to be the case and what they think it ought to be, there can be rapid and very dramatic changes in the DSP. During these periods, the *perceived* nature of physical and social worlds, the problems seen to be in need of solution, and the values and ethics guiding human behavior may be completely transformed in a very short period of time.

Each of the two previous great revolutions in human history was defined by major shifts in the existing social paradigm. The components of the dominant social paradigm in most hunting and gathering societies did not have much in common with the dominant paradigm that evolved along with the Agricultural Revolution. And the dominant social paradigm of industrial societies shares little with the dominant social paradigm of agrarian ones. The third great revolution in human history will foster a predominant view of the world that is as different from the present DSP as the industrial one was from its agrarian predecessor.

A Third Revolution: Some Evidence

Shifts in dominant social paradigms result from social anomalies or dilemmas, conditions for which the prevailing DSP cannot provide an explanation. These shifts can be minor or major, rapid or slow, objectively destructive or constructive, depending upon the rate at which anomalies accumulate and the incentives that individuals have to alter their views of the world. Minor shifts in components of dominant social paradigms have not been infrequent occurrences, especially since the beginning of the Industrial Revolution. But major, rapid, and thorough transformations of basic world views have been rare. In the case of the Agricultural Revolution, diffusion of new agricultural technologies was very gradual, as were the ensuing changes in norms, values, beliefs, and survival rules. During the Industrial Revolution, by contrast, the changes in norms, values, ethics, and survival rules were very rapid, and industrial technologies and related changes in dominant social paradigms were diffused throughout most of the world in only a two or three hundred year period.[6]

In the early stages of a paradigm shift, it is not easy to detect the changes that are taking place. That a transition is now imminent might not immediately be obvious to many persons, because early in a revolutionary period most are still very much captive of the old way of looking at things. But evidence is beginning to mount that a period of transformation of great consequence has now begun. It is similar to the previous revolutions in that it will result in an entirely new way of looking at the world and a new set of values, ethics, and survival rules.

Willis Harman has suggested that there are four key dilemmas (anomalies) within the DSP of industrial societies that may not be resolvable without a system transformation. He labels these *the growth dilemma* (we need continued growth but can't live with its consequences), *the control dilemma* (we need more guidance over technological innovation but shun centralized control), *the distribution dilemma* (rich individuals and rich nations find it too costly to share wealth with the poor but failure to do so can lead to disaster), and *the work roles dilemma* (society cannot provide enough legitimate roles to keep up with expectations being instilled in the young). He links these dilemmas that are intrinsic to the present DSP with a "new scarcity." The old scarcity involved shortages of things that were required to meet basic human needs. These old shortages could be overcome by improving technology and using more territory—traditional economic solutions. The new shortages, however, result from approaching planetary limits to growth.[7]

There is a long list of interrelated new scarcity problems that are now beginning to slow growth on a planetary scale and shake some of the fundamental assumptions in the present social paradigm. Central to all of them is the dwindling global supply of petroleum and natural gas. In 1974, the world found out what it is like to cope with energy shortages and higher prices. On that occasion, scarcity was brought on by the actions of a cartel of energy exporters. But several studies indicate that projected energy shortages in the latter years of the 1980s and early years of the 1990s might well result from lack of reserves and capacity rather than from any contrived scarcity.[8]

There is also a growing global water shortage, which represents another potential limit to growth. Additional potential shortages exist in food production, production of nonfuel minerals, and in the ability of natural waste disposal systems to absorb pollution created by industrial progress.[9] Energy lies at the center of all these new scarcity problems, however, because if abundant energy is available it can help ameloriate the other problems.

There are many other aspects to the argument that a new revolution is imminent. In The End of Progress, Edward Renshaw has argued that a law of diminishing returns governs many of the processes responsible for progress within the industrial paradigm. Speed in transportation, for example, has been pushed to a point where it is no longer economically practical to move faster, especially given higher prices for fuels. This results from a rapidly rising cost curve for moving things faster. In many cases, each additional mile per hour now costs more than any related increase in human productivity. Similar relationships operate in automation and increased scale of production and distribution. Huge, automated, multinational corporations have, in many cases, reached the point of diminishing returns in the scale of their centralized international operations. Increasing transportation costs now make decentralization and duplication of facilities a preferable alternative. And an unemployed pool of laborers numbering as high as one-third of the work force in many less developed countries makes labor-intensive rather than energy-intensive growth a preferred development strategy for the future.[10]

There is a continuing debate over the meaning of these new scarcities for the future quality of life on a planetary scale. One side in the debate claims that the resilience of industrial society will lead to new technological innovations and energy alternatives that will solve new scarcity problems.[11] At the other extreme, there are many who see conservation, a more frugal lifestyle, and new social institutions as essential to maintaining a minimally acceptable quality of life.[12] The significance of the debate is not that one side or the other will be proved wrong. Regardless of which vision of the future turns out to be more correct, the present dominant social paradigm in industrial societies will be transformed as the rapid growth associated with fossil fuels either comes to an end or assumes a radically different shape.

The Changing Paradigm in International Relations

There are many different levels on which—and area in which—paradigms and paradigm shifts may be studied. In the physical sciences, for example, there is one general paradigm that dominates most scientific inquiry. Within this paradigm, assumptions are made that physical events are predictable, that there are physical laws that can be discovered by human efforts, that a set of rules called scientific method best guides inquiry, and that deductive reasoning leads to accumulation of knowledge within the paradigm. The more general scientific paradigm, however, is very complex, and there are many different subparadigms representing different segments of the physical world. Thus, astronomy, physics, and biology each have their own paradigms containing rules of inquiry very similar to those governing all science but with a content and perspective that are discipline-specific. A paradigm shift can occur in any discipline, and the effect on the general scientific paradigm can be greater or lesser depending upon its linkage with the discipline.

Similar complexities are found in dominant social paradigms. Just as there are subparadigms that are component parts of the scientific paradigm, there are also subparadigms applicable to different areas of social life and social inquiry. People share certain perspectives and beliefs about the economy, politics, and social life, as well as about other nations and international affairs.[13] A revolutionary shift in the DSP affects all of these subparadigms, but a shift in a subparadigm can take place and have a greater or lesser effect on the DSP depending upon how integral it is to the entire predominant way of looking at things.

This book focuses upon changes in that subparadigm of the DSP called international relations. This is the part of the DSP that deals with relations among actors in the international system. These actors may be individuals, groups, subnational units, nations, international nongovernmental organizations such as multinational corporations, or international organizations. The old dominant paradigm in international relations contains a view of international reality, defines issues that divide and unite actors within the international system, and provides a frame of reference through which actors can interpret the flow of international events.

The dominant paradigm in international relations is changing in response both to changes in dominant social paradigms and to the realities governing relations among actors in the international system. The Agricultural Revolution was responsible for the birth of something resembling an international system as well as the creation of small empires. The Industrial Revolution gave birth to the European state system in international affairs, more communication among nations, colonialism, world wars, and interdependence, as well as supporting ethics and ideologies. The third great revolution is creating an ecopolitical paradigm in international relations based upon recognition of the finite nature of the planet and the inextricable interdependence of the states making up its territory. Concepts, scholarly purposes, research agendas, and methods of inquiry are now changing in response to perceived inadequacies in previous ways of looking at the world.

Harman has suggested three types of conditions that indicate that a transformation in a paradigm is imperative: (1) the complex of problems, dilemmas, and discontinuities is so great that a change in basic values is required for their resolution, (2) the presence of "lead indicators" is increasingly noted, (3) a competitive paradigm or model can be identified.[14] Each of these conditions can be found in contemporary international affairs. There can be little doubt that the related issues of increased energy prices, high rates of malnutrition or even starvation in many areas of the world, inequities in international trade, failure to meet development targets, unemployment, economic recession, and political instability provide an exceptional challenge to accepted views of global economic and political progress. While these conditions may have existed to a lesser or greater extent throughout history, they now are *perceived* by political leaders as pressing issues, and these leaders are attempting to do something about them. It is also easy to find related lead indicators that reveal an international system undergoing a transformation. Global inflation, commodity speculation, growing insecurity over access to natural resources, collapse of respected banks, and in some cases a near economic collapse of nations, fear of the future, and a growing sense of alienation could be cited as on the basic list of lead indicators. And there is an emerging paradigm, offered by leaders of less developed countries in the guise of a new international economic order, which promises to remedy present social and political ills. Just as an expansionist perspective dominated international affairs during the Industrial Revolution, an ecopolitical paradigm will emerge to make order of the apparent chaos accompanying this third great revolution.

N ECOLOGICAL PERSPECTIVE

In order to understand the dynamics behind the emergence of ecopolitics, it is necessary to understand some basic principles of ecology. *Homo sapiens* is governed by the same physical laws that regulate the growth and development of all other species. And theories explaining how populations of human beings act in relation to other populations are thus best anchored in basic ecological principles that govern interactions among all types of populations.

For much of human history, populations of *Homo sapiens* were directly involved in life and death struggles with populations of many other species. But human creativity as revealed in technological developments has enabled human beings to triumph over other species and escape the extinction that might have occurred in "hand to hand" combat with other carnivores. First the Agricultural and then the Industrial revolutions improved the human competitive position until now human beings perceive themselves, within the industrial paradigm, to be dominant over nature. If necessary, mountains can be moved, rivers redirected, and climates altered to overcome natural barriers to human progress. In the face of all of the contrary evidence inherent in the rise and fall of great empires, this human dominance perspective sees an industrial future of growth without limits.

This dominance perspective was molded by an extended period of technological advance and geographical expansion of the horizons of Western European industrializing nations. The fifteenth and sixteenth centuries marked the beginning of a geographical expansion by virtue of Western European colonization of distant lands that culminated in vast empires that persisted well into the twentieth century. In the United States, abundance was promoted by the westward push of the frontier beginning in the eighteenth century and culminating in Alaska in the twentieth century. In both Western Europe and the United States, a technological revolution made existing land and resources much more productive on a per capita basis with each passing decade. Human populations expanded rapidly in this atmosphere of increasing abundance but food production and manufacturing were more than able to keep up.

In the last quarter of the twentieth century, however this abundance and human dominance perspective is being shaken by the specter of new scarcities. This is in no small part due to the absence of new frontiers. Only the Antarctic and Arctic remain to be colonized, and they promise little relief for growing and restive populations. Attempts to circumvent the new scarcity by creating a new "frontier" in the form of space colonies is taken seriously mostly by a small coterie of science fiction buffs, avante garde social scientists, and vested interests in the aerospace industry.[15] It is in this context that the concerns of demographers and ecologists become relevant to international relations theory.[16]

Populations and Interaction

Populations are central to analysis in building ecological theory. For an ecologist or biologist, a population is technically a group of individuals of the same species. In this general sense, the human population of the world could be said to number approximately 4 billion. But this is not a very valuable way to use the concept. There are subpopulations of almost all species, closely knit groups that interact almost exclusively with each other and almost never with other members of the species. Biologists and ecologists compromise by further restricting the definition of population to a "dynamic system of interacting individuals . . . that are potentially capable of interbreeding with each other."[17] By this definition, the preindustrial world was inhabited by thousands of human populations. Similarly, since almost all human beings are now linked into a global communication system and at least have the potential to interbreed, it could be said that there is now just one population of human beings and that they are all citizens of the world.

Obviously, people generally do not perceive themselves to be citizens of the world but of populations living within various geographical units called countries. Theoretically, every human being—or every white-tailed deer—in the world could, through some conceivable set of circumstances, mate with any other human being—or white-tailed deer—on the planet. But the likelihood of certain persons or deer interbreeding varies according to physical and social distance. Thus, the possibility that a Canadian Eskimo and a Nigerian Ibo would interbreed is almost zero, while the likelihood that a single male and female on Manhattan would do so is very much greater. In defining the boundaries of a population, it is critical to examine the *comparative frequency of interaction*. But when dealing with human populations, as opposed to other species, it is important to keep in mind that interactions can be of a face-to-face nature as well as mediated through mass communications.

Although this application of the formal definition of population to human beings in national units might upset some biologists and ecologists, it is an extremely useful way to begin to understand what an ecological perspective on relations among actors in the contemporary international system can offer. If all of the direct and mediated communications of all of the people of the world could somehow be mapped, it would be clear that there are some clusters of human beings that interact much more frequently than others. These clusters usually are demarcated by the boundaries of nation states. "Peoples are marked off from each other by communication barriers, by 'marked gaps' in the efficiency of communication."[18] In other words, nationality is determined by social communication and economic intercourse among people. People who identify themselves as members of a national population feel that their fortunes "covary" with those of other people within the national population.[19]

An analysis of these interaction patterns would reveal sharp discontinuities representing national boundaries, but also significant differences in interactions among people within national boundaries. This simply means that countries vary in the extent to which all segments of the population have been integrated effectively into national life. While there are certainly difficulties in dealing with marginal or minority populations within nations, the vast majority of the human race can be identified as belonging to national populations through their communication patterns.

Such interacting populations have been the basic units of identification for human beings since the earliest recorded human history. While the principle of in-group identification is at least as old as culture itself, the size of the population units with which individuals identify has increased along with communications capabilities. The size of early political empires was constrained by horse-dependent transportation and primitive communication networks. Preindustrial Europe, for example, consisted of many small populations loosely knit into larger confederations. Relations between centralizing political leaders of the larger confederation and those of the smaller groups in the periphery varied over time in relation to the aggressiveness, power, skill, wealth, and communications capabilities possessed by the core. The technological, economic, and social factors responsible for the unification of contemporary large industrial nations have been well documented elsewhere.[20] The important point here is that the Industrial Revolution as a source of military, transportation, and communications technology aided the transformation of loosely knit confederations into contemporary, integrated nation-states.

Populations and Resources

Whether small principalities or large nation-states, territorial units in isolation have a limited capability to sustain human populations because they are endowed with limited quantities of natural resources. Human populations, just as those of other species, have always pressed against the limitations inherent in the natural resource endowment found within their geographical territory. These natural factors regulating populations have been historically manifest to human beings as tragic "unnatural" events, such as famine and plague, which may well have been related to periodic changes in climate. During periods of relatively favorable crop-growing weather, human populations have grown and flourished only to be cut back during ensuing less favorable decades.[21]

A number of natural resources are essential to the activities of all populations. To an ecologist, "a resource is anything needed by an organism, population, or ecosystem which, by its increasing availability up to an optimal or sufficient level, allows an increasing rate of energy conversion."[22] An abundance of resources in relation to demands guarantees the growth of consumption and expansion of numbers within a population. One of the most basic of ecological principals, Von Liebig's law of the minimum, holds that the life of an individual or the size of a population is limited by the resource necessary for survival that is in shortest supply (see figure 1–1). Thus, even though a population may have plenty of space into which it can expand, lack of available water or other resources can inhibit such expansion.

Paul and Anne Ehrlich have categorized six types of resources essential to the survival of human populations.[23] These include energy,

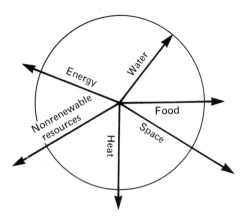

FIGURE 1-1. *Von Liebig's Law and Resource Space.* The arrows represent relative quantities of resources. According to Von Liebig's law, this population can expand only to fill the circle, since water is the resource in shortest supply. This population has more food, space, heat, energy, and nonrenewable resources than are necessary to sustain its present level.

nonrenewable resources, water, food, space, and heat. When taken in combination, these essential resources found on any piece of territory can be called a "resource space" available for expansion of population and consumption. All natural populations tend to expand nearly to fill this available resource space until their expansion is halted by the resource in shortest supply.

The amount of available resource space, then, limits the carrying capacity of any piece of territory. *Natural carrying capacity* is defined by ecologists as the maximum total biomass (the dry weight of all living flora and fauna) that can be supported by any given piece of territory within the constraints of current solar income (sunlight). The mixture of flora and fauna grown within these limits can, of course, affect the maximum dry weight that can be supported. Natural carrying capacity is related to the ability to get energy from food, which is a function of the fertility of the soil, temperature, rainfall, and amount of sunlight available. Under hunting and gathering conditions, the natural carrying capacity of a piece of land sets constraints on the number of human beings that the land can support. A given human population can expand to its maximum size within these constraints by eliminating the competition for available food, by using great skill and new technologies in husbanding needed resources, or by consuming only enough food per capita to meet minimal human needs.

Natural carrying capacity represents a useful point of departure in analyzing the loads that human populations put on existing national territories. It seems obvious, for example, that the human population of Bangladesh is pressing much closer to the limits of natural carrying capacity than is the population of Australia. But, on the other hand, it is not so clear that Bangladesh is closer to these limits than is a country like the Netherlands, a highly industrialized nation that must import considerable quantities of raw materials from other national territories. The key to this distinction lies in the fact that *Homo sapiens* is unique in his use of trade and advanced technologies to enhance the natural carrying capacity of inhabited territories. The food available to a population of deer is determined by natural constraints: sunlight, temperature, and rainfall patterns. The deer have no choice but to rely upon the vagaries of weather, and their numbers are limited accordingly. Human beings, by contrast, use various kinds of institutions and technologies to increase carrying capacity and thereby more effectively use resources.

The two most important sets of technological developments that permitted the world's human population to increase were the domestication of plants and animals during the Agricultural Revolution and the discovery and utilization of energy in fossil fuels on a large scale during the Industrial Revolution. In the first case, the technologies developed within the constraints of current solar income, and related population increases could be sustained indefinitely. In the latter case, however, many of the new technologies were dependent on finite supplies of fossil fuels and the related expanded populations will not be able to exist within the constraints of perpetually renewable current solar income once these supplies of fossil fuels disappear.

Trade is the other main method by which national populations change the carrying capacity of their territory. National populations do not live in complete isolation in the contemporary international system. Resources abundant in one country might be scarce in another and vice versa. Through mutually beneficial exchanges of resources and products, cooperating nations can increase their carrying capacity and hence their populations. The advantages of trade are obvious, but there are also drawbacks. Relying on a trade partner (Country A) for a resource whose lack has previously checked population growth in Country B makes Country B vulnerable to the machinations of Country A. If Country A decides to cut off trade in the essential resource, the population of Country B could collapse back to its original level.

The contemporary international trade system is much more complex than this simple example indicates, however. Returning to the example of the Netherlands and Bangladesh, the population of the Netherlands is sustained by a complex trade network whose tentacles reach to the far corners of the globe to secure the dozens of essential resources not found on Dutch soil. The Netherlands is the second largest importer of protein in the world and imports almost all of its cotton, iron ore, bauxite, copper, gold, nickel, tin, zinc, phosphate fertilizers, and a host of other important commodities.[24] In this respect, the population of Bangladesh could be said to be existing much closer to the constraints of natural carrying capacity. If the world trade system were suddenly to disintegrate, the Netherlands would suffer an economic and demographic catastrophe of great magnitude, while Bangladesh would escape with minor economic damage.

A more useful formulation of the carrying capacity concept as it relates to human populations in a complex industrial world takes into account existing levels of technological sophistication as well as the position of a country in the world trade system. *Current carrying capacity* is the total biomass (or human equivalent) that can be supported by national territorial units given existing levels of technology, a reasonable degree of autarky (self-sufficiency) in essential natural resources, and a reasonably balanced trade profile. Although the current carrying capacity concept is very difficult to define precisely and measure, it is an essential concept to use in building ecopolitical theory in international relations.

Technological sophistication is the primary determinant of current carrying capactiy. Some nations are technologically more developed than others, and the extent of these differences can be at least crudely measured. Higher levels of technological development indicate greater ability to manipulate the natural environment in order to sustain larger numbers of people at higher levels of consumption. More highly developed countries can use existing resources more efficiently. In countries that are less developed, current carrying capacity is usually very close to natural carrying capacity. But in industrially developed countries, there is a large gap between the two. The less developed countries, of course, seek to enhance their current carrying capacity through industrial growth, but this is not easily accomplished. Increasing current carrying capacity through industrialization requires capital, long lead times, and creation of an appropriate technologically sophisticated infrastructure.

A second determinant of current carrying capacity is the domestic natural resource base. Highly industrialized economies require large amounts of energy and a diverse assortment of natural resources. If these are available domestically, current carrying capacity will be restricted only by technological sophistication in using them. But if large quantities of natural resources must be imported, this dependency can act as a brake on growth. Joseph Nye and Robert Keohane have made a useful distinction between the *sensitivity* and the *vulnerability* of one country to the actions of others. This distinction is very helpful in understanding the problems of countries that support populations well in excess of both natural and current carrying capacity. Countries are sensitive to the actions of others when they are in a position of mutual dependence by choice. The United States and Japan are now very sensitive to each other because of existing trade patterns. But this sensitivity could be reduced in either country through deliberate policies designed to redirect the flow of trade to other parts of the world. Vulnerability exists when there are no readily available alternatives to the situation in which a country finds itself. Thus, Japan is extremely vulnerable to the nations in the Organization of Petroleum Exporting Countries (OPEC). A rapid increase in oil prices or a cutoff of exports from the Middle East would have grave consequences for the Japanese economy, since there are no readily available alternative sources of petroleum.[25]

Thus, it is possible for countries to live beyond both their natural and current carrying capacity. But the further beyond current carrying capacity a country strays, the more vulnerable it becomes to the actions of others, although there are strategies for reducing this vulnerability. The primary strategy is to maintain a variety of suppliers and export markets. There is, however, no way to eliminate entirely vulnerability based upon natural resource imports essential to populations living well beyond current carrying capacity.

Any list of countries in which populations could be considered to be living well beyond current carrying capacity and thus vulnerable to the actions of other countries would undoubtedly be headed by Japan. The Japanese import large quantities of food and almost all of the fuels and minerals used by Japanese industry. They pay for these imports by exporting manufactured goods, largely to markets in Western Europe and the United States. Thus, Japan is doubly vulnerable, being dependent on a small list of exporters for essential natural resources and on a limited number of export markets from which Japan must earn foreign currency to pay for mineral and fuel imports.

There is a third kind of carrying capacity, ultimate carrying capacity, which is a hypothetical figure about which only conjectures can be made. It is defined as the biomass or human population that could be sustained by a country or by the planet as a whole given the most optimal development and implementation of new technologies. But no one knows what new technologies can reliably be expected to exist in the future, so this concept is not a very useful one in policy making.

These concepts of natural carrying capacity, current carrying capacity, and ultimate carrying capacity help explain why there are recurring controversies over how many people can or should be sustained on the earth. Some claim that the human population and consumption levels are already too large and will soon collapse, while others claim that 20 or 30 billion persons could ultimately live on the planet's surface.[26] Both sides could be right. It is clear that more than 4 billion people cannot be sustained by the earth's natural carrying capacity, although those 4 billion *can* be sustained at present standards of living given present levels of technological development—at least until reserves of fossil fuels are exhausted. Given certain optimistic assumptions about future technological innovations, it would not be impossible to double or even quadruple the earth's population and sustain it at high standards of living, but it makes much more sense when planning national population policies to begin with technologies that do exist rather than conjecture about those that might exist.

In summary, then, nations are composed of interacting populations of human beings who make different levels and types of demands on the natural resource base of the relevant geographical territory. Each national unit has a natural carrying capacity that limits the biomass that can survive within the constraints of solar energy. Current carrying capacity denotes the biomass that can be supported by present-day technologies combined with a reasonable degree of autarky in natural resources. The number of human beings that can be sustained at present within the limits of current carrying capacity is a function of their basic physical needs; their *perceived* wants, which result from existing systems of stratification; and competition for scarce resources with other species on the same territory. The pressures generated by population growth and technological developments within nations give rise to the interactions among nations that can be explained by ecopolitical theory.

The Global Population Explosion

World population and demand for natural resources have exploded as a result of the social impact of industrial technology. The world population grows exponentially and now doubles very rapidly. Exponential growth occurs when quantities increase by a percentage of the base over a unit of time. In a bank savings account, for example, an annual rate of interest is paid on the amount of money in the account, the base, which is steadily increasing because of interest payments. If there is $100 in the account and interest is paid at the rate of 6 percent per year, at the end of the year there is about $106 in the account. During the second year, interest is paid on the full $106, the expanded base, that exists at the beginning of the year rather than only on $100, and so on. World population growth is the most important example of the dynamics of exponential growth. If each family in the world were to have four children, and if each of these children were to produce four more offspring, it is easy to see how rapidly the world population base could increase. Fortunately, not all families have four children, and world population is now growing at an exponential rate of 2 percent per year.

The best way to contrast exponential growth with the more familiar linear variety is to think of two gamblers agreeing to flip a coin in an attempt to build their fortunes. A gambler who understands the dynamics of exponential growth might suggest to his opponent that he will give the opponent one dollar for each time the coin turns up heads and ask "only" that his opponent give him a nickel for the first tail, double for the second tail, and so on. Under normal conditions, by the twelfth toss the clever player is making $1.60 for each tail while the linear thinker gets only one dollar for each head!

A quantity that is growing in an exponential manner will double its base in a number of time units that is determined by the percentage increase per time unit. Because of the mathematics of compound interest formulas, an approximation of this doubling time can be obtained by dividing the percentage increase per unit of time into the number 70. Thus, a country exhibiting an annual increase of 3 percent in population growth will double its population every twenty-three years. Consumption of a mineral for which demand is increasing at 5 percent each year doubles every fourteen years.

At present, the world population is doubling every thirty-five or thirty-six years. This means that if present trends continue, the earth's 4 billion persons will be 8 billion in number shortly after the year 2015. Another doubling could then be expected by the year 2050. In the sixteenth through the nineteenth centuries, much of the world's growth in population took place in Europe and the United States. But the twentieth century has been the century of non-European population growth. The impact of the Industrial Revolution on the less developed world has been very uneven, leading to discontinuities in established patterns of population growth in less developed countries. At present, the external manifestations of industrialization—factory smokestacks, automobiles, television sets, Coca-Cola bottles, and so on—are obvious around the world, exported by the industrial countries along with the life-prolonging technologies that have accompanied industrialization. But these advances in diet, sanitation, medicine, and hygiene have not been accompanied by changes in reproductive behavior, which is governed by the traditional values of the impacted populations.

Table 1–1 illustrates the unevenness of world population growth and demonstrates that there is a very close relationship between levels of industrial development and rates of population growth. In highly industrialized Western Europe, the rate of population growth is presently only about .1 percent per year, meaning that populations in this region will double only every 700 years at present rates of growth. In the USSR, a relative latecomer to industrialization, the population is growing at about 1 percent annually. In Latin America, by contrast, population is growing at an annual rate of 2.7 percent. In Africa, the figure is 2.6 percent, and in Asia, it is 2 percent. Individual countries show even more pronounced differences. For example, Finland, Luxembourg, and East Germany have almost reached zero population growth. By contrast, Kenya, Rhodesia, Iraq, Jordan, the Philippines, Thailand, Honduras, Nicaragua, and the Dominican Republic are all growing at the rate of 3.3 percent or better annually. Just keeping up with population growth requires that these latter countries double industrial and agricultural production every 20 years, an almost impossible feat.

The table highlights an additional significant fact. In 1970, there were 1.1 billion persons (30 percent of the world's population) living in industrial countries and 2.6 billion persons (70 percent of the world's population) living in less developed countries. If present rates of population growth are maintained until the year 2020, there will be only 1.6

TABLE 1-1. World Population Growth

Ten Most Populous Nations	Population Mid-1977 (Millions)	Annual Growth Rate (Percent)	Population Projection to 2000 (Millions)	Life Expectancy
China	850.0	1.7	1,126.0	62
India	622.7	2.1	1,023.7	50
USSR	259.0	0.9	314.0	69
United States	216.7	0.6	262.5	72
Indonesia	136.9	2.4	226.9	48
Japan	114.2	1.1	133.4	74
Brazil	112.0	2.8	205.0	61
Bangladesh	83.3	2.7	154.9	47
Pakistan	74.5	2.9	145.5	51
Nigeria	66.6	2.7	134.9	41
Regions				
Asia	2,325.0	2.0	3,584	56
Africa	423.0	2.6	811	46
Latin America	336.0	2.7	608	62
USSR	259.0	0.9	314	69
North America	240.0	0.6	294	72
Western Europe	152.0	0.1	169	71
Eastern Europe	108.0	0.7	122	70
Oceania	22.0	1.3	32	67

SOURCE: Population Reference Bureau, 1977 World Population Data Sheet (Washington, D.C., 1977).

billion persons (11 percent) in the industrial world and 12.7 billion persons (89 percent) in the less developed world, a population shift of great ecopolitical significance. Then, inhabitants of the highly industrialized countries will represent a tiny minority of the world's population.

Figure 1-2 summarizes world population statistics for the twentieth century. With the exception of the World War I period, it shows an almost steady increase in rates of population growth, until 1975, when a very slight decrease was noted. The world birthrate remained nearly constant at 35 per 1000 persons over this period of time until the most recent decade, when it tapered off to about 30 per thousand. But due to improved methods of life extension, the death rate has been steadily plummeting from 30 per thousand persons at the turn of the century to only 13 per thousand persons at present. And this is the factor responsible for the contemporary rapid growth of world population.

. The process that explains the uneven patterns of world population growth is called the *demographic transition*. The demographic transition is best described as being composed of three stages. In the first stage, characteristic of preindustrial societies, populations are in equilibrium as high birthrates are matched by high death rates. Pro-

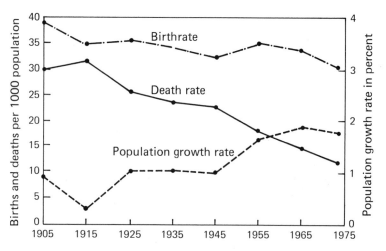

FIGURE 1–2. World Birth, Death, and Population Growth Rates, 1905–1974. Birthrates since 1965 have declined to a greater degree than death rates, possibly denoting the beginning of a down-trend in the population growth rate. [SOURCE: Population Reference Bureau, Washington, D.C.]

natalist norms and values are predominant and are effectively enforced by a variety of social sanctions and economic incentives. The second stage of the demographic transition is characterized by declining mortality as life-prolonging technologies become available. Thus, populations grew rapidly in Europe from 1650 to 1900 because of declining mortality and are now growing in the world's less developed countries. During the second stage of this transition, death rates tumble but conformity with rigid pronatalist norms maintains high birthrates.

Industrialized Western Europe and the United States have now passed into stage three of the demographic transition, which occurs when pronatalist norms, values, and attitudes begin to crumble and are replaced by industrial values and population equilibrium. Parents come to understand that each child born will probably survive and become an adult, which is definitely not the case in the preindustrial setting. The economic value of children also declines along with urbanization. As people move from rural areas, where children are an asset as farm laborers, to urban areas, where large numbers of unemployed children are an economic burden, birthrates drop. Furthermore, the economic cost of educating and raising children compares unfavorably with the washing machines, televisions, or automobiles that can be purchased instead. For these and a number of other reasons, the birthrate has historically fallen at advanced levels of industrialization.[27]

In order for a country to move into stage three of the transition, however, norms and values governing reproduction must change in response to new physical realities. It can take three or more generations for a substantial transformation of these values to take place, and different cultures are characterized by different susceptibility to these industrial values. Before fertility rates will change, potential parents must: (1) find it socially and morally acceptable to assess the costs and benefits of having more children, (2) perceive having children to be less desirable than not having them, (3) have effective techniques for preventing unwanted births available to them.[28]

At the present time in much of the less developed world, pronatalist norms and values still govern reproductive behavior. Economic progress is painfully slow, and there is little incentive to rural populations to have less children, despite the birth control devices lavished on most of the less developed world by foreign aid programs. In many less developed countries, it is now questionable whether economic and social conditions will ever be conducive to movement into this third stage of the demographic transition.[29]

In summary, then, contemporary world population is growing exponentially at about 2 percent each year. This growth is very unevenly distributed. The third stage of the demographic transition has been completed in most industrial countries, and norms and values governing reproductive behavior have changed in response to the economic imperatives of industrialization. The location of the most vigorous present population growth is the less developed countries, where life-prolonging technologies have been introduced while birthrates remain high. Because of great difficulties in changing the syndrome of norms and values anchored in large families and because of the large number of young people in the populations of the less developed countries, populations will continue to grow there for the foreseeable future. Worldwide, if the number of children per family remains the same as it is at the present, there will be at least 12 billion people on the earth around the year 2020. Even if by some miracle all families in the world cut back to two-child families by the year 1990, there would still be nearly 6 billion mouths to feed by the year 2020, and the political and economic pressures rising from the resource demands of this population will shape the content of the emerging ecopolitical paradigm.

IE GREAT TRANSITION: EXPANSION TO ECOPOLITICS

The International Politics of Expansion

The dynamics that underlie an ecopolitical theory of international relations have always been important in determining interactions among nations. But at present these dynamics are becoming much more obvious. For example, in retrospect it is apparent that technology, energy, agriculture, and related factors that determine current carrying capacity have also been important in shaping world economic and political history. The course of human history has been marked by repeated clashes among national populations, the rise and fall of great civilizations, and the expansion and contraction of empires. Historians, political scientists, climatologists, and demographers are now suggesting that an increasing number of historical conflicts, periods of imperialism, and shifts in political and economic organization can be attributed to factors that changed the carrying capacity or population of the relevant political units.[30]

The evolution of the human race has been characterized by expansion and growth. The growth that took place in the days when most human beings lived by hunting and gathering came about at the expense of other species. The more recent and substantial population growth has been sparked by the technologies inherent in the Agricultural and Industrial revolutions. The Agricultural Revolution was based on the domestication of plants and animals, a big step forward over the hunting and gathering societies that previously provided subsistence. Agriculture was accompanied by related social innovations, including settlement in permanent villages, a more complex division of labor within exchange economies, new forms of social and political organization, and eventually organized conquest on a much larger scale. Agriculture also led to a jump in the human population, since abundance of food energy and the predictability associated with regular harvests permitted greater numbers to survive. The productivity of lands brought under cultivation was dramatically increased *within* the energy budget provided by current solar income.

The Industrial Revolution fostered a much greater increase in the number of human beings and also created an international politics of vigorous expansion. Unlike the technologies of the Agricultural Revolution, which increased carrying capacity within the constraints of current solar income, the technologies of the Industrial Revolution increased carrying capacity by tapping into stored solar income found in fossil fuels. This fossil fuel subsidy, the amount of useful energy derived from fossil fuels in excess of the energy used to get them, and related new technologies have expanded current carrying capacity very dramatically, replacing work done by human and animal energy with work done by mechanical equipment. It has been during the Industrial Revolution that many national populations have begun living well beyond the natural carrying capacity of the land.

Thus, historically there has been a slow acceleration of growth in population, in the development of new technologies, in the variety and per capita demands for resources, and in contacts among national populations. But, it has only been during the last three hundred years that extremely rapid and destabilizing growth has become one of the main factors shaping relations among nations. During this period, the population of the world increased eight fold, consumption of fossil fuels increased from almost nothing to current levels of nearly 7 billion metric tons of coal equivalent annually, the quantity and variety of nonfuel minerals used skyrocketed, the size and power of national units grew rapidly, and the frequency and intensity of interaction among national populations greatly increased. The three-hundred-year period between 1650 and 1950 produced not only an industrial revolution but an international political and economic order based on rapid, technology-inspired growth and expansion of national territory.

The historical roots of this economic and political expansion can be traced back to twelfth- and thirteenth-century Europe and an outward surge that accompanied the feeble beginnings of industrialization. Immanuel Wallerstein identifies two major outward thrusts from Western European nations that followed on the heels of innovations in transport and communications.[31] The first occurred between the eleventh and mid-thirteenth centuries. It was marked by the reconquest of Spain from the Moors, the recapture of Sardinia and Corsica by Christians, territorial acquisitions associated with the Crusades, and an English expansion into Wales, Scotland, and Ireland.[32] The second, and better known, outward thrust was the Atlantic expansion of the fifteenth and sixteenth centuries, which was motivated by gold, spices, fuel, and food staples needed in Western European nations.

According to Wallerstein, the pressure for the second outward expansion came mainly from a combination of scarcity and greed.[33] The fourteenth century was not a happy time for the European nobility. Opportunities for internal growth declined as even marginal lands, areas not really fit for optimal production, were planted and harvested to increase income. There are indications that changes in climate also cut deeply into agricultural productivity. Furthermore, a series of small wars made increased taxes a necessity and further cut into the lifestyle of the nobility. Given declining economic growth prospects, rising conspicuous consumption among the nobility, and a need for improved diets for expanding populations, one obvious course of action was a major push outward to the less explored portions of the world.

The Portuguese were the first actively to acquire colonies, a fact that can be largely explained by lack of other expansion opportunities. They were soon followed by the Dutch, British, and eventually other European powers and Japan in securing distant territories. Many of the Atlantic islands thus colonized became sources of wood, cereals, and sugar for European populations pressing close to then-current carrying capacity. The American colonies became sources of lumber, silver, gold, and tobacco. This wave of expansion finally carried European armies into even the most remote corners of Africa and Asia.

During this period of expansion, growing populations, new technologies, and increasing standards of living caused most European countries to move well beyond natural carrying capacity, and there could be no return to the current solar income energy systems. These countries financed growth through technological innovation and used the fossil fuel subsidy to build industrial economies. But they also turned outward, and through trade and conquest began to acquire larger portions of their natural resource needs from colonial empires. At first, this was expansion by choice, moving outward to colonize lands that were capable of providing luxury agricultural commodities. Subsequently, however, the colonizers became locked into an international economy in which a steady stream of raw materials from a colonial empire became essential to their physical and economic well-being. This dependence was particularly pronounced in Spain, where a steady flow of gold from the New World supported lavish lifestyles that could not be sustained when the flow of gold dried up.

This second wave of European expansion was related to technological advances, population growth, rising expectations, and insufficient domestic opportunities. The more industrialized the European nations became, the greater the quantity and variety of resources that was needed to meet domestic demands. Nazli Choucri and Robert North have used the term "lateral pressures" to refer to the dynamics of foreign expansion that resulted from growth pressures within a confined geographical territory: "When demands are unmet and existing capabilities are insufficient to satisfy them, new capabilities may have to be developed. . . . Moreover, if national capabilities cannot be attained at a reasonable cost within national boundaries, they may be sought beyond."[34] Lateral pressures can take several forms. Expansion of trade is one option for a country that possesses natural resources or industrial commodities of value in the international marketplace. Political confederation or formation of common markets is another possible response. Acquisition of colonies is a third option for countries with sufficient military power. The method a country uses to get needed resources beyond its boundaries is determined by domestic economic and military capabilities, technological sophistication, geographic location, and the power, friendliness, and resources of neighboring states.[35]

Thus, much Western European growth associated with the Industrial Revolution led to and was supported by an international expansion that augmented current carrying capacity through colonization of most of the non-European world. There are now more than 165 national populations having sovereignty over their territory; the majority of these countries were colonial possessions as little as two decades ago (see table 1–2). At the beginning of World War II, colonial possessions occupied nearly one-third of the world's population and land area, and these possessions were used largely to meet the resource needs of colonial powers. European countries—Great Britain, the Netherlands, France, Belgium, Portugal, Italy, and Spain—with a combined population of 200 million persons, controlled over 700 million people in their

TABLE 1-2.   States That Have Gained Independence Since 1943

Country	Year of Independence	Former Colonial Status	Population*
Lebanon	1943	French Mandate	2.8
Iceland	1944	Danish	0.2
Syria	1946	French Mandate	7.8
Jordan	1946	British Mandate	2.9
Philippines	1946	United States	44.3
India	1947	British Dominion	622.7
Pakistan	1947	British Dominion	74.5
Burma	1948	British	31.8
Sri Lanka (Ceylon)	1948	British—left British Commonwealth in 1972	14.1
Israel	1948	British Mandate	3.6
North Korea	1948	Japanese—under Soviet occupation	16.7
South Korea	1948	Japanese—under US occupation	36.9
Indonesia	1949	Dutch	136.9
Libya	1951	Italian—under British and French occupation	2.7
Cambodia	1953	French—Associated State in French Union	8.0
Laos	1953	French—Associated State in French Union	3.5
Vietnam	1953	French—Associated State in French Union	47.3
Morocco	1956	French and Spanish Protectorate	18.3
Tunisia	1956	French Protectorate	6.0
Sudan	1956	British-Egyptian Condominium	16.3
Ghana	1957	British—plus portion of former French Togo	10.4
Malaysia	1957	British	12.6
Guinea	1958	French	4.7
Cameroon	1960	French Trust Territory	6.7
Central African Republic	1960	French	1.9
Chad	1960	French	4.2
Congo (Brazzaville)	1960	French	1.4
Cyprus	1960	British	0.6
Dahomey (Benin)	1960	French	3.3
Gabon	1960	French	0.5
Ivory Coast	1960	French	7.0
Malagasy Republic	1960	French	7.9
Mali	1960	French	5.9
Mauritania	1960	French	1.4
Niger	1960	French	4.9
Nigeria	1960	British	66.6
Senegal	1960	French	5.3
Somalia	1960	Italian Trust Territory	3.4
Togo	1960	French Trust Territory	2.3
Upper Volta	1960	French	6.4

TABLE 1-2. (cont.)

Country	Year of Independence	Former Colonial Status	Population*
Zaire (Congo)	1960	Belgian	26.3
Tanzania (Tanganyika)	1961	British Trust Territory	16.0
Sierra Leone	1961	British	3.2
Kuwait	1961	British Protectorate	1.1
Algeria	1962	French	17.8
Jamaica	1962	British	2.1
Burundi	1962	Belgian Trust Territory	3.9
Rwanda	1962	Belgian Trust Territory	4.5
Uganda	1962	British	12.4
Trinidad and Tobago	1962	British	1.0
Western Samoa	1962	New Zealand Trust Territory	0.2
Kenya	1963	British	14.4
Zanzibar	1963	British—merged with Tanganyika in 1964	
Malawi	1964	British Protectorate	5.3
Malta	1964	British	0.3
Zambia	1964	British Protectorate	5.2
Gambia	1965	British	0.6
Maldives	1965	British Protectorate	0.1
Singapore	1965	Part of Malaysia	2.3
Botswana	1966	British Protectorate	0.7
Lesotho	1966	British Protectorate	1.1
Barbados	1966	British	0.2
Guyana	1966	British	0.8
South Yemen	1967	British Protectorate	1.8
Equatorial Guinea	1968	Spanish	0.3
Mauritius	1968	British	0.9
Swaziland	1968	British Protectorate	0.5
Nauru	1968	Australia–New Zealand–British Trust Territory	0.1
Fiji	1970	British	0.6
Tonga	1970	British Protectorate	0.1
Bangladesh	1971	Part of Pakistan (East Pakistan)	83.3
Bahrain	1971	British Protectorate	0.3
Qatar	1971	British Protectorate	0.1
United Arab Emirates	1971	British Protectorate	0.2
Bahamas	1973	British	10.2
Grenada	1974	British	0.1
Guinea-Bissau	1974	Portuguese	0.5
Mozambique	1975	Portuguese	9.5
Angola	1975	Portuguese dependency	6.3
Cape Verde Islands	1975	Portuguese	0.3
Comoro Islands	1975	French	0.3
Papua New Guinea	1975	Australian	2.9
Sao Tome Principe	1975	Portuguese	0.1
Surinam	1975	Netherlands	0.4
Seychelles	1976	British	0.1

Aid–1977 estimate in millions.

SOURCES: Arthur S. Banks, ed., Political Handbook of the World: 1976 (New York: McGraw-Hill,
76), and Population Reference Bureau, 1977 World Population Data Sheet (Washington, D.C.,
77).

colonies. Japan controlled over 60 million people, and the United States about 15 million.[36]

The underlying dynamics of this global expansion are clear in retrospect, but at the time, the colonizers were neither aware of nor honest about their motives. Some justified lateral expansion in the name of religion: bringing Christianity to heathens in Africa and Asia. Others rationalized these pursuits as necessary exploration and discovery. Still others found justifications in commercial and mercantile imperatives. Colonies were taken to be part of a natural state of affairs and essential to economic progress. At the time of the expansion, there were very few moral inhibitions about taking territories from relatively defenseless inhabitants. Might made right, and the pressures for expansion could be halted only by counterforce from another expanding power.

Colonizers and the colonies developed asymmetrical relationships. The colonies served as extensions of national territory. Lumber, cereals, other agriculture commodities, minerals, and even slave labor flowed from them to the mother country. The colonizers, in return, offered "civilization" to the heathen masses. There were limited benefits for the colonies, including, in some cases, improved living standards and a lengthened life-span, but a strong element of economic exploitation overlaid all these relationships.

The Industrial Revolution, then, gave birth to an expansionist international politics accompanied by lateral pressures that forced an outward expansion in trade and development of networks of colonies. National populations and their per capita demands for natural resources soon exceeded the capacity of existing territory. Resource deficits were made up by imports from colonies. Over time, the dependence of colonizers on their colonial empires continued to rise, and they strayed further from their natural carrying capacity. The independence movement of the post–World War II period came as an economic as well as a political shock to these countries, which had come to count on colonies as sources of natural resources. The colonial powers were ill prepared to cope with the independence movements in either a military or an economic sense, since they had depleted their strength in the protracted combat of World War II. And now they must devise new strategies for obtaining natural resources that were once imported from colonies.

The Foundations of Ecopolitics

The international relations of the Industrial Revolution and the period of growth and abundance associated with it are currently being transformed into an international relations of limited opportunities. A central factor in this transition is *perceived* new scarcities. "Ecopolitics" is the term that describes the cluster of economic, ecological, and ethical issues that accompanies these changes in perspective in international relations. Ecopolitics is emerging from a new assessment of remaining resource-intensive growth possibilities in a finite world.

In order to assess better the nature of this transition, it is important to address some of the key questions that have interested scholars in international relations. There are at least four key questions that can be distilled out of the long list of candidates that help describe the nature of the emerging ecopolitics.

1. What are the key issues in international politics that form the basis for unity and division among various actors in the system?
2. Who are the significant actors in the international system, what is the nature of the international system, and what is the nature of the prevailing codes of conduct among major actors?
3. How is power used in relations among actors in the international system and what are its sources?
4. What is the level of interdependence in the international system?

Ecopolitics represents the emergence of broader ecological, ethical, and economic issues and conflicts in international politics as a partial substitute for the narrower military power issues typical of the international politics of the industrial era. Bergsten, Nye, and Keohane have found this new international politics to involve the politization of economic issues as well as changes in the utility of force and economic power for most states.[37] This changing context for international politics now involves a new ecological way of seeing things that stresses international politics as a "system of relationships among interdependent, earth-related communities that share with one another an increasingly crowded planet that offers finite and exhaustible quantities of basic essentials of human well-being and existence."[38]

Serious ecopolitical issues were not totally absent within the old international politics. It is simply a fact that those states in a position to set the international agenda of key issues were not interested in or motivated to discuss them. Thus, many ecopolitical issues that are now coming to dominate international negotiations were then not considered worthy of discussion. Peter Bachrach and Morton Baratz have pointed out that one important aspect of the exercise of power is the ability to keep certain issues from coming to public attention.[39] In international politics, as in other political arenas, dominant forces are often able to mute political conflict by keeping countless potential issues from being placed on agendas. It was a consensus among the major powers that kept these ecopolitical issues from surfacing on international agendas.

It is a clear sign of the growing power of the presently less developed countries that they have been able to shatter this old consensus and thrust the relevant "nondecisions," issues that have previously never been openly debated, onto the agenda of international negotiations. Within the old and established paradigm there was a large consensus, and routine international relations predominated. At present, this consensus is crumbling and, as aspects of the old paradigm are questioned, a new international politics is beginning.[40]

There are many reasons why consensus sometimes breaks down. New actors with different views can obtain a position of power in a relevant political system. Shifts in power relationships can occur among old system members. Or the social or physical environments can generate problems that cannot be solved by old methods. There is an element of all three in the rise of ecopolitics. For example, the advance of technology combined with natural resource limitations has made access to and control over petroleum and natural gas an important issue in contemporary international politics. Two decades ago, control of the world energy industry was firmly in the hands of multinational corporations based in the industrially developed countries, and this situation was quietly accepted within the then-existing consensus. Since then, oil power has elevated Saudi Arabia, Iran, Kuwait—and OPEC collectively—into a much more powerful position in the international system. And dependence on foreign oil and natural gas has differentially weakened the position of formerly powerful industrial nations.

Periods when an existing consensus is called into question in social life are accompanied by changes in morals, as old values and ethics are questioned. Thus, changing definitions of human rights are a central theme in ecopolitics. During the period of rapid industrial expansion and overt colonialism, there was little concern over individual rights of people in conquered territories or even over the rights of other countries. But human rights issues that were formerly settled by benign neglect have now become matters of international debate. Rights to minimal diets, the morality of large income gaps between rich and poor nations—and between the rich and poor within those nations—rights to work, just wages, racism, colonialism, neocolonism, and a number of other moral issues that were largely ignored in the old international consensus now occupy center stage in international politics. In some respects, the "is" of *realpolitic* is being replaced slowly by the "ought" of ecopolitics. This does not mean that all leaders of all nations have suddenly become moralists. It does mean, however, that ethical considerations are now being interjected into the new international politics and could become much more significant as determinants of international behavior.

Finally, a growing realization that all states and individuals share a finite ecosphere* and that there are limits to the burdens that can be

---

*"Ecosphere" is a term used to refer to the global ecosystem, the complex sum of

imposed on that ecosphere has given impetus to new issues of both an economic and a moral nature. Publication of *The Limits to Growth* in 1972 rekindled the debate over growth prospects that began in the eighteenth century with the Reverend Thomas Malthus.[41] But this time the debate is taking place on a planetary scale. Many subsequent studies have further refined the growth debate and focused on the morality of great differences in consumption between rich and poor nations.[42] Irrespective of the accuracy of the world models involved, in political affairs empirical reality is often overshadowed by perceptions of this reality. These perceptions, in turn, are often conditioned by rhetoric instead of fact. The new array of ecopolitical issues has been given a tremendous boost by the limits to growth thesis, and leaders of less developed countries have seized upon it as a potentially powerful moral argument for major programs of global wealth redistribution.

ECOPOLITICS: THE CHANGING SYSTEM, ACTORS, AND RULES

The transition from the politics of expansion to ecopolitics is changing the shape of the international power configuration, the nature of significant actors, and the rules under which international relations take place. Morton Kaplan has outlined the power configurations that can induce stability by studying past international arrangements. He has distinguished six different states of equilibrium that could exist in any potential international system. He labels them the balance of power, loose bipolar, tight bipolar, universal, hierarchical, and unit veto systems.[43] Each of these systems has a different group of key actors and a distinct set of rules for conduct among actors that characterizes it.

The international system of the eighteenth and nineteenth centuries was denoted by a limited number of key participants and use of balance of power tactics. In some respects, it was a nonsystem. The major European powers were the actors in the system. The rules specified that the main actors would attempt to increase their capabilities but would stop short of eliminating other key actors in their quest for power. National actors would also act to constrain those ascribing to supranational organizing principles. Changes in dominating coalitions would take place to keep any actor or group of actors from controlling the system.

The breakdown of the balance of power system in World Wars I and II was followed by the evolution of a tight and then loose bipolar system, with the NATO and Warsaw Pact nations organized around coalition leaders, the United States and the Soviet Union. More recently,

---

many smaller interrelated ecosystems. An ecosystem is a community of flora and fauna combined with its nonliving physical environment.

the rules of Kaplan's unit veto system correspond most closely to many attributes of international politics in the 1960s and 1970s. Within a unit veto arrangement, the key principle is that major actors in the system possess the power to destroy any other actors, so "the unit veto system is a stand-off which, as long as it operates according to its inherent rules, perpetuates the existing state of affairs."[44]

Stanley Hoffman, in turn, has described the power configuration of the present international system on three different levels.[45] At the most fundamental level, it is still a bipolar system, the United States and the Soviet Union being the two anchors on which other states fasten their foreign policies. But this bipolarity has been muted by a number of factors that are changing the rules by which the international game is played. First, the world's landscape has undergone major changes within the last twenty-five years, sparked by an independence movement that transformed the empires of major nations into dozens of smaller countries. And the legitimacy of most of these new national actors is no longer questioned by major powers. Second, major nations are hesitant to use their power in conflicts that have a potential for leading to a nuclear conflagration, which would be totally destructive to all participants. Thus, the two major nuclear powers are tied together by mutual self-restraint, since both of them have an interest in avoiding a nuclear confrontation.[46]

On a second level, however, the present international system is moving toward polycentrism, meaning several different centers of power, because the nuclear powers fear to use their ultimate weapon. The two superpowers are deadlocked by mutual deterrence, and lesser powers are now playing minor games of their own.[47] In other words, while the big cats are locked in deadly confrontation, the mice have more freedom to engage each other in power struggles on a subnuclear level.

On the third level, the nuclear balance of terror between the superpowers creates the potential for a new multipolar power structure. The present terror balance could be disturbed by either of two occurrences. The nuclear stalemate could deteriorate and the two superpowers could engage each other, or lesser actors could develop their own nuclear capacity and use the "impotence of power" created by nuclear deterrence to create their own small spheres of influence.[48]

It is clear, then, that the bipolar power system that emerged on the heels of World War II is giving way to a new type, the shape of which cannot yet be clearly perceived. The key elements, however, are the mutual nuclear deterrence of the two superpowers, leading to the emergence of smaller nuclear actors within the stalemate thus created, and the tendency for lesser military powers to engage each other with conventional weapons because they know that the major powers will be unlikely to intervene. The rules have also changed, and there is now much greater freedom for lesser powers to maneuver without running a risk of being annihilated. Finally, and most important, ecopolitical strategies and tactics are assuming a key role in international politics. The petroleum boycott and price increases of 1973–1974 represented a crystallization of forces that is leading to a new type of international power configuration characterized by a new set of rules. The major powers within the emerging system still possess unit veto capability, but using the veto assures their own destruction. In the new system, formerly minor actors, protected by the nuclear umbrella of major power patrons, have become significant actors in their own right. Furthermore, a multiplicity of new actors has joined the nation-state in the international power game. The United Nations, its specialized agencies, regional political organizations, multinational corporations, and international commodity cartels all play a significant role in ecopolitical maneuvering. The nascent international system is thus characterized by a much greater number of significant actors, a different set of critical issues, and a much more complex set of rules within which power struggles take place.

The extent to which the rules of the game have rapidly changed is illustrated by two events ocurring in the Middle East only seventeen years apart. In 1956, Egypt threatened to seize the Suez Canal. The British quickly dispatched paratroopers to the scene to quell the nationalistic fervor. In 1973–1974, the OAPEC (Organization of Arab Petroleum Exporting Countries) and OPEC nations were able to withhold petroleum and quadruple crude petroleum prices, actions with economic consequences for industrial countries as severe as if war had been declared. None of the major powers intervened to reestablish the old prices. The risks and potential costs of military action were deemed to be too high. Since that time, industrial nations have been extremely careful to tailor many of their political and economic actions so as not to offend the leaders of OPEC nations. Many formerly ignored nations that once had no voice in international affairs are now in a power position that permits them to help shape the international agenda.

New Sources of Power

Power is considered to be the essence of politics and, therefore, more than one hundred definitions of the concept exist in the political science literature. But the power concept is easy to grasp in essence. Richard Adams has defined it as "that aspect of social relations that marks the relative equality of the actors or operating units; it is derived from the relative control by each actor or unit over elements of the environment of concern to the participants."[49] Power is a social, psychological, political, and economic phenomenon, and control is the physical manifestation of power. Amitai Etzioni has written about three aspects of power, coercion, remuneration, and authority.[50] All of these deal with the means by which one actor can induce another actor to behave in a desired manner. In international relations, the induced actor may be coerced by military force, may fear economic consequences for lack of compliance, or may comply because the requests of the other actor are believed to be morally right within a framework of shared values.

Political scientists have spent a great deal of effort attempting to define and measure power in relations among nations. The key questions have been why some nations are able to control the behavior of others in the international system and what are the sources of power leading to this control. Hans Morgenthau has been one of the foremost analysts of power in international politics, and he has come up with a long checklist of factors that increase or decrease it. Among these are geography (isolation, defensible frontiers), natural resources (food, raw materials), industrial capacity, military preparedness, population, national character, national morale, the quality of diplomacy, and the quality of government.[51] Countries with appropriate combinations of these characteristics have been historically powerful in international affairs. Steven Spiegal has suggested a slightly more parsimonious list of types of power that maintain the present international hierarchy. These include material power, military power, motivational power, achievement, and potential.[52] His list overlaps with that of Morgenthau but also provides useful categories to use in analyzing power shifts in the present ecopolitical transition.

Military force has historically been the prime factor in determining power in the international hierarchy. During the period of industrial expansion, it was the superior military force of the European countries, backed by sophisticated technology, that directly led to the conquest of colonial territories. In relations among industrialized nations, it has been largely a matter of mutual fear that has kept the peace during the few periods when major powers have not been at each others' throats. Military strength is dependent upon a nation's level of technological sophistication, industrial infrastructure, quality and quantity of population, access to natural resources, and geographical location. High-technology countries with large and skilled populations having access to abundant natural resources have regularly dominated countries that are less well endowed.

But now the power hierarchy forged out of military conquests is slowly eroding from beneath. In Adams's language, this deterioration can be attributed to a number of factors related to changes in the control of key elements of the environment. Foremost among these was World War II, which sapped the military and economic strength of the European colonial powers. World War II left many European nations in shambles, and they hardly had the political determination, economic wherewithal, or military power to withstand the anticolonial elements seeking self-determination. Protracted guerrilla wars against the French in Indochina and Algeria and disorders in British-ruled India and

Pakistan weakened the resolve of these countries, and others, to rule by force.

The degree of political and economic independence exercised by former colonies has increased slowly over time. Their political maturation has now created an important third world block that previously did not exist as a power in international politics. The initiative for the new ecopolitics has come from this rapidly expanding bloc of Third World countries, and the former colonial powers are now fighting a defensive action.

The development of new military technology resulting in movement from nuclear weapon exclusivity to nuclear weapon oligarchy to nuclear weapon anarchy has also been an important factor in changing the old political power hierarchy. In the contemporary multipolar world, at least six countries—the United States, the Soviet Union, Great Britain, France, China, and India—possess nuclear weapons, and several smaller countries either now possess these weapons or the technology to develop them. It is one of the ironies of history that the development of such overwhelming destructive power and its concentration in the hands of a few nations has created unparalleled freedom for the smaller former colonies, that do not themselves possess nuclear weapons, to use their conventional power in international politics.

A related factor in this erosion and reversal of old power relationships is the increasing cost of conventional warfare. Mature industrial economies are no longer growing at the rates they once enjoyed during the period of rapid industrial expansion. Environmental constraints, higher prices for fuels and nonfuel minerals, capital shortages, slower increases in labor productivity, and a host of other factors makes the guns *and* butter approach to warfare impossible. It is no longer economically feasible for major powers to wage protracted warfare in small, distant countries such as Vietnam. The economics of such warfare place unmanageable demands on the contemporary industrial powers. Military equipment is costly, and heavy military expenditures accelerate already high rates of inflation. Increasingly, nuclear powers are forced into the dilemma of using either their most powerful weapons or refraining from getting involved at all.

In this situation, other aspects of power have become more important in a less rigid international hierarchy. Control over natural resources has now become a source of power quite apart from their consumption in military adventures. Economic power in world trade is also becoming an important source of power in international politics. And even new ideas, values, and ethics are important in the ideological vacuum left by the relative impotency of the nuclear powers. Failure to recognize the significance of these new sources of power can lead to rather absurd conclusions. Spiegal used his five sources of power to create a power hierarchy of nations. It consisted of two superpowers, five secondary powers, seventeen middle powers, and thirty minor powers. Saudi Arabia and Kuwait were not even included in his select list of fifty-four countries. Venezuela and Cuba were not considered to be middle powers while Argentina was. And key proponents of the new international economic order were almost completely ignored.[53]

None of this means that military force is no longer important in international politics. In fact, Klaus Knorr has found evidence that a recent decline in the use of force is too ambiguous to be called a trend. Between 1965 and 1974, military expenditures in constant dollars rose by 28 percent, military manpower by 24 percent, and arms imports by 60 percent.[54] What these figures indicate is that military expenditures have been increasing among minor powers and disputes among them might become more frequent, while major powers will be much more hesitant to get involved in such disputes. But most important, ecopolitical factors have emerged as new sources of power and as supplements to and replacements for the use of coercive force in maintaining the international hierarchy.

The Impact of Interdependence

The preindustrial world was divided into many semiisolated kingdoms, each of which was reasonably self-sufficient and autonomous. In a primitive world with very little economic intercourse among national populations, it was impossible for human populations to grow much beyond natural domestic carrying capacity. Furthermore, in this world the fortunes of all human populations on the planet were not closely linked. Wars could be fought among distant kingdoms and would pass unnoticed in the rest of the world. There was no danger of escalation of such encounters into a world war that could destroy all civilization. When famines occurred, and there have been significant numbers of them throughout history, they were largely localized affairs. A famine in Africa, for example, had no impact on food prices in France. The spread of disease was inhibited by rudimentary transportation systems and resulting lack of contact among human populations. When populations that previously had no contact encountered each other, however, epidemics were very likely because of lack of resistance to strange diseases. An epidemic of smallpox may explain how the Spanish conquered fierce Indian tribes in Latin America during the colonial period.

The expansion of the industrial world and the accompanying development of an international trade system, however, have integrated all parts of the globe into one increasingly interdependent whole. "Interdependence" is a much-used term that has different meanings for different people. Put most simply, it describes a situation in which two actors become mutually dependent. In the case of nation-states, it means that national populations become closely linked through international transactions. Interdependence usually leads to mutually beneficial outcomes, although changing distributions of benefits over time may make the outcome more favorable for one actor than another.[55] Classical economists operate from a positive perspective, claiming that interdependence thrives on comparative advantage and leads to overall net benefits for all involved. The perspective of the emerging new international economic order, however, stresses distribution issues in interdependence, such as questions of who benefits the most in these situations.

There is a generally accepted belief that global interdependence has been increasing and is leading to identification with a global community, but attempts to measure this phenomenon have yielded ambiguous results. Karl Deutsch, for example, has found that national self-preoccupation has recently become much more pronounced. His data show that foreign economic involvement of nations in relation to the size of the domestic economy over the last century has been declining.[56] Using more contemporary data, however, Peter Katzenstein has found a reversal of these trends and claims that international transactions have been increasing in relation to size of domestic economies over the most recent two decades.[57]

The problem lies in inadequate conceptualization. Measuring interdependence is an extremely difficult task, and relating it to domestic economic growth may not be meaningful. Oran Young, who has suggested seven conditions that should exist in a more interdependent world, concludes that "the phenomenon of interdependence in sociopolitical systems is considerably more complex than it is often thought to be. Interdependence involves numerous dimensions that may vary asymmetrically, and it is frequently difficult to find operational indicators in terms of which the level of interdependence in a global system can be measured accurately."[58] It is clear, however, that the *absolute* level of transactions among nations has been rising along with the establishment of a global system of economic relations. It is less clear (and less important) that transactions among nations have been rising faster than transactions within nations. The economic fortunes of many countries are at present inextricably interlinked. This does not mean that all countries profit or profit equally from this interdependence, but it does mean that if all transactions among countries were suddenly to cease, the economies of many countries living beyond current carrying capacity would be seriously affected.

The spread of industrialization and the accompanying development of an international system have integrated most parts of the planet into a system in which the fortunes of all actors are intertwined. On the most basic physical level, all national populations share one ecosphere, which is now recognized to be relatively finite and fragile. What one nation does to it has an impact on all other countries. Industrial pollution on the European continent, for example, can lead to acidic rain in Scandinavia. Furthermore, almost all industrial countries depend on others for the vast quantities of natural resources that are essential to industrial production. And finally, no longer can any developed nation "opt out" of the international economic system. Economic conditions in the United States have an impact on Western Europe and vice versa.

There are several factors that account for this new state of interdependence in the international system, and all of them are results of the new energy-related technologies spawned by the Industrial Revolution.[59] The most important is a dramatic acceleration in global communication and transportation. In the preindustrial world, transportation was based on current solar income; people walked, depended on beasts of burden, or sailed the oceans courtesy of the winds. The invention of the steam engine led to the "iron horse" and rail travel, then to the private automobile, then to the airplane, and eventually to the supersonic transport. Countries that were previously weeks or even months apart are now separated by only a few hours' travel. Progress became synonymous with size and speed. Ironically, this "progressive" movement in world transportation became increasingly inefficient in consumption of energy. On a passenger-mile basis, travel by plane is much less energy efficient than travel by automobile, which is much less efficient than travel by rail or water!

A simultaneous revolution occurred in the global flow of information. The telephone, radio, and finally television brought previously isolated parts of the world into a global communications network. Now earth satellites can instantaneously transmit images from one part of the world to another, and there is no such thing as an "isolated" political event. Political events in China or Africa are subjects for discussion on the evening news in the United States.

The spread of economic activity and the emergence of a global marketplace is another factor that has caused increased contact in the international system. Expanding industrial economies require fuels, a wide variety of nonfuel minerals, and, most important, markets for their products. Large multinational corporations now dominate an international economy in which the economic affairs of all nations are tightly interwoven. Depressions or recessions in important industrial countries can cause a more general decline in the world economy.

A final technology-related factor responsible for the changed international system is the increasing scale of warfare. Wars are no longer fought by men on horseback or even in trenches, and the scope of a conflict cannot be limited to small geographic areas. World War I was really a continental war, and World War II involved half the world. A World War III would undoubtedly involve the whole world, and few national populations would escape unscathed. Contemporary warfare is push-button warfare, with intercontinental ballistic missiles poised to carry their payloads thousands of miles in a matter of minutes. Fallout from nuclear weapons cannot be contained by national boundaries. The present generation is the first to possess the knowledge to build the ultimate weapon: bombs that are capable of destroying all human life on the face of the earth.

Thus, the international politics of the previous great transformation involved the creation of a "world" economy dominated by a few powerful industrial nations. The contemporary transition is being accompanied by the emergence of ecopolitics, the dismantling of old dominance patterns, and their replacement by interaction patterns having their underpinnings in interdependence among a much greater number of sovereign national populations. Recognition of increased interdependence is a key aspect of the ecopolitical transition. Countries now recognize their mutual dependence and relative vulnerabilities and will not hesitate to use them to their advantage. This raises a new agenda of international issues of cooperation and suggests the need for a new code of conduct in international politics that will permit interdependent, but competing, national units from destroying each other through nonmilitary types of conflict.

In summary, in the language of conventional international relations analysis, the development of global ecopolitics is being accompanied by changes in the nature of the international system, including a change in the number of significant actors, a shift in the types and sources of power that are exercised by these actors, changes in the ethics governing the international agenda of issues, and increasing interdependence among all significant international actors. In the following chapters, the most significant items on the emerging ecopolitical agenda are analyzed in greater detail.

ENDNOTES

1. See Paul Ehrlich and Anne Ehrlich, *Population, Resources, Environment* (San Francisco: W. H. Freeman, 1972), pp. 6–7. See also Paul Ehrlich, Anne Ehrlich, and John Holdren, *Ecoscience* (San Francisco: W. H. Freeman, 1977), chap. 4.
2. See the discussion of exponential curves and "deflection points" in Jonas Salk, *The Survival of the Wisest* (New York: Harper & Row, 1973), chap. 3.
3. Thomas Kuhn, *The Structure of Scientific Revolutions* (Chicago: University of Chicago Press, 1962), chap. 2.
4. Ibid., chap. 4.
5. See Dennis Pirages and Paul Ehrlich, *Ark II: Social Response to Environmental Imperatives* (San Francisco: W. H. Freeman, 1974), p. 43.
6. The impact of the Industrial Revolution on the shaping of the present dominant social paradigm is discussed in Karl Polanyi, *The Great Transformation* (Boston: Beacon Press, 1957).
7. Willis Harman, "The Coming Transformation," *The Futurist* (February 1977), See also Willis Harman, *An Incomplete Guide to the Future* (San Francisco: San Francisco Book Co., 1976), chap. 2.
8. See, for example, Organization for Economic Cooperation and Development,

World Energy Outlook (Paris, 1977); Central Intelligence Agency, *International Energy Situation: Outlook to 1985* (Washington, D.C., April 1977); and Carroll Wilson, *Energy: Global Prospects 1985–2000* (Cambridge, Mass.: MIT Press, 1977).

9. See Donella Meadows, et al., *The Limits to Growth* (New York: Universe Books 1972), and Ehrlich and Ehrlich, *Population, Resources, Environment*, chaps. 4–7.

10. Edward Renshaw, *The End of Progress* (North Scituate, Mass.: Duxbury Press, 1976).

11. The best examples of the "technological optimist" position are offered by Herman Kahn, William Brown, and Leon Martel, *The Next 200 Years* (New York: William Morrow, 1976), and Wilfred Beckerman, *In Defence of Economic Growth* (London: Jonathan Cape, 1974).

12. See William Ophuls, *Ecology and the Politics of Scarcity* (San Francisco: W. H. Freeman, 1977), and Herman Daly, ed., *Toward a Steady-State Economy* (San Francisco: W. H. Freeman, 1973).

13. An early attempt to gauge these perceptions of other nations is found in William Buchanan and Hadly Cantril, *How Nations See Each Other* (Westport, Conn.: Greenwood Press, 1972).

14. Harman, "The Coming Transformation," *The Futurist* (April 1977).

15. See Gerard O'Neill, "Space Colonies and Energy Supply to the Earth," *Science* (December 5, 1975), and Jack Salmon, "Politics of Scarcity vs. Technological Optimism: A Possible Reconciliation?" *International Studies Quarterly* (December 1977).

16. See, for example, Harold Sprout and Margaret Sprout, *Toward a Politics of the Planet Earth* (New York: Van Nostrand Reinhold, 1971), and Nazli Choucri, *Population Dynamics and International Violence* (Lexington, Mass.: D. C. Heath, 1974).

17. Kenneth Watt, *Principles of Environmental Science* (New York: McGraw-Hill, 1973), p. 1.

18. Karl Deutsch, *Nationalism and Social Communication* (Cambridge, Mass.: MIT Press, 1953), p. 100.

19. Karl Deutsch, "Communication Theory and Political Integration," in Philip Jacob and James Toscano, eds., *The Integration of Political Communities* (Philadelphia: J. B. Lippincott, 1964).

20. See Barrington Moore, *Social Origins of Dictatorship and Democracy* (Boston: Beacon Press, 1966), and Charles Tilley, ed., *The Formation of National States in Western Europe* (Princeton: Princeton University Press, 1975).

21. The influence of weather and plagues on human populations is documented in William McNeill, *Plagues and Peoples* (Garden City, N.Y.: Anchor Press, 1976).

22. Watt, *Principles of Environmental Science*, p. 20.

23. Ehrlich and Ehrlich, *Population, Resources, Environment*, p. 59.

24. Paul Ehrlich and John Holdren, "The Impact of Population Growth," *Science* (March 26, 1971).

25. Robert Keohane and Joseph Nye, *Power and Interdependence* (Boston: Little, Brown, 1977), pp. 12–13.

26. See S. Fred Singer, Ed., *Is There an Optimum Level of Population?* (New York: McGraw-Hill, 1971).

27. Thomas Espenshade, *The Value and Cost of Children* (Washington, D.C.: Population Reference Bureau, April 1977). See also Michael Teitelbaum, "Relevance of Demographic Transition Theory for Developing Countries," *Science* (May 1975), and Jay Weinstein, *Demographic Transition and Social Change* (Morristown, N.J.: General Learning Press, 1976).

28. Ansley Coale, *Proceedings of the IUSSP International Population Conference* (Liege, Belgium: 1973), p. 65.

29. See S. E. Beaver, *Demographic Transition: Theory Reinterpreted* (Lexington, Mass.: D. C. Heath, 1975); Robert Cassen, "Population and Development: A Survey," *World Development* (October-November 1976); and Timothy King, *Population Policies and Economic Development* (Baltimore: Johns Hopkins University Press, 1974).

30. See Immanuel Wallerstein, *The Modern World System* (New York: Academic Press, 1974), pp. 33–37; Stephen Schneider, *The Genesis Strategy* (New York: Plenum Press, 1976); and McNeill, *Plagues and Peoples*.

31. Wallerstein, *The Modern World System*, pp. 38–39.

32. Archibald Lewis, "The Closing of the European Frontier," *Speculum* (October 1958).

33. Wallerstein, *The Modern World System*, pp. 39–48.

34. Nazli Choucri and Robert North, *Nations in Conflict* (San Francisco: W. H. Freeman, 1975), p. 16.

35. Ibid., p. 15.

36. David Finlay and Thomas Hovet, Jr., *7304: International Relations on the Planet Earth* (New York: Harper & Row, 1975), pp. 22–23.

37. C. Fred Bergsten, Robert Keohane, and Joseph Nye, Jr., "International Economics and International Politics: A Framework for Analysis," in C. Fred Bergsten and Lawrence Krause, eds., *World Politics and International Economics* (Washington, D.C.: Brookings Institution, 1975), pp. 6–7.

38. Sprout and Sprout, *Toward a Politics of the Planet Earth*, p. 14.

39. Peter Bachrach and Morton Baratz, "Decisions and Non-Decisions: An Analytical Framework," *The American Political Science Review* (September 1963).

40. For more detail on nondecisions and stability, see Dennis Pirages, *Managing Political Conflict* (New York: Praeger, 1976), pp. 81–88.

41. Malthus's original work, *An Essay on the Principle of Population as It Affects the Future Improvement of Society with Remarks on the Speculations of M. Goodwin, M. Condorcet and other writers*, was published anonymously in 1798.

42. See Mihajlo Mesarovic and Eduard Pestel, *Mankind at the Turning Point* (New York: E. P. Dutton, 1974), and Jan Tinbergen, et al., *Reshaping the International Order* (New York: E. P. Dutton, 1976).

43. Morton Kaplan, *System and Process in International Politics* (New York: John Wiley & Sons, 1957), chap. 2.

44. Ibid., p. 51.

45. Stanley Hoffman, *Gulliver's Troubles, or the Setting of American Foreign Policy* (New York: McGraw-Hill, 1968), pp. 21–46.

46. Ibid., pp. 21–33.

47. Ibid., pp. 33–43.

48. Ibid., pp. 43–46.

49. Richard Adams, *Energy and Structure* (Austin: University of Texas Press, 1975), pp. 9–10.
50. Amitai Etzioni, *A Comparative Analysis of Complex Organizations* (New York: Free Press, 1961), chap. 1.
51. Hans Morgenthau, *Politics Among Nations* (New York: Alfred A. Knopf, 1948), chap. 9.
52. Steven Spiegal, *Dominance and Diversity* (Boston: Little, Brown, 1972), chap. 2.
53. Ibid., chap. 3.
54. Klaus Knorr, "Is International Coercion Waning or Rising?" *International Security* (Spring 1977), 93–94.
55. Keohane and Nye, *Power and Interdependence*, pp. 8–10.
56. Karl Deutsch and Alexander Eckstein, "National Industrialization and the Declining Share of the International Economic Sector, 1890–1959," *World Politics* (January 1961).
57. Peter Katzenstein, "International Interdependence: Some Long-Term Trends and Recent Changes," *International Organization* (Autumn 1975).
58. Oran Young, "Interdependencies in World Politics," *International Journal* (Autumn 1969): 750. See also Richard Rosecrance and Arthur Stein, "Interdependence: Myth or Reality?" *World Politics* (October 1973).
59. See Eugene Skolnikoff, *The International Imperatives of Technology* (Berkeley: Institute of International Studies, 1972).

SELECTED READINGS

1. Nazli Choucri and Robert North. *Nations in Conflict.* San Francisco: W. H. Freeman, 1975.
2. H. S. D. Cole, et al., eds. *Models of Doom: A Critique of the Limits to Growth.* New York: Universe Books, 1973.
3. Karl Deutsch, et al. *Problems of World Modeling: Political and Social Implications.* Cambridge, Mass.: Ballinger, 1977.
4. Paul Ehrlich, Anne Ehrlich, and John Holdren. *Ecoscience.* San Francisco: W. H. Freeman, 1977.
5. Tomas Frejka. *The Future of Population: Alternative Paths to Equilibrium.* New York: John Wiley, 1973.
6. Willis Harman. *An Incomplete Guide to the Future.* San Francisco: San Francisco Book Co., 1976.
7. Herman Kahn, William Brown, and Leon Martel. *The Next 200 Years.* New York: William Morrow, 1976.
8. Thomas Kuhn. *The Structure of Scientific Revolutions.* Chicago: University of Chicago Press, 1962.
9. Emmanuel Ladurie. *Times of Feast, Times of Famine.* Garden City, N.Y.: Doubleday, 1971.
10. William McNeill. *Plagues and Peoples.* Garden City, N.Y.: Anchor Press, 1976.

11. Donella Meadows, et al. *The Limits to Growth.* New York: Universe Books, 1972.
12. Lewis Mumford. *The Myth of the Machine: Technics and Human Development.* New York: Harcourt, Brace & World, 1967.
13. William Ophuls. *Ecology and the Politics of Scarcity.* San Francisco: W. H. Freeman, 1977.
14. Dennis Pirages and Paul Ehrlich. *Ark II: Social Response to Environmental Imperatives.* San Francisco: W. H. Freeman, 1974.
15. Edward Renshaw. *The End of Progress.* North Scituate, Mass.: Duxbury Press, 1976.
16. Harold Sprout and Margaret Sprout. *Toward a Politics of the Planet Earth.* New York: Van Nostrand Reinhold, 1971.
17. Immanuel Wallerstein. *The Modern World System.* New York: Academic Press, 1974.

2

The Ecopolitical Agenda

Ecopolitics and the related new agenda of issues have emerged from the confluence of two broad trends in international politics and economics. On the political side, the most important trend has been the dismantling of colonial empires and the resultant emergence of more than one hundred newly independent states. As these countries have completed their political revolutions, the concerns of their political leaders have shifted from demands of a political nature to demands of an economic nature. At the same time, a second trend, tremendous growth in the global human population and per capita consumption, has led to a new concern over the rapidly growing number of human beings, the adequacy of the world's food supply to sustain them, the ability of the earth's finite resources to fund future growth in consumption, and future environmental integrity. New economic and ecological issues are driving a wedge between rich and poor countries, who see the future of the world economy from markedly different perspectives.

The emergence of these new political units and the concern with growth issues are not coincidental. The presently industrialized nations partially "solved" their problems of limited carrying capacity through the classic imperialism of the fifteenth through nineteenth centuries. But now the problems of the overextended industrial countries have returned, thanks to the independence movements. Colonies no longer provide industrial countries with basic resources at the command of the colonial masters. Raw materials that were previously taken from them must now be purchased through international trade. The international and domestic consequences of such changes for some countries, such as France, Japan, Spain, and Great Britain, have been extremely severe. In addition, if ambitious industrialization plans succeed in presently less developed countries, additional pressures on supplies of natural resources can be expected to increase future prices and further exacerbate the plight of many of the developed countries.

Concern about limits to growth in the size and consumption demands of the human population are not particularly new: the Reverend Thomas Malthus called attention to the specter of population growth near the end of the eighteenth century, warning that the "power of population is indefinitely greater than the power of the earth to produce subsistence."[1] He saw population to be increasing in an exponential or geometric manner while production of food increased only in a linear fashion. Malthus did not anticipate any new technological breakthroughs in agriculture that would make land much more productive and thus augment global carrying capacity quickly enough to keep pace with an expanding world population. But his concerns have now returned in response to the rapid doubling times of world population in the twentieth century.

The new wave of concern over the impact of growth began to gain acceptability with the 1972 publication of *Limits to Growth*.[2] This study was an attempt to take a holistic look at the interrelationship of population growth, food production, industrialization, consumption of nonrenewable resources, and pollution on a planetary scale. Unlike Malthus, who wrote by candlelight in his solitary study, the research team that carried out this effort had access to a sophisticated computer simulation and a file of data on global economic and environmental trends. The results reported in the book set off a heated debate about the amount of growth the earth could ultimately support, a debate that provides the framework for the emergence of the ecopolitical agenda. The possibilities for future growth are hotly contested between "technological optimists," who see no limits, and those who see a fundamental change in growth opportunities taking place.[3] Whatever the future does hold, population growth, ownership of natural resources, environmental integrity, and a host of other ecopolitical issues increasingly shape interactions among the world's political units.

Population growth is one of the principal trends shaping the ecopolitical agenda and is directly related to increases in consumption of food, fuels, and nonfuel minerals. But human consumption of all of these resources has been increasing even faster than population, which has been increasing at slightly less than 2 percent yearly. With the exception of periods of economic recession, world consumption of energy has been increasing exponentially at about 5 to 6 percent each year, which means that energy consumption now doubles every twelve to fourteen years. Consumption of many other natural resources has likewise been increasing much faster than the rate of global population increase. The reason is that industrialization is characterized by *increased per capita consumption* of natural resources. Persons in industrialized countries require more energy, more iron, more copper, more water, more food, and more of a host of other resources to sustain their high levels of living. Thus, while the twentieth century has been the century of rapid population growth, much of it taking place in the less developed countries, it has also been the century of consumption growth, much of it taking place in the industrially developed world.

The absolute size and rate of increase in human consumption of natural resources is now so great as to raise the possibility that many key raw materials may become exhausted by population pressures in the near future. A critical component of the established dominant social paradigm in industrial societies has been an illusion of environmental plenty as the normal state of humankind. Emile Benoit attributes this aspect of the paradigm to two factors in recent history. The first has been the safety valve migration to fertile areas in North and South America and Australia. And the second has been the large-scale tapping of fossil fuels.[4] New land is now no longer freely available, and recent studies show that supplies of petroleum and natural gas will become more difficult to obtain within two decades.[5] Nor is it certain that non-fuel minerals will remain relatively abundant if supplies of energy needed to extract and process them dry up.[6] It should be obvious, then, that rapid exponential growth cannot be sustained for much longer in a very finite world, particularly since technological innovations on the scale of those that increased global carrying capacity during the early stages of the Industrial Revolution do not appear to be on the horizon.

So it is understandable that exponential growth in population and consumption and the finite nature of natural resources is now seen as an important factor in conflicts among nations. Less developed countries realize that fossil fuels are becoming more expensive or, in some cases, disappearing just as they are embarking on programs of industrial development based upon these fuels. And those countries that have reserves of fossil fuels want to extract as much profit as possible from them. Less developed importers of fuels and nonfuel minerals are concerned that the voracious appetites of industrial countries will exhaust the world's limited supplies before they get a chance to use them. Therefore, a central element in ecoconflict is control of natural resources; prices to be paid for them, access to them, and arrangements for optimally using them to meet human needs and wants.

The other major trend shaping the agenda of ecopolitics and ecoconflict is the stready increase in the number and influence of new actors in international politics. More than one hundred new states have emerged from colonial domination since World War II, and a considerable amount of solidarity now exists among them.

A variety of terms is used to refer to the less developed countries that have recently received independence. None is adequate to describe all of their common characteristics, but the most serviceable one refers to these countries collectively as the "Third World." This term differentiates these less developed countries from the First World, the industrialized capitalist countries, and the Second World, the Soviet Union and industrially developed Eastern European countries. The reasons for distinctions between these two sections of the industrial world are not altogether clear. Questions could also be raised about the appropriateness of lumping nearly one hundred less developed countries, ranging from petroleum-rich Saudi Arabia to poverty-stricken Chad, into the Third World category. But, for lack of an attractive alternative, the term "Third World" is used here to refer to the less developed countries that have painfully attempted to develop solidarity over the past two decades (see table 2–1).

The first attempt at developing Third World solidarity took place

TABLE 2–1. *Major Steps in the Development of the New International Economic Order*

April 1955 — Meeting of 29 African and Asian countries in Bandung, Indonesia, to hasten independence for remaining colonial areas.

October 1960 — OPEC formed.

September 1961 — Meeting of 25 nonaligned nations in Belgrade, Yugoslavia, to discuss relaxation of East-West tensions, colonialism, and neocolonialism.

March 1964 — First meeting of UNCTAD in Geneva, Switzerland.

October 1964 — Meeting of 47 nonaligned nations in Cairo, Egypt, to seek common platform.

February 1968 — Second meeting of UNCTAD in New Delhi, India, leads to moderate agreement on trade expansion.

September 1970 — Meeting of 52 nonaligned nations in Lusaka, Zambia, to discuss common political perspectives on anticolonialism and related matters.

April-May 1972 — Third meeting of UNCTAD in Santiago, Chile, to discuss reform of international monetary system and the problems of the least developed countries.

September 1973 — Meeting of 77 nonaligned nations in Algiers, Algeria, to discuss political liberation movements and economic liberation by means of nationalization.

November 1973 — Arab members of OPEC embargo exports to selected industrial countries; rounds of price increases for petroleum begin.

April-May 1974 — Declaration of the Establishment of a New International Economic Order at the Sixth Special Session of the General Assembly of the United Nations.

December 1974 — Charter of Economic Rights and Duties of States adopted by the Twenty-ninth General Assembly of the United Nations.

February 1975 — Lome Convention between the European Economic Community and 46 less developed countries to provide for price supports for selected basic commodities is signed.

February 1975 — Conference of 110 developing nations in Dakar, Senegal, to draw up an action program on raw materials.

September 1975 — Seventh Special Session of the General Assembly of the United Nations deals with development and international economic cooperation.

May 1976 — Fourth meeting of UNCTAD in Nairobi, Kenya, brings confrontation between North and South countries over commodity markets.

August 1976 — Meeting of 85 less developed nations in Colombo, Sri Lanka, to discuss the new international economic order.

1975–1977 — Negotiations between industrialized and less developed countries over commodity markets take place in Paris.

August 1979 — Special Session of the General Assembly of the United Nations deals with the question of technology transfer.

in Bandung, Indonesia, in 1955. At that time, less than one-half of contemporary countries were politically independent. At the Bandung meeting, twenty-nine leaders of newly emergent African and Asian countries met to discuss ways in which they could cooperate to hasten independence in those territories still held by industrial nations.

The next major event in the political development of the Third World was a conference of twenty-five nonaligned nations that took place in Belgrade, Yugoslavia, in 1961. This conference emphasized political rather than economic matters. The fledgling group of new states had great difficulty in agreeing on an agenda of issues and also had difficulty with the very basic problem of deciding which "nonaligned" nations merited invitations. The twenty-five participant nations were carefully selected in order to minimize disagreements, but significant differences were apparent between countries with revolutionary regimes such as Cuba, on the one hand, and conservative countries such as Saudi Arabia, on the other. The final document, drawn up by the conference after a great deal of internal conflict, contained an appeal to the United States and Soviet Union for a lasting peace, condemnation of imperialism and neoimperialism, and a demand for greater participation by the nonaligned countries in the affairs of the United Nations, a demand that has surely been more than met by subsequent changes in the number of Third World nations.[7]

The next important meeting of Third World countries was held in Cairo in 1964 and attended by forty-seven states, which attests to the rapid strides made by many national independence movements between 1961 and 1964. During this period, thirty-three new territories were given their independence, most of them former French colonies in Africa. But growth in numbers also resulted in more internal political disputes that divided delegates along ideological lines. Presidents Sukarno of Indonesia and Nkrumah of Ghana led a militant faction that included revolutionaries from the new African nations. The militant faction took a very strong line against cooperation with industrial nations. The moderates at the conference, including India, Yugoslavia, Egypt, and Ceylon (Sri Lanka) were able to fend off the radical attacks, and the final conference statement read much like the one that came from the earlier Belgrade meeting. The nonaligned nations could agree only on a mild document calling for nuclear disarmament, elimination of foreign military bases, peaceful settlement of disputes, self-determination for all nations, and acceleration of economic development in the less developed world. Thus, the recommendations of the meeting were mainly rhetorical, as the Third World nations spent most of their time attempting to keep their faction-ridden organization together.[8]

In 1970, fifty-four nonaligned nations met in Lusaka, Zambia. This meeting marked a turning point in the focus of the Third World agenda. By this time, most former colonial possessions had been liberated, leaving little reason for vehement outbursts against colonialists. Tensions among the major powers were also on the wane. Indeed, the arms race by this time was much more heated among the less developed countries than among the major powers. The final resolutions of this 1970 conference focused on world political trouble spots, including Vietnam, the Middle East, and the white minority regimes of South Africa, Rhodesia, Mozambique, and Angola. But the resolutions also called for the economic liberation of developing nations from the control of large economic powers. This marked the introduction of economic issues into Third World solidarity negotiations, and they have now become a critical part of North-South disputes.[9] President Kenneth Kaunda of Zambia injected economics into the meeting in his welcoming address when he called upon all nonaligned nations to establish new means for collective political and economic action in a world dominated by big powers. The main goal for the Third World, according to Kaunda, "must be to reduce dependence on those powerful nations who, for their own interest, expect political and ideological support in return for economic, financial and technical assistance."[10] This theme has been echoed, expanded, and refined in many international meetings since 1970 and has become an important aspect of the conflict between the Third World and industrially developed countries.

The focus of Third World solidarity efforts has shifted rapidly since the 1970 meeting. The size of the Third World bloc has grown to over one hundred, and its political influence is no longer questioned. With the exception of the southern tip of Africa, there are few large former colonies that remain to be politically liberated. With the political issues out of the way, the Third World is now focusing its attention on a long list of economic demands.

This growing list of economic demands was first unfolded at a meeting of seventy-seven Third World nations in Algiers in 1973, which was followed by a direct confrontation with industrial countries at the Sixth Special Session of the General Assembly of the United Nations. At the General Assembly meeting, the *Declaration of the Establishment of a New International Economic Order* was promulgated. This declaration demanded a fundamental revision of the existing international economic system. The Twenty-ninth General Assembly of the United Nations adopted the *Charter of Economic Rights and Duties*, which specified a new list of fundamental economic rights from a Third World perspective. The Seventh Special Session of the UN in 1975 dealt with a long agenda of economic cooperation issues that was shaped largely by Third World initiatives. In 1976, these economic confrontations shifted to the fourth meeting of UNCTAD, the United Nations Conference on Trade and Development.

Each of these meetings and confrontations led to further evolution of both Third World demands and solidarity. At the Algiers conference, Third World nations called for improvement in terms of trade to counteract "economic aggression" from the industrial world, full control over their domestic natural resources, including the right to nationalize foreign holdings and determine appropriate compensation, and a Third World development fund created and controlled by Third World countries.[11] These demands were then elaborated and repeated at the 1974 Sixth Special Session of the United Nations General Assembly and the Seventh Special Session, held in 1975.

Several additional economic demands were voiced at the fourth meeting of UNCTAD in 1976. A proposal for indexing prices of seventeen basic commodities to a collection of eighty-nine industrial products and for the creation of buffer stocks to stop price fluctuations in basic commodities was offered by representatives from the Third World. The question of technology transfer was also raised, and representatives from less developed countries demanded easier access to patents and development of "intermediate technologies" more appropriate to their developmental situation. Finally, a request was made for cancellation or rescheduling of the rapidly mounting public and private debt of Third World countries, which totaled nearly $200 billion by the end of 1976.[12]

As Third World solidarity has grown, so has its power. This power has been used to inject a new set of issues into international affairs. These and related issues make up the current ecopolitical agenda. Issues of political liberation have been replaced by those of economic independence. Economic growth issues have been supplemented by questions of wealth distribution. The East-West military conflict has been replaced by North-South ecoconflict. And, most important, ethical questions and issues of human rights have supplanted the narrow definitions of development characteristic of the post–World War II period.

The Third World has come a long way in developing solidarity since initial attempts at unity in Bandung and Belgrade. But the extent to which this unity can be maintained in the future remains an unanswered question. The number of Third World countries grew from a few dozen in the 1950s to the seventy-seven nations that forged demands for a new international economic order in 1974. This group now totals well over 110 and is composed of many different countries facing many different kinds of problems. This fact may eventually threaten the solidarity built up over the past two decades. The political and economic situations in these countries differ dramatically, ranging from oil-rich conservative regimes in the Middle East to poverty-stricken revolutionary regimes in Africa. Many of the early Third World goals, including independence and reduction of tensions among major powers, have been met, and it will be more difficult to maintain cohesion in the future. Furthermore, the vast wealth accumulated by OPEC countries has not been used to strengthen consensus and has not been redistributed rapidly to other less developed countries. Thus, Nye and Keohane have concluded that in the long run "the danger is not that the rich will depend on the poor in the next decade, but that they [the rich] may ignore them."[13]

But it is also possible to underestimate the solidarity of the Third World. The most obvious factor operating to cement it is a common antipathy toward most countries in the industrialized world. Collectively, Third World countries find the current distribution of global income to be inequitable, and they argue for a greater share for themselves. Confrontation with nonsympathetic industrial countries offers visions of an enemy against which these countries can close ranks. Furthermore, a certain degree of institutionalization has occurred among the Third World countries, and common positions now taken are often the result of compromise within the group. Finally, there can be no question but that basic unresolved economic differences with developed countries are a powerful glue holding Third World nations together.[14]

BASIC ECONOMIC ISSUES

The most fundamental international issue that the Third World nations have forced onto the ecopolitical agenda is a proposed dismantling of the old international economic order and establishment of an entirely new international economy. The existing international economic order is perceived by Third World leaders as an inequitable remnant of the colonial era. They point out that the 70 percent of the population living in less developed countries receives only about 30 percent of world income.[15] The cause of this poverty is taken to be an international economic system in which the industrial countries prosper by keeping the prices of raw materials depressed while simultaneously increasing prices for high-technology items. Empirical data do indicate that, with the exception of the brief worldwide commodity boom of 1972–1973, many of the non–oil-exporting less developed countries have seen a significant deterioration in their terms of trade* over the last two decades.[16]

There is no need for industrial countries to engage in conspiracies on the scale of the OPEC cartel to make the present international economic system work in their favor. Technological innovation is the most important factor that perpetuates old patterns of economic domination. In a relatively unmanaged market, natural resources flow toward those countries in which the greatest amount of value can be obtained from them. The technologically developed countries use natural resources to produce a wider variety of more sophisticated products more

---

*Terms of trade is a measure of the average price received for a unit of a nation's exports compared to the average price paid for a unit of imports.

cheaply than can the less developed countries. The less developed countries, then, are locked into an established international economic system that does not benefit them to the degree that it does the industrial countries. But for most of them, the exploitation losses from relationships with highly industrialized countries are less than what they perceive to be the costs of escape from this system and creation of another type of economic system.[17] Among the less developed countries only Tanzania and Sri Lanka have made modest attempts to break free from the present international economic order.

Since industrial countries produce high-technology labor-saving products that are highly valued on international markets, they are able to pay more for natural resources than the less developed countries. This fact has important implications for the less developed countries as the world economy moves into an era of rising natural resource prices resulting from the dynamics of resource depletion. In any potential natural resource market characterized by actual or structural scarcity, a small number of less developed exporters of raw materials would stand to profit handsomely while the other less developed countries would be extremely handicapped by their inability to pay for higher-priced raw materials.

The international flow of raw materials and unfavorable terms of trade for the less developed countries are reinforced by several other factors. Not only do the high-technology and labor-saving products of industrial countries have a natural appeal to elites and masses in less developed countries, but a worldwide advertising blitz creates new demands for them. The products of industrial economies, ranging from aircraft to Coca-Cola, are kept in demand through constant demand creation. The prices for manufactured goods move mostly in one direction—up, mainly because the high costs of production have become institutionalized in the affluent countries. Wages and fringe benefits, for example, are fixed by negotiations between powerful labor unions and giant corporations. Wage cuts during periods of diminished demand for products have been extremely rare. When price cutting by industries in "nouveau riche" countries such as Japan or Taiwan has an impact on industrial economies, "orderly marketing agreements" are used to curb the importation of cheaper products. In 1977, for example, the United States used such arrangements to curb importation of television sets from Japan and shoes from Korea and Taiwan. Furthermore, there is a tendency for economic activity to be concentrated in fewer and fewer hands in the industrial countries as large multinational conglomerates reduce competition through mergers and unofficial price-fixing agreements.[18]

Thus, while the industrial countries have institutionalized high prices for high-technology products, the presently poorly organized, less developed countries compete with each other to sell their raw materials and relatively undifferentiated products at prices determined either by an erratic and manipulated market or by multinational corporations, which often own wells, mines, and forests in these less developed countries. During the global economic recession of 1974–1975, for example, the price of copper dropped to nearly one-third of its 1973 level. This caused an average decline of more than 2.3 percent in the gross national products of Zambia, Zaire, and Chile—countries highly dependent upon revenues from copper exports.[19]

Organized labor plays no significant role in forcing the prices of exports from less developed countries upward because there are alternative sources of supplies for most raw materials, the extraction of these raw materials is energy- rather than labor-intensive, and the supply of labor in relation to demand for it is overwhelming in most less developed countries. The formal rate of unemployment hovers between 20 and 30 percent of the work force in most of these countries, and wages vary between one-fifth and one-tenth of those paid in the United States and Western Europe.[20]

There are other structural reasons why terms of trade continue to favor the industrially developed countries and why the flow of raw materials will continue to move from South to North. But now the important point is that Third World leaders have begun to understand these dynamics of international trade and have presented the industrial world with a new set of rules by which they think that the international economic game should be played. They see the establishment of a new international economic order as the only way of escaping from an international economic system that keeps them perpetually supplying raw materials to the industrial world at prices that keep the less developed countries from accumulating the capital necessary for further industrialization.

These demands for a fundamental revision of the international economic order and the philosophy that sustains it have been expressed in the *Declaration of the Establishment of a New International Economic Order* and accompanying action program put forward at the Sixth Special Session of the General Assembly of the United Nations held in 1974.[21] The declaration resulted from the negotiations among a group of seventy-seven less developed countries that took place in 1973 and 1974.* The less developed countries were able to maintain their solidarity at the special session and, since they control a majority of the General Assembly votes, were able to pass a slightly modified version of their original declaration and action program over the objections of many industrial countries, including the United States.

The draft of the *Declaration of the Establishment of a New International Economic Order* and accompanying action program out-

---

*Although the group originally consisted of seventy-seven countries, its numbers have now grown to more than 110 countries. The term "group of seventy-seven" is still used to refer to the larger number, however.

lined many essential points of economic contention between the industrial and less developed countries. The most fundamental question is control over natural resources. The draft declaration stated that "every country has the right to exercise effective control over its natural resources and their exploitation with means suitable to its own situation, including the right of nationalization or transfer of ownership to its nationals." Furthermore, the document declared that "nationalization is an expression of the sovereign right of every country to safeguard its resources; in this connection, every country has the right to fix the amount of possible compensation and mode of payment, while possible disputes have to be solved in accordance with the domestic laws of every country."[22]

This latter aspect of the draft declaration struck at the core of the interests of the industrial countries. At the special session, leaders of many industrial countries stated that they could accept the concept of permanent sovereignty over natural resources, even though many of them had interests in natural resources in less developed countries either directly or through multinational corporations. But the nationalization provision was found totally unacceptable because compensation for nationalized property was to be set by the nationalizing countries. The industrial countries wanted any such compensation to be set by international tribunals in accordance with international law. The less developed countries claimed that they had played no role in the formulation of existing international law and therefore found it to be inadequate on matters of compensation since it could hardly be considered to be neutral.

As a result of negotiations, the final declaration omitted any reference to the compensation issue. A new phrase was added to replace the compensation statement. It declared that "no state may be subjected to economic, political, or any other type of coercion to prevent the full and free exercise of this inalienable right [of nationalization]."[23] The United States made a formal objection to this wording at the last minute but was ignored.[24]

The draft declaration by the group of seventy-seven also demanded restitution and compensation for the depletion and exploitation of natural and human resources in all states and territories under foreign domination.[25] This point could easily be extended to cover restitution for *past* as well as *contemporary* exploitation. Needless to say, the industrial countries did not yield on this point, and it was removed from the final document at the Sixth Special Session.

The group of less developed countries further demanded a fundamental change in raw materials markets in their draft. The draft suggested that collective self-reliance should be fostered among these countries and that producers' associations and joint marketing arrangements are necessary to stabilize primary commodity markets. It provided for the establishment of a "just and equitable relationship between prices of raw materials, primary commodities, semi-manu-factured and manufactured goods exported by developing countries and the raw materials, primary commodities, food, manufactured and semi-manufactured goods and capital equipment imported by them" through indexation of the prices of raw materials to those of manufactured goods. Finally, the Third World countries demanded expansion of markets for "natural products in relation to synthetics, taking into account the interests of the developing countries, and to utilize fully the *ecological advantages* of these products."[26]

Reshaping the international economic order involves many other points of ecopolitical contention, most of which were included in the draft declaration. A reform of the international monetary system was called for, including "inflation protection" for currency reserves of less developed countries as well as increased credits to meet their balance of payments crisis. A new code of conduct for multinational corporations that would put an end to interference in the internal affairs of countries in which they operate was suggested. Finally, the document called for a special development program for the thirty-six countries that have been affected most harshly by recent changes in global economic conditions.

These latter suggested changes in the structure of international economics ran contrary to the preferences of industrial countries, but they survived in the final UN document. If they were to be implemented, they would result in a remarkably different type of international economy. Of course, one of the reasons that the industrial countries were willing to compromise on the final declaration of principles is that they realized that there is a big gap between declarations of principles and actual changes in economic behavior. While the UN documents and declarations from meetings of less developed countries all call for co-operation between producers and consumers of primary commodities, these Third World countries have had very little success in implementing these principles. Furthermore, the lengthy North-South negotiations in Paris that broke up in 1977 after two years of talks, officially called the Conference on International Economic Cooperation, made little headway in addressing these basic questions.

These economic issues and related points of ecopolitical contention, however, have set the guidelines for a continuing North-South dialogue. The number of ecopolitical issues has grown, and Third World demands are now being made in a wide variety of international forums. These include meetings of UNCTAD, regular and special sessions of the UN General Assembly, UN-sponsored special conferences on critical issues, and bilateral and multilateral negotiations on economic issues. The Sixth Special Session of the General Assembly marked a turning point in terms of *articulation* of a new set of demands from the less developed countries. But it remains to be seen whether articulation of demands will lead to concrete changes in international behavior.

STEMMING CONSUMPTION: BIRTH CONTROL OR WEALTH CONTROL?

Another area of substantive ecopolitical disagreement between industrial and less industrial countries concerns the question of limits to growth, adequacy of the world's resource base to support future industrial growth, control of remaining resources and their utilization, birth control, and limits on per capita consumption. The conventional perspective on development, widely shared in the industrial world, is that a decline in the rate of population growth is essential to future economic growth in most less developed countries. Without population growth curbs, the immediate consumption demands of a rapidly growing population foreclose the possibility of accumulating the capital for industrialization and sustained economic growth. The less developed countries, however, are much more concerned with industrial country per capita consumption of petroleum, natural gas, and nonfuel minerals. They fear that if predictions of future shortages and price increases are valid, they will never have a chance to attain desired levels of development.

Population growth is recognized as an important problem in almost all less developed countries, although there is no general agreement on its socioeconomic impact or on the actions that should be taken to curb it.[27] The political dimensions of the population problem were clearly demonstrated at the United Nations Conference on Population held in Bucharest, Romania, in 1974. Seven countries, Laos, Malta, Malawi, Niger, South Africa, Saudi Arabia, and Tonga refused even to send representatives. The countries that did attend quickly separated into many different factions.

Representatives from industrial countries, quick to point out their own low rates of population growth, stressed the importance of birth control, particularly in less developed countries having such high rates of population growth, as the key to economic development. Representatives from less developed countries and the socialist bloc quickly countered these arguments. The initial challenge by the Third World countries focused on the assumed causal relationship between population limitation and economic development. Many representatives from less developed countries argued that to expect population growth to level off *before* economic development and redistribution of wealth takes place is to put the cart before the horse. Poverty is the *cause* of population growth. When people perceive no improvement in their living standards they will not change their behavior patterns on the promise of future benefits. These speakers argued that the primary way to solve the problem is through a new international economic order and development of Third World economies.[28]

Representatives from less developed countries also pointed out that population growth is only one component of a more general set of problems linking population growth, economic stagnation, depletion of natural resources, and environmental decay. They pointed out that the one-third of the world's population living in industrial countries consumes 60 to 70 percent of the world's annual production of natural resources. These resources, they argued, are increasingly being used to meet nonessential "wants" in the rich countries, while obtaining raw materials to satisfy basic human needs in the poor countries is becoming much more difficult. Furthermore, it is the developed countries that are increasingly polluting the environment with their industrial wastes. In short, spokesmen from many less developed countries claimed that it is not birth control in the less developed world but wealth or consumption control in the industrial countries that should be the first item on any agenda of population-related problems. Although increases in population may be greater in less developed countries, they countered, the per capita growth in consumption, the real core of the resource limitation problems, is greatest in the more developed world.[29]

Conference host Premier Nicolae Ceauşescu of Romania went so far as to argue that more population *growth* was needed in less developed countries as a precondition for economic development. According to his view, which was shared by representatives from several countries, a large and vigorous population is essential to the development of a powerful nation. Ceauşescu, an advocate of population growth in his own country, argued in his address to the conference that the population question is closely linked to the setting up of a new international economic order and that a correct ratio between prices of industrial products and raw materials favoring a more rapid development of the countries lagging behind must be found. He decried the growing consumption gap between the rich and poor countries, as did many other delegates to the conference. While a majority of conference delegates opposed his position, it is nevertheless significant that, out of 110 surveyed developing nations, only about thirty had active population-limitation programs. Another thirty countries had advice and social welfare type programs, while fifty had done nothing at all.[30]

The recommendations for action coming from the meeting also reflected the great division of opinion that exists between the developed and less developed worlds. There was no consensus on the need for birth control. In fact, the action recommendations simply urged those countries whose leaders think that high birthrates are frustrating development to adopt appropriate population policies that "are consistent with basic human rights and national goals and values." It was recognized that some countries might want population growth, and these countries were encouraged to reduce mortality and to "encourage an increase in fertility and . . . immigration."[31] Another long section of the recommendations concentrated on increasing the life-span by decreasing mortality and morbidity. Little was said about how such rapidly expanding populations would be able to feed themselves.

The recommendations did include, however, a statement that per capita use of world resources is much higher in the developed than in the developing countries. As a remedy, the conference suggested that the developed countries "adopt appropriate policies in population, consumption, and investment, bearing in mind the need for fundamental improvement in international equity."[32] The less developed countries, according to this document, should not be saddled with population control policies since their primary national aspirations require growth. But the industrial countries must limit their impact both through decreased births and limits on individual consumption in the interest of international equity.

These arguments can be backed up by some empirical population and consumption data. Suppose that the People's Republic of China, which contains about one-fifth of the world's population, could miraculously be raised to the United States' level of consumption. At present, it is estimated that there are in excess of 800 million Chinese. This is roughly four times the number of Americans. In 1974, the world as a whole consumed 8 billion metric tons of coal equivalent in energy. Of this 8 billion total, the United States consumed 2.4 billion, or about one-third. China, on the other hand, with a much larger population, consumed only .5 billion. Roughly speaking, each American was sustained by 11 tons of coal equivalent in 1974, while each person in China was sustained by only two-thirds of a ton. Another way of putting this is that it cost the ecosphere about seventeen times as much energy to support one American as it took to support one Chinese.

Sustaining China at the United States' level of development would thus require 9 billion metric tons of coal equivalent in additional energy each year, which would increase present world energy consumption by more than 100 percent. Similar quantities of nonfuel minerals would also be needed to support China at the United States' level of development. And these figures do not even consider the problem of the tremendous quantities of metals and minerals that would be required to develop the industrial infrastructure needed to raise China to these high levels of development.

Thus, wealth control demands by the Third World countries have both a factual and rhetorical aspect. They call attention to the hypocrisy of some of the doctrines of economic development, which were formulated when the abundance of natural resources was unquestioned, and to the impossibility of sustaining an industrial world at the United States' level of consumption. From the Third World point of view, a demand for equity and global redistribution of wealth is long overdue. Furthermore, should leaders in the industrial world retort that massive redistribution of wealth would result in international economic chaos, it is not certain that many of the less developed countries would find this to be an objectionable outcome. From their point of view, economic chaos may be preferable to what they perceive to be a highly inequitable international economic system.

Another area of significant and growing disagreement between the industrial and less developed worlds centers on preservation of environmental integrity. Industrial countries have just begun to develop an appreciation of the finite and fragile nature of the natural waste-disposal systems that they have depended upon to digest industrial and human waste. "Waste disposal" is somewhat of a misnomer because it gives the impression that wastes somehow disappear when they are disposed of properly. In most cases, however, waste disposal simply means "dilution" of concentrated wastes.[33] Thus, air is used to dilute gases associated with industrial processes, and rivers and oceans are used to dilute industrial and human wastes.

After centuries of industrial progress, however, the capacity of these natural waste-disposal systems is being severely taxed. For decades, the atmosphere has been used to disperse smoke, rivers to flush away sewage and industrial effluents, and the oceans as garbage dumps. As a result, many waste-disposal areas shared in common by several countries, such as the Rhine River, have become polluted beyond their capacity to absorb effluents. The Rhine is said to be so filled with foreign substances that it occasionally becomes a fire hazard because of the combustible materials floating on the water. Even the oceans are now clogged with pollutants. Recent reports indicate that 50 percent of the area off the East Coast of the United States, 80 percent of the Caribbean, and 90 percent of the area around the Bahama Islands are contaminated with oil and bits of plastic.[34]

In recent years, the deleterious effects of pollution have become increasingly evident, since pollution has apparently been growing exponentially along with industrialization. But industrial countries have been loath to recognize environmental problems, because preserving environmental integrity cuts back somewhat on economic growth. During the heyday of industrial expansion, wastes from industrial processes could be dispersed virtually without economic costs, since there were so many unspoiled waste-disposal areas into which they could be dispersed. Today, however, industry in developed countries is being forced to "internalize" many of these disposal costs, which were formerly treated as "externalities"—activities that were of no economic consequence.

Preservation of environmental integrity is an ecopolitical issue that has been raised most forcefully by the industrialized countries. Serious differences between economically advanced and less developed countries were first highlighted at the United Nations Conference on the Human Environment, held in Stockholm in 1972. Representatives from industrial countries suggested a variety of plans for the preservation of environmental integrity. The more radical of the environmentalists even offered severe growth-limitation schemes. While there was general agreement among representatives of industrial nations that environmental integrity is an important concern, there was disagreement over growth priorities, and no consistent set of programs was offered by them, save for the fact that the rapid growth of the past stressing *quantity* should be replaced by a future emphasis on *quality*.[35]

Representatives from less developed countries were quick to suggest that the emphasis on environmental integrity was misplaced and that for them economic development must have the highest priority. They attacked the hypocrisy of industrial countries, most of which were aided historically in industrialization by the freedom to pollute air, land, and sea. It seemed to them that, now that the industrial world had attained high levels of development, these countries were attempting to foreclose growth possibilities for others. The representatives from less developed countries emphasized that for two-thirds of the world's population the *human* environment is dominated by poverty, malnutrition, illiteracy, and misery, the elimination of which should surely be of higher priority than *physical* environmental purity. Until the gap between rich and poor nations narrows substantially, they stated, little progress can be expected in protection of the global physical environment.[36]

The more radical speakers at the conference attacked the industrial countries for exporting their environmental problems. Multinational corporations were accused of plundering the resources of less developed countries in order to meet their growing needs for raw materials and of shifting polluting activities from industrial countries with rigid environmental standards to less industrial countries with lower standards. The People's Republic of China led the radical attack and was vociferous in condemning both industrial countries in general and the United States specifically. The Chinese delegate received heavy applause for his attack on the developed world in which he claimed that the Chinese were "firmly opposed to the superpowers subjecting other countries to their control and plunder on the pretext of improving the human environment. Victim countries have the right to apply sanctions against and demand compensation from culprit countries."[37]

Thus, differences over environmental priorities parallel the population control–wealth control controversy. The industrial countries are perceived by the Third World to have "found environmental religion" very late in their respective industrial development programs. Now that they have created comfortable standards of living for themselves, the industrial countries want to slow planetary industrialization in order to replenish the spoiled ecosphere. The less developed countries have no quarrel with the goal of environmental integrity per se, but only with the implications of these environmental policies for their own economic development. They don't want the industrial countries to force environmental standards on them that are tougher than those that existed when the developed countries underwent rapid industrialization. Their concern is that slowed growth, antipollution measures, and increased production costs in the industrial world will be passed on to them in the form of higher prices for imports. They also fear that slowed economic growth in industrial countries will cut back the amount of their economic assistance. The less developed countries affix responsibility for the largest amount of prior environmental pollution on the industrial countries and argue, therefore, that both reparations and developmental aid are now owed to them by these industrial nations.

ASIC HUMAN RIGHTS: BREAD OR BALLOTS?

Issues of human rights and fundamental freedoms have been an important part of the Third World struggle for political liberation and are now an important component of ecopolitics. The *Universal Declaration of Human Rights* was adopted by the General Assembly of the United Nations on December 10, 1948. Since that time, more than thirty other declarations concerning human rights have been made by various UN organs.[38]

The *Universal Declaration of Human Rights* and related documents spell out a common understanding of the inalienable rights of all members of the human family. These documents declare that all human beings are equal, that there should be no discrimination based on race, color, sex, or religion, that torture and slavery are immoral, that freedom of assembly should be preserved, that everyone has the right to a standard of living adequate for health and well-being, and so on. These documents previously were used by Third World leaders as justifications for the anticolonial movements leading to statehood. They are presently being used by Third World leaders against the white supremacy regimes in Rhodesia and South Africa and by the United States as an ideological weapon in foreign policy.

Human rights and fundamental human freedoms raise divisive issues in ecopolitics because they are perceived differently by different political leaders. Revolutionary leaders in the former colonial areas of the world have chosen to emphasize those aspects of human rights declarations that support peaceful assembly and political independence. Other leaders emphasize the types of human rights that serve the political purposes of regimes in power. Political leaders in the Soviet Union, for example, emphasize the economic and educational aspects of universal human rights while forgetting about political freedoms. The Carter administration in the United States has chosen to emphasize political freedoms while ignoring many of the economic rights implied in these documents. The thirty-year history of human rights declarations is thus checkered with many subjective interpretations. In this respect, human rights are certainly not universal but represent ammunition used in ideological struggles.

The Third World interpretation of human rights has shifted over time. When the primary task was one of gaining political independence, revolutionary leaders extolled the virtues of self-determination and other political freedoms. Once independence was gained, however, maintaining domestic order became paramount, and in most Third World countries, political rights and individual freedoms have been severely curtailed.[39] This schizophrenia has also been apparent in North-South conflicts. In the early years, the Third World emphasis was almost solely on human rights related to political independence. Subsequently, however, basic human economic needs for food, clothing, and shelter have been stressed by Third World leaders, while political freedoms and different types of economic rights have been stressed by leaders of industrial countries.

Conflicting views over the meaning of human rights declarations have most recently crystallized around the issue of world food supplies. Starvation has been common throughout world history, but starvation, malnutrition, and the right to an adequate food supply have only recently emerged as divisive human rights issues between rich and poor countries. Starvation and malnutrition are most frequently encountered in the less developed world where, because of the lack of purchasing power, necessary imports of food, fertilizers, and pesticides cannot be financed. Excess food consumption in the industrial world combined with malnutrition in the less developed world is becoming an increasingly important source of ecopolitical tension in a world in which total population is pressing closer to global limits on food production.

A number of events culminated in obvious and sharp conflict between industrial countries, chiefly the United States, and the less developed countries at the World Food Conference held in Rome in 1974. The call for a world conference on food problems had originated at the meeting of nonaligned nations in September of 1973. The nonaligned countries were most concerned with trade, hoping to stabilize prices for their agricultural export commodities and to open up new markets. The United States responded with its own call for a food conference two weeks later in the General Assembly of the United Nations. The conference envisioned by the United States, however, was seen as dealing with questions of increasing world agricultural productivity, adequate food reserves, and striking a balance between population and food production in the long term. The United States' proposal totally ignored trade issues.

The final conference agenda included trade issues, problems of increasing food production, and questions of food aid. The latter item became of particular importance to many less developed countries in the face of a 1974 grain shortage estimated by the United Nations Food and Agricultural Organization at between 7 and 11 million tons, most of it occurring in South Asia and the sub-Saharan region of Africa.[40] In his speech to the conference, however, former Secretary of State Henry

Kissinger ignored the matters of immediate food aid and better terms of trade for exporters of basic agricultural commodities. He offered more developmental assistance in the long run and suggested that the oil-rich OPEC countries might do likewise.[41]

A substantial number of Third World delegates took issue with the United States' emphasis on long-term research and development while so many were starving in less developed countries. Representatives from less developed countries reckoned that the 7- to 11-million-ton 1974 shortfall meant that 500 million people would starve before the spring harvest of 1975. The problem of meeting this deficit became one of the most prominent issues of the whole conference, and food-surplus countries were repeatedly entreated to pledge surplus grain for immediate relief. The countries holding surplus grain at the time were the United States, Canada, the European Economic Community, Australia, and Argentina, and they were urged by the conference to earmark these grain reserves for the less developed countries. Further, industrial countries were encouraged to cut back meat consumption and feed cattle less grain so that more could be sent to poor countries.[42]

Although United States' food policy has changed with a new administration, the US emerged from this confrontation as the most intransigent of the industrial countries and needlessly alienated the leaders of many less developed countries. US leaders refused to make any short-term aid commitments to help alleviate the starvation problem, largely on the grounds that such actions would interfere with *normal market mechanisms*. The United States was unwilling to disappoint cash customers who were waiting in line for future grain shipments. Furthermore, the American representatives argued, sending food to less developed countries would create inflationary pressures in the exporting countries as well as drive up prices for other less developed countries. Under heavy pressure from conference delegates, the United States representatives cabled President Ford, requesting an immediate doubling of the United States food aid. He refused the request.

Secretary of Agriculture Earl Butz emerged from the conference as a crusty and straightforward apologist for the conservative United States point of view. Food was seen as a "tool in the kit of American diplomacy." It was to be used to further foreign policy objectives and humanitarian needs were to be only a secondary consideration.[43] (The 1974 United States budget included $1 billion for food aid, but only 20 percent was ticketed for the hungriest nations, while the rest was aimed at particularly important targets of American foreign policy.) Thus, Butz and the Ford administration obviously had learned their lessons from the Organization of Petroleum Exporting Countries. While complaining about the use of petroleum as a weapon in international economics, the United States was treating food in the same way.

Although the United States' position on food aid has mellowed with the removal of food conservatives from power, fundamental differences of opinion persist between rich and poor countries over the vital role of food in the world economy. To the poor countries, food represents the most basic of human rights, and aid and trade in food should be above normal economic and political considerations. To many industrially developed countries, food is a commodity like any other. It is to be sold at the highest price in the world market and used as an instrument of economic warfare when necessary.

In summary, the issue that divides rich and poor countries is the mechanism and the rationale by which the world's supply of food should be apportioned. The industrial countries, led by the United States, prefer to rely heavily upon market mechanisms and work with established patterns of purchasing power. The less developed countries, however, argue that food is the most basic of human rights and should not be handled simply as another commodity. For them, at least rhetorically, available food should be apportioned to meet the nutritional needs of people and not primarily for profit.

THE FUTURE OF ECOCONFLICTS

These three main areas of disagreement between the Third World and industrial countries—birth vs. consumption control, environmental integrity vs. industrial growth, and human rights and food—will persist and be supplemented by new points of contention if current projections of increased demand in the face of natural resource constraints are valid. Within the present world food system, for example, a string of two or three bad harvests in key countries would accentuate the right-to-food debate. Environmental disruptions will undoubtedly worsen as a result of continued efforts to apply more fertilizers and pesticides to increase agricultural production in less developed countries and as a result of continued world industrialization. And control of international common waste disposal areas will become an issue of increasing importance as larger quantities of raw materials are transported (and spilled) in the oceans and as seabed mining becomes practical.

Nor will the economic issues that split the developed and less developed world lessen in intensity. Controversy over fair prices for raw materials and the organization of international raw materials markets could worsen as additional groups of commodity exporters attempt to form new producer cartels. The tighter the world's population, with its growing per capita demands, presses against the world's supply of food, fuel, nonfuel minerals, and natural waste-dispersal systems the more intense the arguments between the "have" and "have-nots" could become.

In the chapters that follow, an attempt is made to analyze the empirical, as well as political, basis for several of these major ecopolitical disputes in greater detail and to suggest what impact they may have on shaping the nascent ecopolitical paradigm. The physical environment clearly sets constraints on the rapid growth that has permitted human beings to ignore these critical problems up to now. Coming to terms with them sets an international political agenda that will occupy center stage in international negotiations for at least the next century.

ENDNOTES

1. Thomas Malthus, *An Essay on the Principle of Population as It Affects the Future Improvement of Society with Remarks on the Speculation of M. Godwin, M. Condorcet and other writers* (published anonymously, 1798).
2. Donella Meadows, et al., *The Limits to Growth* (New York: Universe Books, 1972).
3. See, for example, Herman Kahn, William Brown, and Leon Martel, *The Next 200 Years* (New York: William Morrow, 1976); H. S. D. Cole, et al, eds., *Models of Doom: A Critique of the Limits to Growth* (New York: Universe Books, 1973).
4. Emile Benoit, "The Coming Age of Shortages," *Bulletin of the Atomic Scientists* (January 1976).
5. See, for example, Organization for Economic Cooperation and Development, *World Energy Outlook* (Paris, 1977); Central Intelligence Agency, *International Energy Situation: Outlook to 1985* (Washington, D.C.: April 1977); and Carroll Wilson, *Energy: Global Prospects 1985-2000* (Cambridge, Mass.: MIT Press, 1977).
6. See Meadows, et al., *The Limits to Growth*, pp. 58–59, for estimates of non-fuel mineral availability under differing assumptions.
7. Conference results reported in the *New York Times* (September 6, 1961).
8. Results reported in the *New York Times* (October 11, 1964).
9. Reported in the *New York Times* (September 11, 1970). Also see Karl Sauvant and Hajo Hasenpflug, eds., *The New International Economic Order* (Boulder, Colo.: Westview Press, 1977), part 2.
10. Kaunda's remarks reported in the *New York Times* (September 9, 1970). © 1970/72 by The New York Times Company. Reprinted by permission.
11. Demands reported in the *New York Times* (September 10, 1973).
12. Meeting reported in the *New York Times* (May 17, 1976). The debt estimate is from David Beim, "Rescuing the LDC's," *Foreign Affairs* (July 1977). See also Sauvant and Hasenpflug, *The New International Economic Order*, part 4.
13. Robert Keohane and Joseph Nye, Jr., "World Politics and the International Economic System," in C. Fred Bergsten, ed., *The Future of the International Economic Order: An Agenda for Research* (Lexington, Mass.: D. C. Heath, 1973), p. 156. See also Roger Hansen, "The Political Economy of North-South Relations: How Much Change?" *International Organization* (Autumn 1975).
14. See C. Fred Bergsten, "The Threat from the Third World," *Foreign Policy* (Summer 1973), and Karen Hudes, "Towards a New International Economic Order," *Yale Studies in World Public Order* (1975).

15. David McNichol, *Commodity Agreements and the New International Economic Order* (Pasadena: California Institute of Technology, Social Science Working Paper No. 144, 1976), p. 4.

16. A complete record of these relationships can be found in *The Handbook of International Trade and Development Statistics 1976* (New York: United Nations, 1976), pp. 56–57.

17. For greater detail on this point, see Benjamin Cohen, *The Question of Imperialism* (New York: Basic Books, 1973), pp. 213–216.

18. One of the best examples of this is the international uranium price-fixing agreement that operated in the early 1970s. The nature of conglomerates is a complex issue. The best places to start are Richard Barnet and Ronald Muller, *Global Reach* (New York: Simon & Schuster, 1974), and Richard Barber, *The American Corporation* (New York: E. P. Dutton, 1970) and references cited therein.

19. These figures are taken from *World Bank Atlas 1976* (Washington, D.C.: World Bank, 1977).

20. Barnet and Muller, *Global Reach*, pp. 127–128. See also David Blake, "Trade Unions and the Challenge of the Multinational Corporation," *The Annals of the American Academy of Political and Social Science* (September 1972).

21. See *Official Record of the General Assembly, Sixth Special Session* (New York: United Nations, 1974), Annex.

22. Ibid., p. 18.

23. Ibid.

24. For a general discussion of these debates, see Hudes, "Toward a New International Economic Order," pp. 106–122.

25. *Official Record of the General Assembly, Sixth Special Session*, Annex, p. 18.

26. Ibid., p. 200. Italics added.

27. See Nazli Choucri, *Population Dynamics and International Violence* (Lexington, Mass.: D. C. Heath, 1974), and Michael Teitelbaum, "Population and Development: Is Consensus Possible?" *Foreign Affairs* (July 1974). For a report on the Bucharest meeting, see W. Mauldin, et al., "A Report on Bucharest," *Studies in Family Planning* (December 1974).

28. *Report of the United Nations World Population Conference, 1974* (New York: United Nations, 1975), pp. 68–70.

29. Ibid., p. 70.

30. Reported in the *New York Times* (August 18, 1974).

31. *Report of the United Nations World Population Conference, 1974*, p. 9.

32. Ibid.

33. For more explanation, see Gerald Garvey, *Energy, Ecology, Economy* (New York: W. W. Norton, 1972), chap. 6.

34. Mentioned in "Report to the Congress on Ocean Dumping and Other Man-Induced Changes to Ocean Ecosystems, October 1972–December 1973" (Washington, D.C.: NOAA, March 1974). See also John Colton, Jr., Frederick Knapp, and Bruce Burns, "Plastic Particles in Surface Waters of the Western Atlantic," *Science* (August 9, 1974).

35. See *Report of the United Nations Conference on the Human Environment* (New York: United Nations, 1973).

36. Ibid.

37. Reported in the *New York Times* (June 11, 1972). © 1972 by The New York Times Company. Reprinted by permission.
38. These are found in *Human Rights: A Compilation of International Instruments* (New York: United Nations, 1967).
39. For an assessment of Third World progress, see Rupert Emerson, "The Fate of Human Rights in the Third World," *World Politics* (April 1975).
40. *Report of the World Food Conference* (New York: United Nations, 1975), p. 32.
41. Reported in the *New York Times* (November 6, 1974).
42. *Report of the World Food Conference*, pp. 33–35.
43. Cited in the *New York Times* (November 17, 1974).

SELECTED READINGS

1. Jagdish Bhagwati, ed. *The New International Economic Order*. Cambridge, Mass.: The MIT Press, 1977.
2. C. Fred Bergsten, ed. *The Future of the International Economic Order: An Agenda for Research*. Lexington, Mass.: Lexington Books, D. C. Heath, 1973.
3. Benjamin Cohen. *The Question of Imperialism*. New York: Basic Books, 1973.
4. Branislav Gosovic. *UNCTAD: Conflict and Compromise*. London: A. W. Sijthoff, 1972.
5. Amilcar Herrera, et al. *Catastrophe or New Society: A Latin American World Model*. Ottawa, Canada: International Development Research Center, 1976.
6. Helge Hveem. *The Political Economy of Third World Producer Associations*. Oslo: Universitetsforlaget, 1977.
7. Wassily Leontief, et al. *The Future of the World Economy*. New York: Oxford University Press, 1977.
8. David McNichol. *Commodity Agreements and the New International Economic Order*. Pasadena: California Institute of Technology, Social Science Working Paper No. 144, 1976.
9. Mihajlo Mesarovic and Eduard Pestel. *Mankind at the Turning Point*. New York: E. P. Dutton, 1974.
10. Robert Rothstein. *The Weak in the World of the Strong*. New York: Columbia University Press, 1977.
11. Karl Sauvant and Hajo Hasenpflug, eds. *The New International Economic Order*. Boulder, Col.: Westview Press, 1977.

3

The Politics of Food

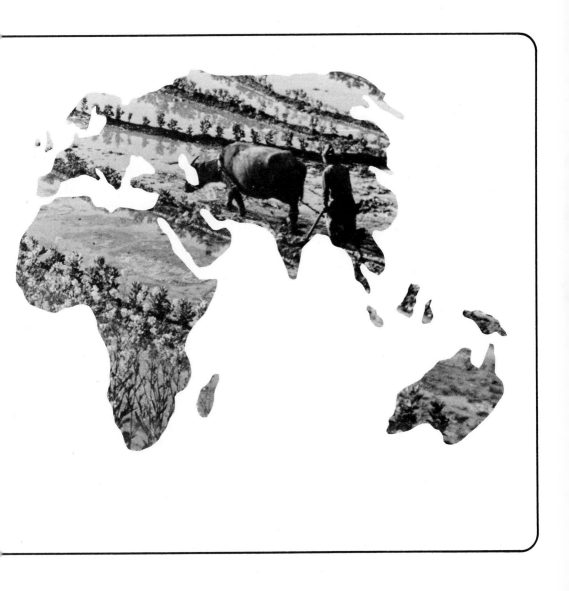

The ability of the world's land to provide food for a rapidly growing population is one of the most important problems in contemporary ecopolitics. Moreover, the food problem now is linked to questions of basic human rights. People in Third World countries are most often afflicted by starvation and malnutrition, and their leaders argue for an adequate food supply as a basic human right. The industrial countries are depicted by Third World leaders as "overconsuming" the world's food just as they "overconsume" energy and nonfuel minerals.

The food problem is also closely linked to the energy problem, since an increasing share of the world's annual agricultural productivity is dependent upon the use of energy-intensive production techniques. Increasing energy prices have led to increased prices for fertilizers, pesticides, farm equipment, and so on. And the food problem is related to more general issues of political economy, including the immense gap between the rich nations and the poor. The rich nations have the purchasing power to dominate the world food market and to engage in conspicuous consumption, while the masses in many poor countries do not have adequate purchasing power to buy food in order to avert starvation. They are caught up in a vicious circle of chronic poverty, poor prospects for economic development, and lack of needed foreign exchange reserves.

The essence of the present world food problem can be found in the interplay of at least three sets of factors: objective need, effective demand, and production possibilities.[1] Objective need for food on a global scale is a function of basic dietary requirements, the size of world population, and its composition. The availability of food for purchase in a world food market has permitted many national populations to grow well beyond the current carrying capacity of their land, thereby increasing global objective need to the point where it has begun to approach production capacity. In some cases, an imbalance between population and food production has been the direct result of the introduction of lifesaving technologies into less developed areas of the world. Death rates have been cut back, birthrates have remained stable, and agricultural production has risen very slowly. In other cases, political and economic decisions have been made to forsake agricultural self–sufficiency in order to put land to more economically lucrative uses.

A growing objective need for calories and protein does not completely explain existing starvation and malnutrition. Objective need must be translated into effective demand in the world food market before it can have any impact on future food production decisions. Farmers make decisions to bring land under cultivation and to buy fertilizers based upon their market expectations. If high prices are expected, it seems worthwhile to the farmers to plant more land, use more fertilizer, or irrigate more acreage. Objective need for food can influence farmers' production decisions only through the marketplace, and the marketplace is organized around purchasing power in the form of dollars, pounds, marks, yen, and other currencies. Objective need becomes effective demand only when hungry people have currency that can be used in the world food market and thereby indirectly influence producers' behavior. It is entirely conceivable that in some future world a large portion of the population could be starving at the same time that idle land remains untilled. If the starving have no purchasing power with which to influence prices and production decisions, their demands go unheard in the market. This situation has been true of the world food market of the recent past to a certain extent. Many Africans and Asians have been starving while idle land could have been put into production in some industrially developed and developing countries.

Finally, the world food problem is also a result of a number of physical and economic limits to growth in agricultural productivity. There is a finite supply of usable land, which appears smaller all the time in relation to world population. Fresh water for drinking and irrigation is limited, and there are many competing uses for it. Prices for nitrogen fertilizers, pesticides, and herbicides move higher with energy prices. Weather patterns influence productivity, and some experts now argue that the world climate is changing gradually to one that is less favorable for global agricultural production. All of these constraints shape future production possibilities.

The interplay of these three factors will continue to govern the emergence of the world food problem as a key issue on ecopolitics. Each of them is discussed in greater detail in the sections that follow.

THE WORLD FOOD MARKET

Formerly, agriculture was not considered an important component of international relations. There have always been some agricultural products crossing national borders, but prior to the global expansion accompanying the Industrial Revolution, the quantities traded were small and limited largely to gastronomic delicacies. Historically, relations among nations have not been determined by trade in food. It has only been recently that food demand in many industrial countries has exceeded domestic production capabilities and that these countries have begun to meet this demand by importing substantial quantities of agricultural commodities.

In preindustrial societies, availability of food from a territory was the most important factor determining the numbers of human beings that could survive there. Factors such as soil fertility, rainfall, available sunlight, and temperature determined the quantity of food that could be produced without the technological aids characteristic of industrial societies. Human populations tended to grow in size until they approached the natural carrying capacity of the land and then stabilize at an equilibrium point slightly below the maximum. This equilibrium was maintained by such natural and social mechanisms as periodic famines, during which the rich usually survived and the poor died, and infanticide.

In the preindustrial world, when harvests fell short of food requirements there was no recourse to an international market, grainery, or relief agencies. Since the world food market was decentralized, famines were frequent but localized affairs. Many of them passed unnoticed to Western historians because they occurred in remote and largely unknown parts of the world, although extremely large famines in more accessible regions have been chronicled by historians. In 1878, Cornelius Walford published a study that listed more than two hundred famines in Great Britain between the time of the birth of Christ and A.D. 1850, as well as a hundred and fifty major famines in other parts of the world.[2] Another study records nearly one famine per year in China for the two-thousand-year period preceding 1911.[3]

In 1798, Thomas Robert Malthus published his famous work, *An Essay on the Principle of Population as It Affects the Future Improvement of Society*. Malthus was familiar with the historical record of population growth and famine and was alarmed by the population explosion that was increasing objective need for food. In his essay, he argued that when population grows unchecked it increases geometrically (exponentially), but that the production of food can at best increase arithmetically. His "Malthusian" future was one in which life always would be short and nasty, as human populations would press against current carrying capacity, unless a rational method could be devised to curb population growth.[4]

Given the information with which he worked, Malthus was not erroneous in making his dire projections. He could not foresee the technological developments that would have a tremendous impact on both population growth and food production. Medical care, antibiotics, pesticides, improved sanitation, and other "death control" measures have increased world population much more rapidly than Malthus would have thought possible. Simultaneously, new technological innovations have increased agricultural productivity at a rate that has approximated the rate of population growth. Technology and the global spread of the Industrial Revolution have changed the nature of world agricultural production and marketing. The world is increasingly united in an integrated global food marketplace, and famines are no longer isolated events without impact on international politics.

But even though new agricultural technologies are available, the actual numbers who are starving or malnourished are probably worse than Malthus foresaw. The magnitude of starvation and malnutrition in the contemporary world has never been adequately surveyed. The two-thirds of the world's population living in the less developed world consume only one-quarter of the world's protein. In India, per capita consumption of grain is around 400 pounds per person per year. This contrasts with 1800 pounds per person in West Germany, France, and the United States. (Part of the reason for such differences is the tremendous emphasis on eating meat in the industrially developed countries. The wealthier a country becomes the greater the emphasis on red meat, and it takes nearly seven pounds of grain to produce one pound of beef.[5]) It has been estimated that almost 900 million people fall at least 250 calories short of an adequate diet each day and that 1.3 billion are chronically undernourished.[6] Of the less developed countries, Africa and Asia are in the worst shape in terms of adequate calories, while Latin America and the Middle East fare best.

The creation of a world food market has exacerbated existing differences among countries in food consumption patterns. Some national populations historically have pressed much closer to their food production capacity than others. The population of the United States, a country with a historically expanding western frontier, never pressed close to capacity because additional agricultural land was freely available. In China, however, population has continuously pressed against food production capacity because there has been no idle land. But the beginning of large-scale trade in food made it possible for the wealthy countries to import food to meet their growing appetites, and often this food has been imported from countries where starvation is common. Poor harvests in the Soviet Union have, on occasion, led to large grain purchases on the international market, thus driving up prices beyond the reach of the poor in many countries.[7] There is no protection for the poor in a free agricultural marketplace, and there are no guarantees that each country will feed its neediest citizens before exporting to others.[8]

Rural starvation and malnutrition in less developed countries often result directly from cultural and economic inequalities. The poor in rural areas don't own enough land to meet their own nutritional needs. They have no capital with which to buy the fertilizers, equipment, and seeds that would increase yields. In many less developed countries, prices paid to farmers for agricultural commodities are carefully controlled in order to provide subsidies for politically powerful urban workers. And finally, in many of these countries much of the land is owned by the wealthy, who grow export crops for the world market.[9] At least fifteen of the poorest less developed countries devote more acreage to export crops than to those for domestic consumption. Thus, wealth determines which crops get planted in most countries. The poor, having little effective purchasing power, farm the areas and eat the foods that market-oriented entrepreneurs find to be marginal or unattractive.[10]

The emergence of a world agricultural market has helped to create additional problems. Combined with a related decline in food self-sufficiency, the global market has significantly changed the scope of world food shortages. A very bad harvest in only two geographical regions, the grain-producing area in the Soviet Union and the rich agricultural land in midwestern United States, could throw the world food market into turmoil. Two or three such bad years in a row could lead to global starvation on an unprecedented scale. Given such unfavorable developments, food-importing countries would vie economically and perhaps militarily for available food. Food imperialism, the rich industrial countries buying or taking food from less developed countries unable to feed their own populations, would not be an unlikely outcome.

Even worse global famines could be triggered by events similar to those that have occurred in the recent past. A volcanic eruption on the scale of the Krakatoa explosion, not an extremely remote possibility, could spew volcanic ash into the atmosphere and reduce sunlight and global temperatures for as long as three years.[11] The effects on world agricultural production could be devastating. Having made no plans for such a contingency, the nations of the world would collectively experience severe famine and associated political and economic dislocations, as food-deficient nations would desperately attempt to meet their needs at any cost.

Thus, food now plays an important part in the emerging ecopolitics, and it is essential to understand the dynamics of world food production, consumption, and trade, including both the physical and socioeconomic dimensions of food problems.

Food: Production and Consumption

Some knowledge of the types of crops that are grown and dietary patterns is essential to understanding world food trade. An adequate human diet is usually defined by the number of calories and the amount of protein consumed. A calorie is formally defined as the amount of heat necessary to raise the temperature of a gram of water one degree centigrade. When speaking of dietary requirements, the term "calorie" usually means "kilocalorie," the amount of heat necessary to raise the temperature of one kilogram of water one degree centigrade. It is estimated that the average person needs between 2223 and 2656 kilocalories of food energy per day to be adequately fed. The lower figure is the estimate for Asia and the Far East, while the higher figure applies to Australia and New Zealand. More specifically, it is estimated that the average North American needs 2642 kilocalories per day, the average Western European 2565, the average African 2335, and the average Latin American 2383.[12] In the industrially developed market economies, people consume an average of more than 500 excess kilocalories per day. In the less developed market economies, the average consumption falls about 75 kilocalories short of meeting minimum requirements. And this shortfall is accentuated by the unequal distribution of kilocalories within countries.[13]

The amount of protein consumed is perhaps more important than the number of calories, since protein is essential for bodily growth and development. It is essential to maintain and repair tissues, and disease and retardation of growth result from protein deficiency. Since foods vary in the quality and usefulness of the protein contained in them, it is difficult to specify the exact minimum daily amount required. If a standard quantity of eggs, for example, is indexed at 100 in terms of net protein usability for human beings, fish then averages 83 on this scale, meat 82, milk 75, vegetables 70, grains 56, and peanuts 48 for similar quantities consumed. Thus, a person eating a diet with emphasis on eggs would require less gross protein intake than a person eating mainly grains. When all of these factors are considered, however, the minimum amount of protein needed by the average citizen of the world is about 57 grams per day.[14] In 1970, protein consumption in the United States and Western Europe was about 95 grams per person per day, while the average in the world's less developed countries was only 58 grams. This means that about one-half of the people in these countries received less than the requisite minimum. In the Far East, average protein consumption was only 51 grams, and in Africa it was 56 grams.[15]

World food production that provides calories and protein can be divided into five categories: cereals, legumes, fruits and vegetables, roots and tubers, and meat and fish. The first four categories of crops result in about 90 percent of the calories consumed and between two-thirds and three-quarters of world protein consumed. The remaining calories and protein are derived from the fifth category, meat and fish (see table 3–1).

About 56 percent of world calorie consumption comes from cereals such as rice, wheat, and corn. About 10 percent of total calories consumed comes from each of the other four categories of foods.[16] While meat, fish, and legumes contain relatively more protein than calories, almost half of the world's protein consumption still comes from cereals. The bulk of world food trade thus takes place in cereals. Rice and wheat are the most important cereals and have been produced in similarly large quantities, although in the 1970s, wheat surpassed rice in quantity produced.

Wheat is the dietary staple for people in temperate climates. It grows well where winters are cool and wet and summers are hot. It does not grow well in the tropics, where plant diseases that attack wheat thrive. For the period 1973–1976, annual world wheat production aver-

TABLE 3-1. *Patterns of Food Consumption in 1970*

	Consumption of Principal Foodstuffs (Kg Per Capita)				
	Cereals for Direct Consumption*	Starchy Roots	Sugar and Sugar Products	Meat	Fish
North America	90.3	55.1	56.0	109.5	10.7
Western Europe	123.6	88.3	39.5	68.0	17.6
Oceania	106.9	58.8	52.8	114.1	6.8
Others	178.5	32.8	30.0	25.6	51.6
Total Developed Countries with Market Economies	122.6	67.4	43.3	74.4	21.3
Africa	138.4	177.4	9.2	12.8	6.9
Latin America	126.9	100.8	43.8	36.8	6.9
Near East	185.7	23.4	19.1	14.9	2.2
Asia and Far East	193.7	25.5	28.5	4.5	7.8
Total Developing Countries with Market Economies	173.3	61.6	27.0	12.1	7.0
Asian Countries with Centrally Planned Economies	206.7	101.7	5.6	18.7	9.2
USSR–Eastern Europe	207.2	120.3	40.9	48.8	18.6
World	173.8	77.2	26.9	29.5	11.5

*Excluding cereals used for animal feed and industrial purposes.

SOURCE: *Unpublished FAO estimates.*

aged just under 353 million metric tons. The USSR is the world's biggest producer of wheat; it averaged 25 percent of world production for the period 1971–1976. The United States produced about 14 percent of total world wheat during the same period. China, India, and Canada each produced between 4 and 9 percent of the world total. These five countries account for almost two-thirds of world wheat production.

Wheat is the most important agricultural commodity in international agricultural trade. Between 1971 and 1976, almost one-fifth of world production was exported across national boundaries (see figure 3–1). World trade in wheat is more highly concentrated than production. The United States is responsible for almost half of the world's exports. Canada and Australia–New Zealand account for more than one-quarter of the remaining exports. In the decade 1960–1970, France and the USSR also normally exported a substantial portion of their wheat. But the Soviet Union has been plagued with erratic weather and was not among the top five exporters in 1964–1966 and again in 1972–1975.[17] It appears that greater domestic consumption and more emphasis on meat produc-

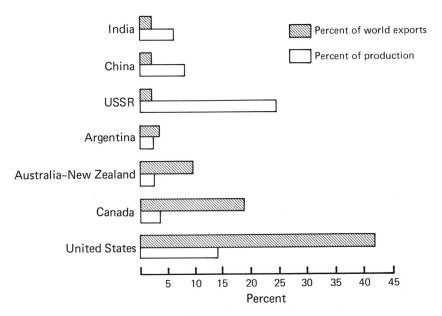

FIGURE 3-1. World Wheat Exporters [SOURCE: United States Department of Agriculture, figures averaged for 1971–1976.]

tion has switched the USSR from the position of net exporter to net importer of wheat.[18]

Rice is perhaps the most important of the cereals, since it is central to the diet of almost half the world's population. Rice production varied considerably in the early 1970s but averaged about 315 million metric tons in the 1972–1974 period.[19] China grows about one-third of annual world production, and India and Pakistan together produce about one-quarter. Usually less than 5 percent of this staple enters into international trade, reflecting both the fact that it is critical to the diet of those in the less developed countries where it is grown and that there is little excess production in those countries.

Figure 3-2 reveals average world rice exports for the period 1972–1974. Slightly over 9 million metric tons were exported annually during this period, which compares with the nearly 70 million metric tons of wheat that were exported. China was responsible for one-third of these exports, followed by the United States and Thailand. Taken together with Pakistan, these countries accounted for nearly three-quarters of all world rice exports.

Corn is the third large cereal crop and the only major one indigenous to the Western Hemisphere. Corn grows well in the midwestern part of the United States, and just under half of world production comes from there. The rest of world production is scattered among a number of smaller producers, including China, Brazil, the USSR, and South Africa. Trade in corn is also highly concentrated, with only three countries ac-

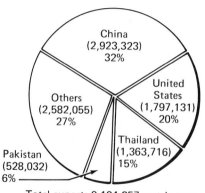

Total exports 9,194,257 metric tons

Gross exports averaged for 1972–1974.

FIGURE 3-2. World Rice Exporters [SOURCE: Food and Agricultural Organization of the United Nations, Trade Yearbook, 1974 (Rome, 1975).]

counting for more than three-quarters of all exports. The United States accounts for 63 percent of the total, Argentina for 10 percent, and South Africa for 6 percent.

These three cereals make up nearly one-half of world total cereal production. The other half is composed of a number of minor grains, including oats, rye, barley, millet, and soybeans. Figure 3-3 indicates that the United States produces nearly one-quarter of the world's total grain and the Soviet Union one-fifth. But world exports of grain are concentrated in only five countries: the United States (47 percent), Canada (12 percent), Argentina (7 percent), and Australia–New Zealand (7 percent).

In summary, both world production and export of cereals, which account for one-half of world food energy and nearly one-half of world protein supply, are highly concentrated. There are two large export crops, wheat and corn. In both cases, the United States dominates the market with 42 percent and 63 percent of total exports, respectively. Rice is not exported in large quantities. Although the climate in the United States is not ideal for growing rice, it is the world's second largest exporter. Canada varies considerably from year to year as an exporter because of the short growing season and unpredictable precipitation. In this respect, Canada is somewhat similar to the Soviet Union in dependence on marginal land. Argentina has only limited possibilities for increasing agricultural production, and political unrest and economic uncertainty combine to reduce that potential. Only the United States and Australia–New Zealand have the potential to increase grain exports. As world demand for food continues to grow, Australia and New Zealand will undoubtedly become a source of expanded agricultural exports.[20]

The residual half of world food production is composed of a wide

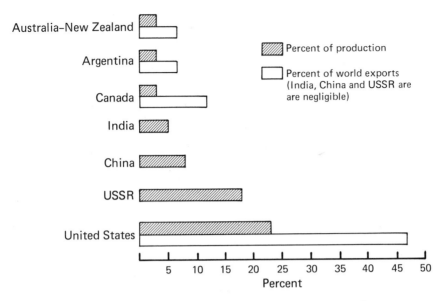

FIGURE 3-3. World Cereal Exporters [SOURCE: United States Department of Agriculture, figures averaged for 1971–1976.]

variety of crops, none of which approaches cereals in signficance. A large quantity of potatoes is grown, but their high water content (75 percent) and great bulk normally restrict international trade. Also, they have a very low protein content and thus are not among commodities that are desired in protein-deficient countries. In 1976, however, a protracted drought in Western Europe led to a large jump in potato trade. The USSR, Poland, and West Germany account for over half of world potato production. Other forms of roots and tubers, including yams, cassava, and sweet potatoes, are important to the diets of people living in poorer countries.

Legumes are another important source of protein. Two of them, soybeans and peanuts, are grown primarily as sources of oil for industrial processes as well as for margarine and similar food products. Processed soybeans are increasingly making their way into human diets as protein supplements. The United States produces most of the world's soybeans and is also the world's largest exporter. The export market is highly concentrated. Between 1957 and 1973, the United States and the People's Republic of China accounted for about 95 percent of all exports. More recently, domination of the soybean market by the US has been challenged by Brazil, which has expanded soybean sales to Japan.[21] The primary importers of soybeans have consistently been Japan and West Germany.

Vegetables, fruits, and sugar are also important to the world's diet. Production of vegetables and fruits is well dispersed, and international trade in these commodities is not significant. Sugar cane is produced in tropical climates and is an important export in many less developed countries. It assumed exaggerated importance in trade in 1973–1975, when crop failures caused a dramatic surge in sugar prices. More recently, however, prices have fallen, and US farmers have demanded higher price supports.

Livestock products and fish are the remaining major world food items. Both are important in providing protein, but they don't make up a significant portion of world food trade. While animals may be turned loose to graze on land that cannot support other crops, intensive livestock production is dependent upon legumes, such as clover and alfalfa, and grains, such as corn. Thus, the world's major producers of livestock also tend to be the world's major producers of cereals and legumes. On a per capita basis, New Zealand produces the most meat, over 800 pounds per year, followed by Denmark, Australia, Ireland, Uruguay, Argentina, and the United States.[22] World trade flow in livestock products is insignificant compared to cereals.

Ghost Acreage

International trade in agriculture is one way that countries can sustain populations beyond their carrying capacity. Fish from the world's oceans represent another method of gathering protein to supplement crops grown on land. Becoming overly dependent on trade partners or fishing, however, is not good political strategy, since competition for crops and fish can be expected to intensify. Industrial nations are now using ever more sophisticated equipment to catch smaller and more elusive fish left in the oceanic commons. Each hard-pressed country attempts to harvest as many fish as possible while commercial fishing is still feasible. Furthermore, in world agricultural trade those countries that are exporters today may have nothing to export tomorrow, as domestic demand or poor weather may make exports unavailable. In 1974, for example, the United States embargoed exports of soybeans when domestic supplies ran low. This embargo became a major irritant in Japanese-American relations. Wheat exports from the United States to the USSR also receive close scrutiny and would be cut off if domestic wheat crops fell far short of domestic demand.

Georg Borgstrom has coined the term "ghost acreage" to describe patterns of dependence on fishing and agricultural trade. This term refers to the amount of land that would have to be brought under cultivation in each importing or fishing country for it to reach a level of net agricultural self-sufficiency. Borgstrom has used imports of protein as his ghost acreage indicator. By adding the protein content of fish caught in international waters to the protein content of net agricultural imports, a "protein deficit" has been figured for each net importer. Borgstrom then has calculated how much land would be required to produce this protein under ideal conditions. The result has been called ghost acreage.[23]

Although Borgstrom undertook these calculations for major agricultural exporters and importers in the mid-1960s, his findings are reinforced by similar data for the mid-1970s. He found the big protein exporters to be the United States, Argentina, Australia, and Canada. The big protein importers, on the other hand, were several Western European countries and Japan. Nearly 16 million hectares of land would have been needed to reach protein self-sufficiency in Great Britain in the mid-1960s, and 10 million hectares would have been needed in West Germany and Japan at that time to reach protein self-sufficiency.*

Borgstrom also found great differences among industrial countries in agricultural self-sufficiency. Canada, Ireland, the United States, and Denmark were the only industrial countries producing more food than they consumed. Norway, the United Kingdom, Belgium, West Germany, and the Netherlands all were producing only between one-third and one-half of their food consumption from domestic agriculture. Japan was producing only 17 percent of domestic requirements.[24]

More recent data, although lacking the complexity of Borgstrom's analysis, indicate that a similar situation exists in the late 1970s. Although not a perfect measure of the protein or calorie content of international food trade, the dollar value of agricultural exports and imports gives a good estimate of the flow of world food. Table 3–2 indicates the extent to which countries depend upon trade to augment their domestic agricultural production. In quantity terms, these listed countries are the "superimporters" of agricultural commodities and correspond to Borgstrom's protein-deficient countries of the 1960s. Japan, West Germany, and Great Britain import several billion dollars' worth of agricultural commodities annually. These three nations are joined by Libya, Belgium, and Norway as the largest agricultural importers on a per capita basis. In 1973, Japan imported $79 worth of agricultural commodities for each of 110 million Japanese citizens, West Germany, $133 worth for 60 million citizens, and Great Britain, $114 worth for 55 million citizens. While other countries show very high per capita imports, their populations and their overall impact on the world food market are much smaller.

Countries such as India, Bangladesh, and, more recently, the USSR commonly are considered to have populations far exceeding agricultural production possibilities. Yet none of these countries is listed as a major importer of agricultural commodities. In each, it is yearly harvest fluctuations that determine import patterns. In 1975, for example, Bangladesh experienced a bumper harvest that was so large as to exceed storage capacity. In 1973, India was a net exporter of agricultural commodities. In 1976, the Soviet Union experienced an excellent harvest

---

*A hectare is equal to 2.47 acres.

TABLE 3-2. *Major Food-Deficient Nations**

| | Net Agricultural Imports (Thousands of Dollars) | | Net Imports Per Capita (Dollars) | |
	1973	1974	1973	1974
Libya	314,435	325,720	146	138.8
West Germany	8,253,120	8,080,250	133	130.2
Great Britain	6,378,413	7,561,650	114	135.1
Norway	366,553	464,270	93	116.5
Belgium	807,614	1,008,485	83	103.2
Japan	8,577,047	10,543,110	79	96.1
Austria	531,762	528,690	71	70.1
Finland	207,158	295,730	44	63.1
Lebanon	128,383	179,600	43	64.5
Portugal	380,892	692,390	42	79.3
Chile	413,768	608,170	41	60.4
Israel	125,970	251,380	39	76.2
Trinidad-Tobago	40,097	49,630	38	—
Jordan	80,176	103,110	32	39.4

*Data for 1973; excludes nations with less than 1 million population.

SOURCES: *Food and Agricultural Organization of the United Nations,* Trade Yearbook 1974 *and* Trade Yearbook 1975 *(Rome, 1975, 1976).* United Nations, Statistical Yearbook 1975 *(New York: 1976).*

and imported only a small quantity of grain.

In addition to agriculture, another source of protein is fish. The oceans are a gigantic common area to which many nations have turned to supplement their diets. Unfortunately, intense competition for fish, increasing oceanic pollution, and the new 200-mile territorial limit are making fishing a less viable option for food-deficit nations. World fish catch reached a high point of 70 million metric tons in 1970 and 1971 but dropped back to between 65 and 66 million metric tons in 1972 and 1973.[25] This figure has not increased much since then, giving cause for alarm in the major fishing nations. This decline has been attributed to a number of factors, including heavy pollution of offshore areas where most fish live and spawn, the use of more sophisticated equipment and finer mesh nets to take younger fish, and an unexplained decrease in the Peruvian anchovy fishery, which is a significant portion of the world fish catch.[26]

Table 3-3 lists the world's most important fishing nations in both quantity terms and on a per capita basis. Japan is responsible for one-sixth of the world's fish catch, which is used to augment its very small domestic production of protein. The average Japanese consumes one-tenth of a metric ton of fish each year. The USSR and China follow closely behind Japan. In both cases, the fish catch is significant largely because of total population size, although three times more fish are caught on a per capita basis in the USSR than in China. Norway and

TABLE 3–3.   *Major Fishing Nations*

	Quantity (1000 tons)		Metric Tons Per Capita	
	1973	1974	1973	1974
Japan	10,702	10,773	.10	.10
USSR	8,619	9,236	.03	.04
China	7,574	6,880	.01	.01
Norway	2,975	2,645	.75	.66
United States	2,670	2,744	.01	.01
Peru	2,299	4,150	.15	.27
India	1,958	2,253	.00	.00
Thailand	1,692	1,626	.04	.04
South Korea	1,655	2,001	.05	.06
Spain	1,570	1,511	.04	.04
Denmark	1,465	1,835	.29	.36
South Africa	1,332	1,415	.06	.06
Indonesia	1,300	1,342	.01	.01
Philippines	1,249	1,291	.03	.03
Canada	1,152	1,027	.05	.05
Great Britain	1,144	1,086	.02	.02

SOURCE: *Food and Agricultural Organization of the United Nations.* Yearbook of Fishery Statistics 1975 *(Rome, 1976).*

Denmark are the most dependent upon protein from the sea on a per capita basis. The average Norwegian is supported by a catch of nearly three-quarters of a ton of fish, most of which is consumed domestically. The statistical Dane is supported by nearly one-third of a ton of fish annually, which helps explain the "cod war" that took place between Denmark and Great Britain in 1975–1976 over fishing rights in the North Sea.[27]

The large per capita dependence upon fish in many protein-deficient countries underscores the seriousness of negotiations over territorial limits and the seabed. While population continues to grow rapidly in many of these countries, world fish catch can be expected to increase only very slowly, if at all. Thus, management of the oceans has become one of the most pressing contemporary ecopolitical issues. The 200-mile territorial fishing limit is now the accepted international norm, and fishing within these boundaries is closely regulated by the relevant countries. Control of this additional territory can become politically important. One example: Angola promised to give Cuba preferred fishing rights in its 200-mile offshore zone in 1976 as a reward for helping in the Angolan struggle for independence. The rising price of fish in countries such as Norway, the USSR, and Japan, which have traditionally fished in open waters around the world, also could have serious domestic political and economic implications.[28]

The characteristics of world food production, consumption, and trade can be concisely summarized because the patterns are so clear-cut. Grains are by far the world's most important source of protein and calories. Rice is produced and consumed mainly in tropical countries with dense populations, and relatively little enters international trade. World exports of other grains are centered in only a very few countries, the United States, Canada, Argentina, and Australia–New Zealand. The flow of food is basically from these countries, as well as from some less developed countries that produce specialty products, to a few protein- and calorie-deficient industrial nations, mainly West Germany, Great Britain, and Japan, and sporadically to food-deficient less developed countries, such as Bangladesh and India. The former have the effective demand (purchasing power) to import large quantities of agricultural commodities, while the latter live at much lower levels of consumption and depend on food aid. A few nations, such as Japan, supplement their diet with considerable fishing, but with the world fish catch declining and territorial limits expanding, this is not a viable option for added food production in the future.

It has been suggested that food could be used as a weapon in the future to counter OPEC or other cartels.[29] The preceding data suggest that attempting to use food in such a way would be a major mistake. Just as in the case of petroleum, those countries that are most susceptible to a food embargo are industrial countries, particularly Japan, West Germany, and Great Britain. The USSR enters the food market on an irregular basis, largely to supplement periodic poor harvests. It is debatable whether an embargo on food shipments to the USSR would be more damaging to the Russians or to American farmers, who would suffer economically. The members of OPEC are not among the world's major food importers. Even on a per capita basis, their net imports amount to only a few dollars per person. This amount of food could easily be transshipped to them by sympathetic countries with only a minimum of economic dislocation in OPEC countries. The other potential victims of a food embargo are the world's poor and undernourished countries. Any direct attempt to use a food embargo to gain political leverage in these countries would be roundly condemned on humanitarian grounds.

FOOD PRODUCTION: ULTIMATE CONSTRAINTS

The crux of the *present* world food problem is an international food market in which potential buyers, many of whom are living close to starvation, have no purchasing power with which to influence the behavior of sellers. It is a problem in political economy having close links to the global distribution of wealth and opportunities.[30] But in the near future, the growing world population will run up against real constraints on the amount of food that can be grown at acceptable prices.

There are three sets of factors that represent *ultimate* constraints on growth in agricultural productivity. The first set of growth-limiting factors is the amount of available land and water. There is only a relatively small unused quantity of both available at anything resembling present prices. Opening new land is an expensive and often risky proposition. Water is usually needed for irrigation when marginal land is brought into production. Additional fresh water for irrigation is scarce, and desalinization is expensive. Furthermore, in many industrializing countries, industry is competing for the same water that is needed to grow more food.

The second set of limiting factors is technological in nature. Most recent increases in agricultural productivity, especially in industrial countries, have taken place with the aid of technologies dependent upon an adequate supply of fossil fuels. Energy-intensive fertilizers, pesticides, and herbicides have been largely responsible for per acre increases in yields. But increasing world energy prices and the law of diminishing returns in fertilizer application make continued increases in per acre yields doubtful in many countries.

Finally, there is a set of climatological constraints that can affect the whole world food production system. Temperature and rainfall patterns change over time and can cause dramatic shifts in regional and even global food production. Some respected climatologists and geologists argue that the human race has just passed through one of the most propitious periods for world food production in recent history. One of the implications of their argument is that climatological conditions will fluctuate much more violently in the future and adversely affect world food production.

The recent record of the race between food production and population growth indicates that preventing future starvation will not be a simple matter. In many areas of the less developed world, there is now more starvation than there was one decade ago. Although world food production increased 31 percent over the decade ending in 1974, on a per capita basis the increase was only 7 percent, less than 1 percent per year.[31] But most important, the global increase in per capita production was not evenly distributed. The industrial countries increased per capita food production by 14 percent. The less developed countries, by contrast, were faced with a per capita food production *decrease* of 2 percent during the decade. In Africa, per capita production declined by 6 percent during this period, and production in the Far East declined by 4 percent.[32] Large increases in population combined with relatively stagnant agriculture and investment in Latin America and Africa produced some dramatic results for individual countries. In 1974, Chile, Colombia, Ecuador, Paraguay, Peru, and Uruguay were all producing food at much less than the per capita level of a decade earlier. In Africa, the figures are much more startling. Mali was producing at 72 percent, Niger at 70 percent, Senegal at 75 percent, the Congo at 81 percent, and Chad at 58 percent of the per capita figure of a decade earlier.[33]

Thus, even during the recent period of favorable economic and climatological conditions, per capita food production declined in many countries. As the constraints on world food production become more obvious, starvation and malnutrition will become even more common and much more pressing as ecopolitical issues.

The Basics: Land and Water

Arable land is the most obvious factor limiting increases in food production. There has been repeated concern about running out of room to grow additional crops since 1798, when Malthus called attention to the seemingly limited supply of land in relation to growing populations. With the passage of the years, our ability to assess potential for additional agricultural production has grown. The earth is now photographed from orbiting satellites, and there is much less mystery about the quantity and quality of unfarmed land. Furthermore, judgments about technological developments and time horizons required for increased yields are much more sophisticated than they were when Malthus made his dire projections.

Most studies of land availability come to the seemingly optimistic conclusion that only about one-half of the world's potentially arable land is now being cultivated. In 1967, the President's Scientific Advisory Committee estimated the amount of potentially arable land in the world to be 7.86 billion acres.[34] A more detailed study of world land availability carried out by agronomists and economists at Iowa State University estimated that 7.8 billion acres of land are available for growing crops or raising livestock. Of these 7.8 billion acres, only 3.4 billion are now being farmed.[35]

More recently, using liberal definitions of arable land, the Organization for Economic Cooperation and Development (OECD) made an estimate of potentially arable land by continent and also projected the amount of land to be under cultivation by 1985. The report concluded that only one-quarter of the potentially arable land is being farmed in Latin America, slightly more than one-third is being farmed in Africa, two-thirds is being farmed in Asia, three-quarters is being farmed in the Soviet Union, and about one-half is being farmed in the United States. All of the arable land in Western Europe is considered to be under the plow, and more than nine-tenths of such land is being cultivated in Eastern Europe. Significantly, the amount of land actually being farmed was projected to decline in the United States, Eastern Europe, and Western Europe by 1985 because of urbanization.[36] The Food and Agricultural Organization of the United Nations undertook an exhaustive study of land reserves in less developed countries in the mid-1960s. On the average, 26 percent of the land in those countries was found to be suitable for cultivation. Of this, 45 percent was actually being farmed. The portion of this suitable land being farmed varied from 100 percent in northwest Africa and 84 percent in Asia to only 23 percent in Latin America.[37]

Table 3–4 summarizes land availability by continent. There are clearly great differences in future production potential. In Europe, almost all the land that can be farmed is being farmed, and there is less than one acre of arable land per person. A similar situation exists in Asia. In Latin America and in Australia, by contrast, only 11 percent of the potentially arable land is now being used. Very low population density in Australia means that there are 22 acres of land for each person, a stark contrast to the situation in Western Europe.

It is important to keep in mind that studies of land availability tend to overestimate the amount of useful land by underestimating the difficulties involved in bringing it under cultivation. Much of the land that is not being farmed now is marginal land on which farming is not economically viable. Further, more than half of the world's potentially arable land lies in tropical areas. Brazil, for example, is now attempting to create new agricultural areas in the Amazon basin, but much of the poor-quality soil will support only existing plant cover and not agricultural crops. There are great difficulties in transferring agricultural techniques developed in more temperate areas to the tropics. Destruction of the tropical rain forest in the interest of agricultural development is also frequently undesirable from an ecological point of view.[38]

In most countries, the land that is now being farmed is the best portion as determined by farmers' historical experience. Population

TABLE 3–4. *Available Land by Continent* (Billions of Acres)*

	1975 Population**	Total Area	Potentially Arable	Cultivated	Cultivated Acres per Person	Ratio of Cultivated to Potentially Arable
Africa	401	7.46	1.81	.39	4.5	.22
Asia	2255	6.76	1.55	1.28	.7	.83
Australia– New Zealand	17	2.03	.38	.04	22.4	.11
Europe	473	1.18	.43	.38	.9	.88
North America†	296	5.21	1.15	.59	3.9	.51
South America	265	4.33	1.68	.19	6.3	.11
USSR	255	5.52	.88	.56	3.5	.64
	3962	32.49	7.88	3.43	2.0	.44

*Estimates are for the mid–1960s.
**In millions
†Includes Mexico.

SOURCES: *Population Reference Bureau,* World Population Data Sheet 1975 *(Washington, D.C., 1975)* and *President's Scientific Advisory Committee,* The World Food Problem, *(Washington, D.C., 1967), II, 434.*

pressures have led to the use of all the land that can be farmed economically at farm prices close to those offered at present. Dramatic increases in food prices would undoubtedly increase the amount of land under cultivation, but the overall additions would not be great. Marginal land is costly to bring into production and to maintain. In the 1960s, the cost of opening new land in unsettled areas ranged between $85 and $2100 dollars per acre, with the average being around $450.[39] The United Nations figure given for opening land to meet production targets in the less developed countries is about $4 billion annually in 1973 dollars.[40]

There are many other reasons why much of this potentially arable land will never be brought into production. Most marginal land is found in areas where erratic rainfall patterns or temperature variations make farming a risky proposition. Two or three years of good harvests may be followed by a protracted drought, bankrupting the farmers who settle there. In large stretches of Africa, the tsetse fly would devastate human beings attempting to farm the land.[41] In addition, much of this marginal land is mainly suitable for grazing, having a much lower potential productivity than land that is currently being cultivated. To bring this land up to present standards would require heavy inputs of fertilizer, which is also expensive. Finally, a great deal of marginal land is geographically remote from markets and population centers. Developing transportation networks to move produce from these remote areas to markets would require a heavy capital investment, which is well beyond the reach of many less developed countries.

There are also political risks inherent in relying heavily on marginal land. Greater dependence on crops from marginal land increases the risk of periodic shortages or even famines. The leadership of the Communist party of the Soviet Union has seen this happen repeatedly since Nikita Khrushchev opened up the "virgin lands" in western Siberia in the 1950s. While this action increased gross Soviet food production over time, it also introduced serious fluctuations in production and upset agricultural planning. In good years there has been an abundance of grain. But in less propitious years, lack of rainfall has dramatically affected crops in the marginal lands, leading the Soviet Union to supplement domestic production by sporadic international purchases. These, in turn, have introduced uncertainty into the international market. In 1973, for example, the Soviet Union purchased 28 million tons of grain from abroad, which is more than any other country imported.[42] The domestic and international economic and political consequences of these boom and bust cycles can be serious. Khrushchev was ousted from his party and governmental positions in 1964 because of his alleged bungling of agricultural policy. In 1976, Dimitri Polyansky was removed from the Politburo for similar agricultural mismanagement.

Because of the expense of bringing new land under cultivation, the lack of economic incentives to do so, possibilities for increasing yields on acreage already being farmed, and the loss of arable land to urbanization, the total amount of land under cultivation worldwide has been expanding only very slowly. The area planted in grain increased by only .3 percent annually from 1960 to 1971.[43] At this rate, the amount of land under cultivation would double in 230 years. Since world population is doubling approximately every thirty-six years, either a tremendous investment in opening new land or a similar investment in increasing yields on land already in production will be required to meet world food needs.

A recent estimate of future availability of arable land based upon accepted worldwide land reserve figures comes to pessimistic conclusions. Taking the present world average of one acre of cultivated land per person as a point of departure, an MIT research group projected future land requirements necessary to feed the world's increasing population. They came to the conclusion that all of the world's available land would be utilized shortly after the year 2000 if present per acre yields are maintained. If present per acre productivity is doubled, additional farmland becomes scarce around the year 2025.[44]

Water places additional limitations on the amount of land that can be put into production. Rainfall is scarce in most of the presently untilled regions of the world, and irrigation potential is limited. In Egypt, for example, 100 percent of all farmland is under irrigation, and in China, Pakistan, Taiwan, and Japan, more than half of all cropland is now being irrigated.[45] An adequate water supply is essential to the success of the miracle grains associated with the green revolution, the much-praised panacea for solving food problems through technology. But irrigation is expensive, and fresh water is in increasingly scarce supply. Particularly in industrial countries, there is intense competition between agriculture and industry for potential irrigation water. And industry usually wins because of its ability to pay higher prices for the water.

The crux of the water problem is that dependable streamflow in many parts of the world is not great enough to meet the projected needs of those dependent on the streams. In the United States at present, more than one-third of all streamflow is withdrawn and used at least once. It is estimated that by 2000, all US streamflow will be used at least one time on its way to the oceans. Water that is withdrawn is not necessarily completely consumed, although it is usually returned to streams in polluted condition. In commercial and residential use, about 90 percent of used water is eventually returned to streams. When used for irrigation, however, only 40 percent of water withdrawn makes its way back into streams. On the average, about one-third of all water withdrawn is actually consumed.[46] Energy is needed to purify polluted water, and, as a greater portion of streamflow is used, there are greater constraints on the availability of pure water for agriculture.

Protracted droughts in the United States and Western Europe upset food production and established living patterns in the late 1970s. In Western Europe, the summer of 1976 brought severe drought, which increased food prices dramatically. In 1977, a similar drought in the western part of the United States led to water rationing. In most parts of the industrial world, the needs of affluent populations and growing industries are putting great pressure on available water, and future abnormal rainfall patterns could lead to local disasters.

Irrigation water is the source of potential conflict among countries. For example, Colorado River water has been a source of countroversy in American-Mexican relations. Farmers in the United States have been withdrawing increasing amounts of Colorado River water to irrigate their crops, leaving only saline water for irrigation in Mexico. Likewise, many European rivers flow through several countries, and treatment of the water by upstream countries determines possible uses for it downstream.

Much of the world's irrigated agricultural land is supplied by wells. Well water is similar to petroleum. It is not available in infinite quantities. Continued pumping of wells lowers the subsurface water table much faster than natural processes replenish it. In India, tube wells used for irrigation often have a very short useful life, as underground water resources quickly dry up. This necessitates the drilling of many more new wells just to keep even.[47]

The global thirst for more water has led to many schemes for acquiring new supplies. One of the most farfetched is a proposal, originally authored by John Isaacs, to capture icebergs in the Antarctic and tow them to California. The oil-rich Arab countries have seized upon this idea, and they have held major conferences to discuss the feasibility of such a project. Although three-fourths of the world's fresh water is locked in polar ice caps and glaciers at present, the costs, energy requirements, and technical difficulties of transporting this water would be tremendous. Furthermore, the impact of transported icebergs on the worsening world food problem would be minimal, and political disputes over control of drifting icebergs could be expected.

Technology and Food

Land has not been the most important factor in recent expansion of world food production. Instead, added output per acre of land already under cultivation has accounted for most of the increase. On a worldwide basis, for example, the output of grain per hectare of land increased from 13.9 quintals* in 1960–1961 to 19.4 quintals in 1973–1974, an increase of 40 percent in yield.[48] At the same time, the amount of land from which grain was harvested increased by only 6 percent. In the

---

*A quintal is 100 kilograms.

United States, there has been a much greater increase in yield. In 1950, for example, the average corn yield was 38 bushels per acre. Over the next twenty years, the yield increased to 81 bushels per acre.[49]

Increased yield per unit of land under cultivation has resulted from the application of new technologies to agricultural production. Biological research has yielded more productive strains of crops that can make optimal use of fertilizers. Large-scale use of fertilizer and irrigation has, at least in the short run, improved the productivity of the soil. Pesticides have cut down considerably on insect damage. Finally, machinery has replaced human labor in many processes. In the United States at present, only a little over 4 percent of the population lives on farms, and it produces more food than is necessary to feed the entire population.

The introduction of the industrial revolution into agriculture around the world has been very uneven. The highly industrialized countries, understandably, have been first to mechanize and energize agriculture, and the less developed world has trailed far behind. At present, agriculture in the United States and Western Europe is equipment-, pesticide-, and fertilizer-intensive. In Western Europe, for example, 182 kilograms of fertilizer are used per hectare of arable land, while 66 kilograms per hectare are used in the United States. In Africa, by contrast, only 9 kilograms of fertilizer are used per arable hectare. There are even greater differences among individual countries. In the Netherlands, 709 kilograms of fertilizer are used per hectare, which partially explains how such a densely populated country can be a net exporter of agricultural products, while more than one dozen less developed countries apply less than 1 kilogram of fertilizer per hectare.[50] Thus, the industrially developed countries not only have an edge in using fossil fuel–based technology in industry but they also have a competitive edge in applying fossil fuels to agricultural productivity through fertilizers, pesticides, and mechanical equipment.

World agricultural production has increased by virtue of better yields, and thus food production has become less related to current solar income and more dependent upon fossil fuels. As the natural carrying capacity of land has been technologically increased, the risks associated with relying upon cheap fossil fuel energy in agriculture are becoming apparent. The global energy crisis is also a food crisis. Rising fuel prices increase the prices of energy-intensive fertilizers, pesticides, and irrigation. Particularly in less developed countries, these increases can lead to decreased yields per acre, as poor farmers cut back on application of high-priced nitrogen fertilizers.

Data on the changing energy requirements of global agriculture are impossible to obtain because of tremendous difficulties in collecting and aggregating so many figures. Studies of the energy requirements of United States agriculture, which is typical for industrial countries, can serve as surrogates, however, and the results of such studies highlight some of the problems of mechanized agriculture. One relevant study has examined the changing fossil fuel component of corn production since 1945.[51] Between 1945 and 1970, the labor component of corn production was cut in half, while energy use by machines nearly doubled. Use of nitrogen fertilizers increased from 7 pounds per acre in 1945 to 112 pounds per acre in 1970. No insecticides or herbicides were used in 1945, but 1 pound of each was used on an average acre of corn in 1970. In addition, much more energy was needed for electricity, drying crops, and transportation in 1970 than was needed in 1945.

The energy content of these inputs into American corn production has been converted into standard figures, and the results are shown in figure 3–4. The total fossil fuel energy required per acre of corn was 935,514 kilocalories in 1945 and grew to 2,879,986 kilocalories in 1970. Fuel accounted for 58 percent of the energy input into corn production in 1945 but only 28 percent in 1970 because of the much more rapid increase in other inputs. The fossil fuel energy represented by nitrogen fertilizer, for example, increased from only 6 percent of the total input in 1945 to 31 percent in 1970. When total fossil fuel input is compared with total per acre yield of corn, the results are quite informative. Yield per acre doubled during the twenty-five-year period, while energy input tripled. In 1945, 3.26 kilocalories of food energy were produced by each kilocalorie of fossil fuel energy. By 1970, this figure had dropped to 2.52 kilocalories of food energy for each kilocalorie of fossil fuel energy required by American agriculture.

These figures hold several very serious implications for the future of world food production. The first is that food prices can be expected to increase in tandem with rising energy costs. Farmers will pro-

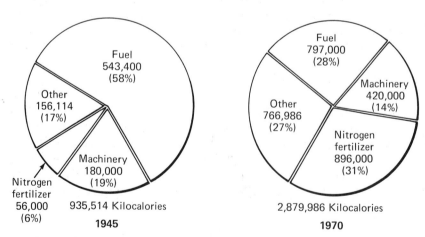

FIGURE 3–4. *Fossil Fuel Energy in Corn Production. Data are in kilocalories per acre of a typical US farm.* [SOURCE: After David Pimental, et al., "Food Production and the Energy Crisis," *Science* (April 19, 1974).]

duce additional crops only when it is profitable to do so. With the prices of all energy-intensive inputs rising, there are two alternatives for farmers: increase food prices or take marginal land out of production, thereby cutting back on production costs. Either way, the world's malnourished will continue to suffer.

The second set of implications of these figures concerns agricultural limits to growth. If the world's 4 billion people are to be fed in the future by agriculture patterned after that developed in Western Europe and the United States, the world's energy shortage will be compounded. It is estimated that for every American 336 gallons of gasoline per year is used just for food production, transportation, and processing. Assuming that petroleum would be the energy source for world agriculture, using 336 gallons of gasoline per person for agricultural purposes would use up known world petroleum reserves in only twelve years—just to meet these agricultural needs.[52] The green revolution represents the export of high-energy American agriculture to the less developed world. To the extent that it is successfully exported, the world energy dilemma will be increased by added energy requirements.

Finally, these figures also indicate that fertilizer application is subject to the law of diminishing returns. Maximum yield of corn, for example, occurs when about 200 pounds of nitrogen are applied per acre.[53] Yield per acre actually stops increasing if more nitrogen is applied. The same is true of other energy inputs. Given the declining ratio between food return and fossil fuel input shown in figure 3-4, it is clear that solar income is now playing a much less important role in food production. It is not impossible that, under some conditions, more net fossil fuel energy would go into the production of crops than would be returned in the form of food energy.

Steinhart and Steinhart have argued that this is already the case for the United States food production system viewed in its entirety.[54] Their definition of the food production system includes not only those things that are directly related to crop production, such as fuel, fertilizer, and irrigation, but also the energy cost of food processing, transportation, and cooking (such as the energy used by the food processing industry, the energy represented by packaging materials, the energy used in various stages of transportation, and the energy used in refrigeration and cooling). They have found that the present United States food production system now requires between 8 and 9 kilocalories of fossil fuel energy per kilocalorie of food put on the dinner table. This requirement leads to both energy-expensive and economically expensive food. The average annual per capita food expenditure in the United States is now much more than $600. It is obvious that the American food production and distribution system cannot be successfully exported to less developed countries, where per capita gross national product is often much less than $600.[55]

In summary, technological developments in food production have led to increased intensity of fossil fuel energy use in farming. Higher prices for energy now cause higher prices for food. There are economic limits to the kilocalories of fossil fuel that can be put into food production in most countries. Furthermore, the green revolution, which is heralded as the answer to world food shortages, represents the exportation of energy-intensive agriculture to less developed countries that cannot afford it. Beyond these economic limits, however, there are important natural limits to technology-intensive agriculture. Dwindling petroleum supplies set limits on the amount of fossil fuel that can eventually be used by global agriculture. In the United States, cost-benefit analyses of the total food production and distribution system lead to questions about the efficacy of using more kilocalories of increasingly scarce fossil fuels to produce only marginally more food kilocalories. At this point, the distributional aspects of the world food problem intersect with technical and natural constraints. If there were enough purchasing power in the hands of farmers in the poor countries, they could make better use of some of the fertilizer now being used in the industrial countries, where the small increments in production make additional fertilizer application relatively unprofitable. And this takes place while the world fertilizer industry operates at much less than capacity because the world's poor cannot buy the expensive fertilizer that could greatly increase their crop production and reduce world hunger.

Changing Climates

The factors previously discussed that shape the global hunger problem are to a certain extent under human control. The causes and consequences of population growth are well understood. Most of the world's marginal land has been investigated, and the costs and risks of bringing it into production can be calculated. Improved yields from existing acreage are a matter of science and economics. And redistribution of purchasing power could alleviate much starvation. But the big factor in future world food production that is not subject to human control is a possible change in world climates. Climatic conditions establish the physical limits on food production. These conditions determine length of seasons and rainfall patterns and thus the regions of the earth where crops can be grown. Since much of the world's food is now grown on marginal land where a slight shift in temperatures or rainfall can turn bumper harvests into agricultural disasters, any major change in climate could seriously disrupt future food production.

Trying to ascertain the historical record of climatological shifts is very much a detective game. Some evidence of change is found in contemporary polar ice caps and glaciers. Many of these ice sheets are thousands of feet thick and contain within them evidence of snowfall, atmospheric dust, volcanic activity, and so on, from thousands of years in the past. By drilling into the ice, core samples can be taken that reveal much about the climate at the times the various ice sheets were formed. Other evidence is found by drilling into the ocean floor for similar samples. A climate record can be pieced together by examining the remnants of animal and plant life deposited over time in layers on the ocean bottom. There is also more direct evidence of recurring ice ages that is manifest to geologists in rock formations left behind by retreating glaciers. Finally, more recent records of climatological conditions in specific areas can be found by examining annual tree rings, which vary in width with temperature and rainfall patterns.[56]

Information about long-term climatological change is difficult to gather, and theories about it are not yet well tested. Climatologists have found abundant evidence of periodic temperature shifts in the changing tree line in subarctic regions. These shifts have been correlated with significant droughts in other areas of the world. Experts now think that enduring mean temperature differences of as little as three or four degrees centigrade can make the difference between global agricultural abundance and an ice age.[57]

As evidence is gathered, it seems to indicate that the last few decades of rapid growth in food production have been the result of an unparalleled period of global good weather. Many areas of the planet that are now prime agricultural production areas were frequently covered by glaciers during the past.

There is additional historical evidence of an impending shift away from an ideal agricultural climate. Studies of mean annual temperatures in Iceland indicate that the period 1931–1960 was the most propitious for agriculture there in the last thousand years. Since Iceland has a "marginal" agricultural climate, mean temperature shifts can easily be seen in periodic changes in agricultural productivity. Additional indirect evidence of long-term temperature changes comes from studies of Kirchner Marsh in Minnesota.[58] They indicate that future shifts in average temperature in a downward direction can be expected. It is possible to interpret these data as indicating future perturbations in what we have come to regard as "normal" climate and much more drastic temperature and rainfall extremes.[59]

Aside from these more speculative long-term shifts in climate, there are well-established short-term cyclical changes that can also disrupt world food production. Sunspot activity, for example, varies in ten- to eleven-year cycles. Every second low point in these cycles seems related to significant droughts and drops in agricultural productivity.[60] The dynamics behind these relationships are not yet understood. But there are clearly boom and bust cycles in world agriculture triggered by solar activity.

There are at least three sets of factors operating to determine climate and thus global food production. These are the solar constant, radiation transmittance in the atmosphere, and changes in the earth's albedo.[61] It seems that the so-called "solar constant," the amount of energy given off at the surface of the sun, is not really constant. Very small changes in this figure could be responsible for triggering changes in the earth's climate. Furthermore, the different values published for the solar constant vary more than the estimated shifts that would be necessary to change climate and weather conditions rather dramatically. At present, appropriate measurements are being made, and there is good evidence that the surface temperature of the sun changes over time.

The earth's albedo refers to the amount of sunlight reflected back into outer space by clouds, dust, and the earth's surface. Slight changes in this albedo can account for significant changes in temperature and rainfall. At present, approximately 30 percent of incident solar energy is reflected back into space and 70 percent is absorbed. A change of as little as one percentage point in albedo could significantly affect weather and climate.[62]

The transmittance of the earth's atmosphere is a little more difficult to understand. Most of the 70 percent of solar energy that is not immediately reflected back into outer space is absorbed, and eventually a part of it is reradiated back into outer space as infrared radiation. But changes in particulate matter in the atmosphere, whether from natural or human causes, can alter normal patterns of absorption and reradiation and thus the earth's temperature. If the absorbed portion of solar energy is not reradiated into outer space at an adequate rate, global temperatures can slowly rise. There is now considerable concern that additional atmospheric carbon dioxide from the combustion of fossil fuels might be creating a "greenhouse effect" by cutting down on infrared reradiation to outer space while not affecting the inward transmittance of high-frequency radiation from the sun. In the last century, the carbon dioxide content of the atmosphere has increased from 292 to 320 parts per million. In isolation from other changes in global temperature, it is estimated that this increase alone could have caused a temperature increase of .25 degrees centigrade.[63]

Many future changes in climate will be affected by human activities. But others could result from natural phenomena. For example, there is a significant possibility of a volcanic eruption triggering short-term changes in world climate and adversely affecting food production. A major volcanic explosion on the scale of the famous Krakatoa eruption, which occurred in 1883, can spew so much particulate matter into the atmosphere as to overwhelm other change factors. The Krakatoa explosion lowered global temperatures significantly and adversely affected harvests for more than two years—the approximate length of time that it took the particulate matter injected into the atmosphere to settle back to earth. It is speculated that global volcanic eruptions are cyclical and correlated on a global scale.[64] Serious earthquakes and volcanic eruptions, which have occurred in the 1970s in various parts of the world, attest to the possibility that global volcanism may be on the upswing. Given current global population pressures against limited food reserves, a Krakatoa-type eruption could cause two years of global famine and hundreds of millions of deaths.

In summary, there are many contradictory forces operating to change world climate. The geological evidence indicates that the world is due to enter another ice age very shortly. But, on the other hand, the buildup of carbon dioxide in the atmosphere is known to be causing a global warming trend. No one can predict which forces will be predominant over the next few decades. But there is general agreement that this combination of factors will produce *temperature and rainfall extremes* much greater than those that have been experienced over the last fifty years.[65]

Weather has now become of great interest to specialists in international politics. After evaluating climatological evidence, a recent CIA report concludes that if pessimists are right, the grain produced at higher latitudes in Canada, the USSR, and China might not be available to the future world market. This could mean that many persons in import-dependent countries could starve as world trade in agricultural commodities might decline dramatically. Although the United States would not be affected too adversely by these developments, political leaders would be forced to choose between domestic consumption of available food, foreign sales for profit, or nonprofit aid to starving countries.[66]

Even if a shift toward a cooler and wetter climate takes place only over an extremely long period, important short-term shifts within the longer trend will create significant world food problems. At best, the world agricultural market will be a victim of more serious boom and bust cycles related to weather conditions. These cycles will be exacerbated by the need to bring more land in marginal areas under production to feed additional billions of people. Marginal land combined with climatic shifts and changing weather patterns could lead to tremendous variations in production, in world food prices, and most important, in global starvation and malnutrition.

Shifting climate patterns could also have varying political effects on different types of countries. Global food shortages would have a most serious impact on the world's large food importers, Japan, Great Britain, and West Germany. Soaring food bills could disrupt trade balances and damage foreign exchange positions. The great drought in France in 1976, for example, eliminated the prospect of French wheat exports and a potential trade surplus for that country in that year. The value of the franc fell accordingly.

Changing patterns of rainfall could also affect many less developed countries in which the green revolution has created a tremendous demand for water. Drier years could seriously reduce agricultural yields in those countries. Finally, relations between the United States and the Soviet Union could be affected by these changes. The USSR has much more marginal land planted in crops than does the United States. Cooler, drier weather in these marginal regions could transform the Soviet Union into a permanent customer for United States grain.

At present, the world food market is not prepared to deal with these climatic fluctuations. During good years, when harvests may be excellent, storage and transportation facilities are frequently overtaxed. Bumper harvests in two widely separated parts of the world in 1975 illustrate the point. In the United States, a significant portion of a near-record corn crop in the Midwest was destroyed because there were not enough railroad cars to move the corn to markets. Much corn was left exposed to rodents and the weather as local storage facilities became filled to capacity.

A more tragic and ironic situation occurred in Bangladesh, a country that normally suffers from chronic food shortages. A bumper rice crop was produced, but a substantial portion was damaged by rot and vermin because there were inadequate storage facilities. Food politics compounded the problem. Bangladesh imported an average of 2.2 million tons of grain each year between 1972 and 1975. The United States supplied about half of these needs through its "Food for Peace" sales. Not expecting a bumper harvest, Bangladesh officials requested significant imports from the United States at the beginning of 1975. The farm lobby in the United States geared up to make certain that Bangladesh would accept this surplus grain and honor the agreement. The result was that warehouses already jammed with domestic rice had to make room for imported American grain. And limited storage capacity meant that very little reserve was left for 1976. In addition, the glut of grain depressed the price of domestic rice, meaning that farmers planted less the next year. This made the prospect of future famines even more likely.

New international institutions obviously are needed to develop a more rational global agricultural policy to deal with future uncertainties. Food could very easily play a role as an ecopolitical weapon in the near future. Failure to store grain in the good years in anticipation of the bad makes the food problem even more serious. The reserves that have been accumulated in the past have resulted from government price support programs and lack of available markets. The reserves of the future must be accumulated as part of a more rational world food strategy designed to eliminate starvation during the lean years that are likely to come.

ENDNOTES

1. See Cheryl Christensen, "International Dependencies in Food Transactions," paper delivered at annual meeting of the American Political Science Association (September 1975), p. 2.
2. Cornelius Walford, "The Famines of the World: Past and Present," *Royal Statistical Society Journal*, vol. 41 (1878).
3. Cited in Paul Ehrlich and Anne Ehrlich, *Population, Resources, Environment* (San Francisco: W. H. Freeman, 1972), p. 13.
4. Thomas Malthus, *An Essay on the Principle of Population as It Affects the Future Improvement of Society with Remarks on the Speculations of M. Godwin, M. Condorcet and Other Writers* (published anonymously, 1798).
5. Lyle Schertz, "World Food: Prices and the Poor," *Foreign Affairs* (April 1974): 513.
6. Figures are the estimates of Schlomo Reutlinger and Marcelo Selowsky, *Malnutrition and Poverty: Magnitude and Policy Options* (Baltimore: Johns Hopkins University Press, 1976).
7. See Fred Sanderson, "The Great Food Fumble," *Science* (May 9, 1975).
8. See Schertz, "World Food," pp. 512–515.
9. See Radha Sinha, *Food and Poverty* (New York: Holmes & Meier, 1976); Keith Griffin, *The Political Economy of Agrarian Change* (Cambridge, Mass.: Harvard University Press, 1974); and Frances Lappé and Joseph Collins, *Food First* (Boston: Houghton Mifflin, 1977), chaps. 11, 23–28.
10. Schertz, "World Food," p. 512.
11. See James Kennett and Robert Thunell, "Global Increase in Quaternary Explosive Volcanism," *Science* (February 14, 1975), and Reid Bryson and Thomas Murray, *Climates of Hunger* (Madison, Wis.: University of Wisconsin Press, 1977), pp. 145–148.
12. Organization for Economic Cooperation and Development, *World Supply and Demand of Major Agricultural Commodities* (Paris, 1976), pp. 29–30, and United Nations, *Assessment of the World Food Situation* (Rome, 1974), p. 36.
13. Organization for Economic Cooperation and Development, *World Supply and Demand of Major Agricultural Commodities*, p. 31.
14. President's Science Advisory Committee, *The World Food Problem* (Washington, D.C., 1967), II: 50–59.
15. United Nations, *Assessment of the World Food Situation*, p. 36.
16. Georg Borgstrom, *The Hungry Planet* (New York: Collier Books, 1972), chap. 3.
17. Christensen, "International Dependencies."
18. See Schertz, "World Food," pp. 514–515.
19. Food and Agriculture Organization of the United Nations, *Production Yearbook 1974* (Rome, 1975), p. 46.
20. See Georg Borgstrom, *Focal Points: A Global Food Strategy* (New York: Macmillan, 1973), part 2.
21. Food and Agricultural Organization of the United Nations, *Production Yearbook 1974*, p. 86.
22. Figures are for 1970. Taken from Earl Cook, *Man, Energy, Society* (San Francisco: W. H. Freeman, 1976), pp. 230–231.
23. Borgstrom, *The Hungry Planet*, chap. 5.
24. Ibid., chap. 2.

25. Food and Agricultural Organization of the United Nations, *Yearbook of Fishery Statistics 1975* (Rome, 1976).

26. See C. P. Idyll, "The Anchovy Crisis," *Scientific American* (June 1973). See also Lester Brown, *By Bread Alone* (New York: Praeger, 1974), chap. 11.

27. See Richard Tomasson, "Iceland's Survival and the Law of the Sea," *Current History* (April 1976).

28. In the summer of 1977, Japanese fish prices rose dramatically, making already high food prices even higher.

29. See William Schneider, *Food, Foreign Policy and Raw Material Cartels* (New York: Crane, Russak, 1976), chap. 3.

30. See Cheryl Christensen, *World Hunger: A Structural Approach* (New York: The Free Press, forthcoming), for further development of this theme.

31. Food and Agriculture Organization of the United Nations, *Production Yearbook 1974*, pp. 27–30.

32. Ibid., p. 30.

33. Ibid., p. 29.

34. President's Scientific Advisory Committee, *The World Food Problem*, II: 434.

35. Cited in Economic Research Service, United States Department of Agriculture, *The World Food Situation and Prospects to 1985* (Washington, D.C., 1974), p. 59.

36. Organization for Economic Cooperation and Development, *World Supply and Demand of Major Agricultural Commodities*, pp. 48–54.

37. Food and Agricultural Organization of the United Nations, *World Indicative Plan* (Rome, 1967), I: 49.

38. See Paul Richards, "The Tropical Rain Forest," *Scientific American* (December 1973), and Daniel Janzen, "Tropical Agroecosystems," *Science* (December 21, 1973).

39. Donella Meadows, et al., *The Limits to Growth* (New York: Universe Books, 1972), p. 48.

40. United Nations, *Assessment of the World Food Situation*, p. 7.

41. William McNeill, *Plagues and Peoples* (Garden City, N.Y.: Doubleday, 1976), p. 21.

42. Lester Brown, "The Next Crisis? Food," *Foreign Policy* (Winter 1973): 6.

43. Economic Research Service, United States Department of Agriculture, *The World Food Situation and Prospects to 1985*, p. 59.

44. Meadows, *The Limits to Growth*, p. 50.

45. Economic Research Service, United States Department of Agriculture, *The World Food Situation and Prospect to 1985*, p. 71.

46. Cynthia Hunt and Robert Garrels, *Water: The Web of Life* (New York: W. W. Norton, 1972), p. 54.

47. See Ehrlich and Ehrlich, *Population, Resources, Environment*, p. 77.

48. Food and Agricultural Organization of the United Nations, *Production Yearbook 1976*, (Rome, 1977), p. 89.

49. David Pimental, et al., "Food Production and the Energy Crisis," *Science* (November 2, 1973): 444.

50. Food and Agriculture Organization of the United Nations, *Annual Fertilizer Review 1972* (Rome, 1973), pp. 48–49.

51. Pimental, et al., "Food Production and the Energy Crisis."

52. Ibid., p. 448.

53. Brown, *By Bread Alone*, p. 117.

54. John Steinhart and Carol Steinhart, "Energy Use in the U.S. Food System," *Science* (April 19, 1974).
55. Ibid., pp. 307–308.
56. See, for example, Valmore La Marche, Jr., "Paleoclimatic Inferences from Long Tree Ring Records," *Science* (March 15, 1974).
57. Reid Bryson, "A Perspective on Climatic Change," *Science* (May 17, 1974). See also Bryson and Murray, *Climates of Hunger.*
58. Studies cited in Bryson, "A Perspective on Climatic Change."
59. These arguments are presented in great detail in Stephen Schneider, *The Genesis Strategy* (New York: Plenum Press, 1976), chap. 3.
60. See Virden Harrison, "Do Sunspot Cycles Affect Crop Yield?" (Washington, D.C.: U.S. Department of Agriculture, Economic Research Service, 1976).
61. Schneider, *The Genesis Strategy,* chap. 5.
62. Ibid., pp. 122–123.
63. Bryson, "A Perspective on Climatic Change." See also P. V. Hobbs, H. Harrison, and E. Robinson, "Atmospheric Effects of Pollutants," *Science* (March 8, 1974).
64. Kennett and Thunell, "Global Increase in Quaternary Explosive Volcanism."
65. These general conclusions are substantiated by the Research Directorate of the National Defense University, *Climate Change to the Year 2000* (Washington, D.C., 1978). See also J. D. Hays, John Imbrie, and N. J. Shackleton, "Variations in the Earth's Orbit: Pacemaker of the Ice Ages," *Science* (December 10, 1976).
66. Central Intelligence Agency, *Potential Implications of Trends in World Population, Food Production, and Climate* (Washington, D.C., 1974).

SUGGESTED READINGS

1. Philip Abelson, ed. *Food: Politics, Economics, Nutrition, and Research.* Washington, D.C.: American Association for the Advancement of Science, 1975.
2. American Association for the Advancement of Science. *Food.* Special Edition of *Science,* May 9, 1975.
3. Georg Borgstrom. *Focal Points: A Global Food Strategy.* New York: Macmillan, 1973.
4. Georg Borgstrom. *The Hungry Planet.* New York: Collier Books, 1972.
5. Lester Brown. *By Bread Alone.* New York: Praeger, 1974.
6. Reid Bryson and Thomas Murray. *Climates of Hunger.* Madison, Wis.: University of Wisconsin Press, 1977.
7. Commission on International Relations, National Academy of Sciences. *World Food and Nutrition Study: The Potential Contributions of Research.* Washington, D.C.: National Academy of Sciences, 1977.
8. Committee on Climate and Weather Fluctuations and Agricultural Production. *Climate and Food.* Washington, D.C.: National Academy of Sciences, 1976.
9. Economic Research Service, U.S. Department of Agriculture. *The World*

Food Situation and Prospects to 1985. Washington, D.C.: USDA, 1974.

10. Maurice Green. *Eating Oil: Energy Use in Food Production.* Denver: Westview Press, 1978.

11. Cynthia Hunt and Robert Garrels. *Water: The Web of Life.* New York: W. W. Norton, 1972.

12. Frances Lappe and Joseph Collins. *Food First: Beyond the Myth of Scarcity.* Boston: Houghton Mifflin, 1977.

13. George Lucas, Jr., and Thomas Ogletree, eds. *Lifeboat Ethics: The Moral Dilemmas of World Hunger.* New York: Harper & Row, 1976.

14. William McNeill. *Plagues and Peoples.* Garden City, N.Y.: Anchor Press/Doubleday, 1976.

15. National Defense University. *Climate Change to the Year 2000.* Washington, D.C., 1978.

16. Organization for Economic Cooperation and Development. *World Supply and Demand of Major Agricultural Commodities.* Paris, 1976.

17. William Paddock and Elizabeth Paddock. *We Don't Know How.* Ames, Iowa: Iowa State University Press, 1973.

18. David Pimentel. *World Food, Pest Losses, and the Environment.* Denver: Westview Press, 1978.

19. Schlomo Reutlinger and Marcelo Selowsky. *Malnutrition and Poverty: Magnitude and Policy Options.* Baltimore: Johns Hopkins University Press, 1976.

20. Stephen Schneider. *The Genesis Strategy.* New York: Plenum Press, 1976.

21. Radha Sinha. *Food and Poverty.* New York: Holmes & Meier, 1976.

22. Radha Sinha, ed. *The World Food Problem: Consensus and Conflict.* Special Edition of *World Development,* May-July, 1977.

23. Transnational University Program, Institute for World Order. *World Food/Hunger Studies.* New York: Institute for World Order, 1977.

4

Global Energy Politics

There are four basic sources of energy for human activities: the sun, fossil fuels, nuclear and thermonuclear fission and fusion, and gravity. The sun has been the primary source of energy during most of human evolution. Energy from it is captured directly through photosynthesis, which creates the food that permits human beings to do work. Currently, solar energy is being used increasingly to heat homes. The advantage of solar energy is that it is almost infinitely renewable. From the present human time perspective, a similar amount of energy can be expected from the sun each year. Thus, growth that takes place within the constraints of current solar income is *sustainable* growth because it does not depend on finite and nonrenewable energy sources.

The energy that has driven the Industrial Revolution, however, has come largely from fossil fuels. Most of the technological successes of the Industrial Revolution have involved learning to use fossil fuels as substitutes for human labor. Agrarian societies are notable for the proportion of work that is done by human beings and draft animals. In industrial societies, by contrast, most of the work that is done is accomplished with the aid of fossil fuels. But the world's supply of fossil fuels is limited by the slow and rare processes by which they have been formed, and industrial growth that depends upon fossil fuel technologies may be of an ephemeral nature. At the present turning point in world history, a search is under way for alternative sources of energy to replace the energy presently produced by burning fossil fuels, and the shape of the "postindustrial" society will be determined by the chosen alternatives. A partial solution to the world energy problem is to harness solar energy more effectively. But gravitational sources of energy, such as the tides, are also promising possibilities. Nuclear energy, created by the splitting of heavy atoms, is now playing an important role in many industrial countries. And on the distant horizon is the possibility that fusion of hydrogen atoms will offer a longer-term solution to the energy crisis.[1]

All industrial countries are now living well beyond their natural "solar income" carrying capacity. Fossil fuel–related technological developments have created the gap that exists in these countries between natural and current carrying capacity, and nonsolar energy sources are now essential to maintaining these large populations and their affluent lifestyles. Industrialization is synonymous with complicated systems of production and distribution that require a constant injection of energy to keep them operating. Even agriculture in industrial countries requires a tremendous amount of fossil fuel, which is constantly being transformed into food in a complex system that requires fertilizers, pesticides, and mechanized equipment. The economies of scale, mass production, and centralization that are now part of the industrial way of life are very expensive in terms of energy consumption.

Historically, fossil fuel reserves have been abundant relative to rather modest demands for them, and depletion of fossil fuels was considered to be beyond the realm of possibility. But the historical pattern of world energy consumption shows an annual increase of about 5 percent during times of economic prosperity, which means that global consumption doubles every fourteen years during "normal" times. In summary, all of the world's currently proved reserves of petroleum will be used up in only twenty-six years at 1976 levels of production and consumption.[2] The situation is, however, much more complicated than these rough figures indicate. New reserves are being constantly discovered, and, simultaneously, world consumption continues to increase. But the point has now been passed at which yearly additions to reserves exceed or match yearly production figures, and reserves are expected to decline gradually. And the mathematics of exponential growth in consumption are such that even if five times present known reserves are discovered, a highly unlikely prospect, only twenty-three more years' supply would be added.[3]

While depletion of fossil fuels is the ultimate constraint on consumption, the crisis of 1973–1974 represented a case of contrived scarcity of petroleum, since it was triggered by the actions of an international cartel of petroleum-exporting nations. This period of contrived constraint and ecoconflict may have been only a precursor of more serious political problems soon to come. Most studies of future energy availability indicate that global demand for fossil fuels will begin to exceed available supplies sometime in the mid to late 1980s.[4] At that time, the actions of only one or two oil exporters will be able to disrupt seriously the world economy.

The crucial political component of the energy problem is that there are no backup energy systems to keep the complex industrial economies operating should the flow of fossil fuels be drastically reduced. Most industrial countries import in excess of one-half of the energy consumed domestically, largely petroleum from the Middle East, and are thus vulnerable to initiatives taken by these countries. Their dependence upon these imports was dramatically demonstrated when the Organization of Arab Petroleum Exporting Countries (OAPEC), the Arab exporter organization, decided to embargo shipments of petroleum to selected industrial countries in 1973–1974. Near panic followed in those countries. Had the embargo been honored by all members of the larger Organization of Petroleum Exporting Countries (OPEC) and been rigidly enforced, there can be no question but that leaders of some industrial countries would have engaged in military action rather than watch their economies slowly disintegrate.

Energy has now become the major element in the emerging eco-politics. And real and contrived shortages of fossil fuels are the most important aspect of energy politics right now. The fossil fuels are the key to most economic activity and a major item in international trade, presently accounting for nearly one-half of all imports and exports of raw materials.[5] The persistence of the Organization of Petroleum Exporting Countries as a functioning cartel underscores the importance of fuels to the international economy. Importers cannot long resist price increases by cutting back their petroleum consumption. And leaders of the small number of oil-exporting countries know that they can use petroleum as a weapon.

Real and contrived scarcity of fossil fuels and the higher costs of obtaining them are now central issues in international relations and domestic politics. Meeting energy demands is now an expensive proposition, as locating, drilling for, and transporting new reserves of fossil fuels are difficult and costly. It has been estimated that obtaining necessary fossil fuels will require an investment of nearly $1 trillion in the world petroleum industry in the 1975–1985 period, which represents over four times the amount spent during the previous decade.[6] Meeting total domestic energy needs in the United States through 1990 will cost between $790 billion and $1 trillion. This amount represents between 22 and 26 percent of all projected available capital during that period.[7] The greater the amount of capital invested in the energy industry the less will be available for other essential activities.

On a more abstract level, the available amount of the fossil fuel subsidy (the amount of energy obtained in excess of the energy costs of obtaining it) is steadily diminishing. Increased capital costs of finding, drilling for, transporting, and processing fossil fuels are a reflection of the increasing amounts of energy that must go into getting them. In the near future, the energy subsidy in petroleum could disappear entirely as the amount of energy required to obtain a barrel of oil begins to exceed the energy found in that barrel.

Contrived scarcity is also becoming a much more serious threat to industrial countries as world consumption approaches production capacity. It has been estimated that contrived scarcity induced by cutbacks in production in only one country, Saudi Arabia, could throw the industrial world into turmoil by the early 1980s.[8] And a concerted withholding action by OPEC could, at present, easily lead to a major international conflict.

These scarcity problems become even more significant because of the tremendous political and economic importance of the world petrol-automotive complex. Nine of the ten largest companies in the world, with combined sales of $250 billion in 1975, sell either petroleum or automobiles.[9] The sales, assets, income, jobs, and so on, associated with this complex make up the backbone of contemporary industrial economies. If the petrol-automotive complex goes under, it might well take the advanced industrial economies along with it. It is for these reasons that understanding the nature and distribution of the world's fossil fuels is important to understanding the future of international relations, as well as the future of industrial civilization.

OSSIL FUELS: BASIC CONSTRAINTS

There are two basic principles that restrict possible solutions to the present energy problem. They are called the first and second laws of thermodynamics. The first law of thermodynamics simply states that energy can neither be created nor destroyed. The amount of combined energy and matter in the universe remains the same, although the forms and usefulness of this energy and matter may change. In other words, within human experience there is no possibility of making an energy-creating device to solve the impending energy problem.

The second law of thermodynamics is more relevant to the energy problem, although difficult to grasp. In general terms, it states that in closed systems there is a tendency to move from less probable to more probable configurations of matter. If a quantity of gas is confined to a jar, for example, and then is suddenly released into the atmosphere, the densely packed molecules move toward randomness. Fossil fuels represent highly ordered or less probable configurations of molecules with great potential to do work. This order is destroyed and the molecules move toward a more probable configuration while the work is being done. The molecules then exist in a more random, disorganized, and less useful form. Thus, when fossil fuels are burned and work is done, the matter is degraded from more organized and potentially useful into disorganized and less useful forms. The second law of thermodynamics is also called the entropy law. Entropy is a measure of disorder, randomness, or inability to do work. A system characterized by a high degree of entropy is a system with very little potential for doing any work.[10]

The second law of thermodynamics cautions human beings to take an inventory of available fuels, because once fuels are used to do work they can never be used again. They become transformed into ashes, gases, and heat. The second law indicates that whenever work is done, fuels are degraded from more useful to less useful forms. A lump of coal, for example, represents highly organized matter. When the lump of coal is burned, however, this organization is destroyed, and the resulting heat, gases, and waste products have little capacity to do work. In this respect, entropy has increased, and the dispersed products cannot be reconstituted into the lump of coal.

The history of industrial civilization is one of increasing entropy as the molecules in highly organized and useful fossil fuels have been constantly degraded toward randomness through industrial processes. Continued industrial prosperity has led to the large-scale transformation of such matter and a related release of waste heat into the atmosphere while work has been done. Thus, technology may permit fossil fuels to be used more efficiently, but once a barrel of oil is burned it is no longer available, and significant environmental pollution results.

In addition to these restrictions, the world's supply of fossil fuels is limited by the manner in which they have been created. Fossil fuels are the result of unique geological processes that have created copious quantities in relatively few geographic locations. In this respect, they are much different from the nonfuel minerals that are found throughout the earth's crust. All fossil fuel represents stored solar income from millions of years in the past. Solar energy has been converted into plant life in large quantities through photosynthesis for about 300 million years. Over that time, an exceedingly small fraction of this plant life has been preserved through specialized processes that have resulted in the creation of coal, petroleum, and natural gas. These processes that create fossil fuels work very slowly. In relation to present demand for them, creation of new fossil fuels is insignificant.

Coal was the first fossil fuel to be used in significant quantities. Most coalfields are composed of seams found at varying depths and widths, indicating repeated incidence of plant growth, water coverage, and burial of matter beneath the waters. Because of these special geological conditions that formed them, coalfields have well-defined boundaries. Coal is the most abundant fossil fuel but the least desirable to use because of environmental pollution problems. Current world coal reserves are about 600 billion tons of hard coal equivalent, enough for well over two centuries' consumption at current rates of usage.[11]

Petroleum and natural gas are formed from organic remains in much the same manner as coal. These fuels are usually found together in areas called fields and in accumulations called pools. Most fields encompass only a few square miles in area, and the largest fields seldom exceed more than 100 square miles. As in the case of coal, oxidation of dead plants is prevented and accumulation and concentration are facilitated by an unusual set of circumstances. When petroleum and natural gas are produced, compacting shale squeezes organic matter into liquid and gas hydrocarbons rather than into coal. Petroleum and natural gas are not often found in the areas in which they were formed, for they are squeezed through the earth and move from areas of high pressure to those where pressures are much lower. In general, they move toward the surface, where gravitational pressures are lower. Pools are formed when a "geologic trap," an impermeable rock formation, halts the upward progress of petroleum and natural gas and traps it. Traps may be created by several different conditions, but these conditions do not occur very frequently. The joint occurrence of trapping conditions and abundant migrating liquid and gas hydrocarbons is an exceedingly rare event, which explains the world's limited number of major petroleum and natural gas producing areas.[12]

Petroleum and natural gas are much rarer than coal because of the greater complexity of the processes by which they have been formed. But because they are cleaner and more efficient than coal they are preferred fuels in home heating, transportation, and industrial processes. Although oil and gas will never disappear entirely from the earth's surface, presently known reserves can be economically exploited only for another thirty to fifty years given different assumptions about future consumption and discovery patterns. Long before the wells run dry, however, rising prices and imbalances between supply and demand will upset the world economy.

If increases in consumption follow historical patterns, the peak of world consumption in both petroleum and natural gas will take place within the next twenty-five years. M. King Hubbert has done some of the most accurate estimates of petroleum reserves, and he has projected that world production will peak just before the year 2000. According to his estimates, the *world* will have consumed 80 percent of all reserves in a period of only sixty years. According to this same estimation procedure, the *United States* has passed through its peak of petroleum production and will rapidly taper off in the 1980s.[13]

World reserves of petroleum in 1976 were estimated to be about 550 billion barrels.[14] This figure is based upon then available technology and prevailing market prices; improved technology and higher prices will undoubtedly increase these figures somewhat. The *ultimate* amount of recoverable petroleum has been the subject of many estimates over the last thirty years. They range from a low of 400 billion barrels (1946) to a high of 2480 billion barrels (1965). Most recent estimates have centered on about 2000 billion barrels.[15] Although new reserves are being discovered, the rate at which they are being located has been falling over the last fifteen years. In the period 1960–1965, about 18 billion barrels of petroleum were discovered each year. In the 1965–1970 period, this figure dropped to about 17 billion barrels a year. The figure has since dropped even further, to 15 billion barrels per year for the five-year period ending in 1975.[16] Yearly *production* of petroleum, however, is now in excess of 22 billion barrels, which means that reserves are being slowly drained down.

Natural gas is in similarly short supply. 1975 proved reserves of natural gas were estimated at 386 billion barrels of oil equivalent, which represents between one eighth and one-third of the estimates of ultimately recoverable reserves.[17] It is difficult to determine precisely world yearly consumption of natural gas because so much is consumed in the Soviet Union. But production of natural gas will probably peak in the late 1980s, and production in the major consuming countries will be at only two-thirds of the 1972 level by 2000.[18]

Regardless of which estimates are taken to be authoritative, it is clear that only a few more decades of fossil fuel consumption remain. Furthermore, world distribution of known reserves is neither random nor egalitarian. Fields are concentrated in those few areas that have historically experienced the peculiar combination of conditions necessary to form petroleum and natural gas reservoirs. And this concentration of world reserves has serious consequences for the global distribution of power and the future of ecopolitics.

Nearly 60 percent of the world's known reserves of petroleum are concentrated in the Middle East. Saudi Arabia possesses one-fifth of all known reserves, an awesome total of more than 110 billion barrels of petroleum. Kuwait and Iran have also been blessed with tremendous petroleum reserves. In fact, about 40 percent of total world petroleum reserves are accounted for when reserves in Saudi Arabia are combined with those of Kuwait and Iran (see table 4–1). Iraq is the fourth Middle Eastern country with sizable reserves, 35 billion barrels, which exceed the known reserves in the United States. Of the Middle Eastern countries, only in Iran is there any real danger of depletion in the middle

TABLE 4–1. World Petroleum Reserves

	Reserves* 1974	Reserves* 1976	Percent of World Reserves, 1976	Percent Increase/Decrease 1974–1976	Annual Production 1976†
Saudi Arabia	103.5	110.2	20	+6.5	3,053
Kuwait	70.9	69.5	13	−1.0	700
USSR	56.3	59.9	11	+6.4	3,794
Iran	68.0	48.1	9	−29.3	2,153
Iraq	35.1	35.2	6	0.0	835
United States	34.2	30.9	6	−9.6	2,972
Abu Dhabi	23.8	24.9	5	+4.6	572
Libya	23.0	24.5	4	+6.5	707
Venezuela	18.6	18.3	3	−1.6	840
China	14.8	18.0	3	+21.6	622
Nigeria	13.7	12.2	2	−10.9	758
Indonesia	12.0	11.5	2	−4.2	550
Great Britain	7.7	10.0	2	+29.9	90
Algeria	9.0	9.6	2	+6.7	384
Mexico	3.1	8.0	1	+158.1	181
Neutral Zone	6.8	6.5	1	−4.4	167
Canada	7.2	6.3	1	−12.5	459
Norway	5.5	5.8	1	+5.5	102
Qatar	5.4	5.1	1	−5.6	181
World	570.0	550.0		−3.5	21,016

*Billions of barrels.
†Millions of barrels.
SOURCE: Derived from World Oil (August 15, 1976), and World Oil (August 15, 1977).

term. The other two Middle Eastern petroleum powers have secure reserves for some time to come.

The Soviet Union and the United States rank third and sixth, respectively, in proven petroleum reserves. But the United States meets only about half its domestic demand for petroleum from the 3 billion barrels of petroleum produced annually and known reserves have been on the decline since the Alaskan discoveries were added to reserves in 1970. There seem to be no short-run alternatives to increased US dependence on foreign oil.[19] The Soviet Union, by contrast, is the world's top producer of petroleum. It meets all of its own domestic demand from domestic production and even exports considerable quantities to Eastern Europe and some Western countries.

Of the remaining large petroleum producers, only Iraq and Abu Dhabi (the United Arab Emirates) possess in excess of 5 percent of world reserves. Libya, Nigeria, and China, taken together, control a total of less than 10 percent of proved reserves, although in each country there is a possibility of additional significant discoveries. Venezuela is the world's fifth largest producer of petroleum but possesses only 3 percent of world reserves. Even at reduced production rates, Venezuela has only enough petroleum, given present technology, to export for about another twenty years. Canada basically produces petroleum to meet her own needs and has cut back exports to the United States drastically. Of the Western industrial countries only Norway and Great Britain have untapped export potential in new North Sea fields. Some of this oil will make its way into Western European markets, but conservative government policies combined with the small size of the reserves will keep production and exports at modest levels.

The picture of world petroleum reserves that emerges from these data is one of high concentration, which explains the ease with which prices could be quadrupled in 1973–1974. Petroleum is found in significant quantities in very few geographical locations. These locations have been well mapped by modern technologies, and the magnitude of ultimately recoverable crude oil can be accurately approximated. The amount of crude petroleum in relation to the demands of a future industrializing world is small, and it is clear that a shift to alternative energy sources must be made within the next three or four decades. Furthermore, only four Middle Eastern countries control over half of the world's proved reserves. The United States and the Soviet Union together control an additional 15 percent, most of which is consumed domestically. Thus, only four countries control most exportable petroleum reserves, and these countries will be in a position to use these reserves as an economic and political weapon against petroleum importers in the increasingly tight petroleum market of the near future.

Natural gas is an alternative to petroleum, but it does not offer a ready solution to depletion problems. Natural gas is not in much greater abundance than petroleum, and nearly 40 percent of natural gas reserves are "associated" with petroleum reserves. In addition, there is only a small interstate market for natural gas because it must be moved by pipeline to contiguous geographical areas. Pressures from energy-hungry industrial countries have led to a search for new ways to transport natural gas. One suggested solution is liquefied natural gas (LNG) tankers, and it appears that a world natural gas market based on tankers could develop. At present, the United States receives liquefied natural gas from Algeria in very small quantities, largely through special facilities in Cove Point, Maryland, and Savannah, Georgia. The more than 400 billion cubic feet of natural gas liquid imports in 1977 is expected to grow to 4 trillion cubic feet by 1985 if trade in natural gas is permitted to develop without government interference. A fleet of more than 120 LNG tankers would be required to meet these projected United States demands. Western Europe and Japan will also require LNG fleets to meet their growing needs for natural gas. It has been estimated that $29 billion would be needed to build LNG facilities by 1985 should current trends continue.[20]

Intercontinental shipment of liquefied natural gas is technologically and politically risky. On the political side, future dependence on a small number of foreign facilities will make importing countries vulnerable to political and economic blackmail that could be as damaging as the petroleum embargo. And shipping the liquefied natural gas is a technological and economic nightmare. Natural gas must be liquefied in the shipping country by cooling it to -161° centrigrade, a process that uses up one-quarter of the amount of energy in the gas. Natural gas tankers then carry this volatile liquid to ports in the importing countries. Any rupture of the gas liquid container could release a plume of lethal gas, as the liquid would rapidly gasify and expand to fill its original volume. The possibility of explosion at sea or in port is not remote. The cost of the new facilities is also staggering. Each ship now runs in the neighborhood of $100 million. The unloading facilities in the United States are estimated to cost more than $.5 billion each. The total bill for US LNG operations will eventually run to tens of billions of dollars.[21]

Natural gas trade raises the same political considerations as petroleum. Table 4–2 reveals that those countries that hold most of the world's petroleum in reserve also control natural gas reserves. The one clear difference is that the USSR has a much stronger reserve position in natural gas than in petroleum. One-third of world proved reserves are found in the Soviet Union, and Iran possesses 17 percent. Algeria and the Netherlands are the only two significant producers of natural gas that are not also major petroleum producers. While the United States controls 11 percent of world reserves, they are declining very rapidly. As of December 1975, reserves were listed at 228 trillion cubic feet, and production was 21 trillion cubic feet annually. With the exception of the Prudhoe Bay, Alaska, discovery in 1970, there has been a

TABLE 4-2. *World Natural Gas Reserves*

	Reserves*		Percent of World Reserves, 1976	Percent Difference, 1974–1976
	1974	1976		
USSR	700	781	35	+11.6
Iran	374	375	17	+.3
United States	237	216	10	−8.9
Algeria	100	115	5	+15.0
Saudi Arabia	60	64	3	+6.7
Netherlands	68	62	3	−8.8
Canada	57	58	3	+1.8
Nigeria	50	51	2	+2.0
Qatar	8	46	2	+475.0
Venezuela	40	43	2	+7.5
Kuwait	38	37	2	−2.6
Great Britain	27	29	1	+7.4
Australia	26	29	1	+11.5
Libya	28	28	1	0.0
Iraq	27	27	1	0.0
World	2,098	2,242	—	+6.9

*Trillions of cubic feet.
SOURCE: Derived from World Oil (August 1976) and World Oil (August 1977).

steady decline in natural gas reserves in the United States since 1967. At present rates of consumption, these known reserves will disappear in only eleven years.[22]

Crude petroleum accounts for more than one-third of world energy consumption and natural gas for about one-sixth. Coal now accounts for one-quarter of world energy consumption, but this portion has been dwindling because of inefficiencies and environmental hazards associated with mining and using coal. With reserves of petroleum and natural gas rapidly disappearing, however, coal is projected to assume a more important role in industrial economies, particularly in the generation of electricity. World coal reserves are more highly concentrated than those of other fossil fuels. The USSR (56 percent) and the US (20 percent) control over three-quarters of known world reserves.[23] The remainder is widely dispersed, mostly throughout the world's northern temperate zones. Coal can never replace petroleum and natural gas in many applications, but its relative abundance in the United States makes it a very attractive alternative energy source if the related environmental pollution problems can be contained.

ENERGY: TRADE PATTERNS AND POLITICAL CONSIDERATIONS

There is a close relationship between economic growth and increased energy consumption. The definitions of progress that are central to the industrial paradigm require substitution of fossil fuels for human labor. People in industrial societies now define progress in terms of numbers of personal automobiles, air-conditioned homes, washing machines, and color televisions. Not to have these things can cause acute feelings of deprivation and perhaps political instability.

Industrial societies also require more energy because of their complexity. Dense populations with high living standards require complex systems of production, distribution, transportation, and waste disposal. And these complex systems require energy and human vigilance if they are to be kept in good order. Freeways must be kept repaired, traffic signals coordinated, produce brought from farm to market, fields fertilized, trains and planes maintained, and electricity supplied to homes and factories. Even short periods without electricity can create chaos in major urban areas.

Figure 4–1 illustrates the close relationship between economic growth and energy consumption. It is obvious that some countries get considerably less economic output per unit of consumed energy than do others. The United States, for example, has been a profligate consumer of energy. Sweden, by contrast, now supports a similar standard of living while using less than two-thirds as much energy per capita.[24] Fossil fuels in the United States have historically been both abundant and cheap, and the patterns of energy consumption that have evolved as a result have been extremely wasteful.[25] Thus, the US is far beyond most other industrial countries in per capita energy consumption. Western European countries, for example, have not industrialized in an atmosphere of fossil fuel abundance. A different set of fuel constraints has led to more frugal patterns of energy usage there.

The transportation sector accounts for a large portion of these differences in consumption. Americans prefer to travel by automobile and plane instead of by rail and bus, which are much more energy efficient per passenger mile. Higher gas prices and the availability of mass transit have kept private automobile ownership and travel much lower in Europe than in the United States.

Given the concentration of petroleum and natural gas reserves in only a few countries and the high energy requirements of industrial countries, there is now substantial trade in fossil fuels. During the early phases of the Industrial Revolution, indigenous supplies of wood and coal were adequate to meet energy needs in many countries. But petroleum and natural gas now are preferred to coal and wood, and nonsolid fuel consumption has increased dramatically in most industrial countries. In Western Europe, coal and other solid fuels accounted for 71 percent of all energy consumed in 1958. By 1974, this figure had dropped to

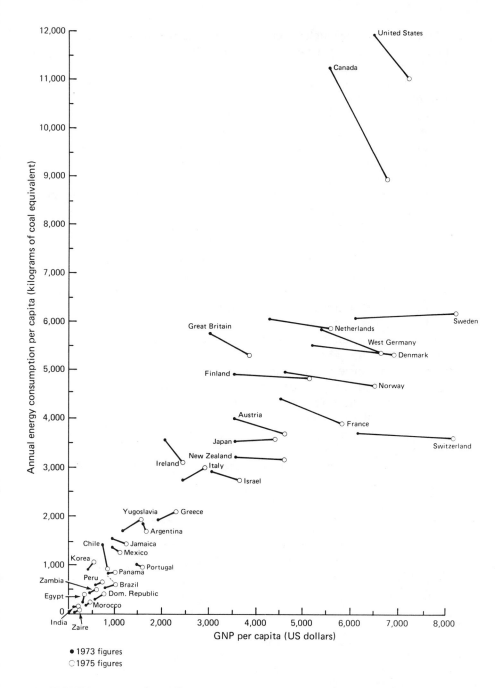

FIGURE 4–1. Industrialization and Energy Consumption [SOURCE: World Bank, *World Bank Atlas, 1975* (Washington, D.C., 1976); Population Reference Bureau, *1977 World Population Data Sheet* (Washington, D.C., 1977); and United Nations, *Statistical Yearbook, 1974 and 1976* (New York, 1975 and 1977).]

22 percent.[26] This switch to imported petroleum and natural gas has left many of these countries extremely vulnerable to political and economic blackmail.

Table 4–3 summarizes the present world flow of petroleum. The United States, with 5 percent of the world's population, accounts for 29 percent of world petroleum consumption. At the same time, the US produces only 16 percent of the world's petroleum, and this percentage is declining. The US is presently meeting half of its petroleum needs through imports, and there is little reason to expect a trend toward more self-sufficiency in the near future.

Western Europe is in even worse shape as a petroleum-deficient area. These countries contain 9 percent of the world's population but consume one-quarter of world production while contributing only 1 percent of world petroleum production. In 1975, Western Europe imported between 12 and 13 million barrels of petroleum per day.[27] This magnitude of imports can have a tremendous impact on balance of payment problems, since these countries must find sizable markets for industrial goods to pay for imported petroleum and natural gas.

Japan is in an even more vulnerable position, since it produces virtually no petroleum but now consumes nearly 10 percent of world production. The Japanese are the most vulnerable of the industrial petroleum importers. Loss of petroleum imports would cause a collapse of Japanese industry, loss of exports, loss of foreign currency, and would hamper the ability to import food and other raw materials. Eventually, there would then be a collapse of the Japanese population. Therefore, Japan has taken a strong position in favor of nuclear power, including breeder reactors.

The USSR first emerged as the world's leading producer of pe-

TABLE 4–3. World Petroleum Demand and Supply

	Consumption* 1975	Consumption* 1976	Percent Increase, 1975–1976	Percent of World Consumption, 1976	Percent of World Production, 1976
United States	16,322	17,180	5.3	29.0	16.1
Western Europe	13,465	14,410	7.0	24.3	1.4
Eastern Europe– USSR	9,078	9,528	5.0	16.1	18.3
Japan	5,025	5,203	3.5	8.8	0.0
Latin America	3,640	3,832	5.3	6.5	7.6
Canada	1,730	1,799	4.0	3.0	2.6
Middle East	1,370	1,443	5.3	2.4	36.8
China	1,143	1,492	30.5	2.5	2.8
Africa	1,043	1,119	7.3	1.9	10.0

*Thousands of barrels per day.

SOURCE: World Oil (August 15, 1977).

troleum in 1974 as a result of rapidly increasing domestic production and a decrease in production in the Middle East because of the petroleum embargo and the world economic recession. With ample reserves, the Soviet Union is likely to remain the top producer for at least the next decade. The USSR contributes only modestly to the international flow of petroleum because of significant domestic consumption. In 1976, the Soviet Union produced 10.4 million barrels per day. Of this, 1 million barrels per day were shipped to Eastern Europe, 1.3 million barrels per day went to hard-currency countries, and 300,000 barrels per day went to Third World countries. These exports netted the Soviet Union more than $11 billion in foreign exchange.[28]

The world flow of exported petroleum originates mostly in the Middle East, which accounts for 37 percent of world production, and moves via tankers to Western European and Japanese customers. New petroleum discoveries have been made in China and Mexico, but there is little indication that significant export capacity will soon exist. While the United States and the Soviet Union are both large producers of petroleum, the United States is becoming a larger net importer by virtue of very heavy domestic demands. By 1985, the US could be importing as much as 60 percent of its petroleum consumption.[29]

Table 4–4 lists the world's major industrial countries and indicates their overall level of energy self-sufficiency. These figures include energy from all of the fossil fuels as well as production from hydroelectric, nuclear, and nonconventional sources. These data highlight the plight of most Western European countries and Japan, all countries that have witnessed a steady erosion of their energy self-sufficiency. One-half of the industrial countries now produce less than 50 percent of the energy consumed domestically from their own sources. Denmark meets virtually none of its energy requirements from domestic sources, Japan only 9 percent, and France 23 percent. In relation to these energy-deficient countries, the United States is in relatively good shape, producing 87 percent of the energy used from domestic fuels.

Some of the industrial countries listed in table 4–4 actually improved their energy self-sufficiency over the ten-year period. Norway experienced a substantial improvement because of petroleum discoveries in the North Sea and may soon be a small net energy exporter. The Netherlands has been blessed with a similar offshore discovery of natural gas, which changed it from a large net importer of energy in 1965 to a significant exporter in 1973. But this bonanza will come to an end in the early 1990s.[30]

Given historical trends toward greater global consumption of petroleum and natural gas and the present production, export, and reserve patterns, the success of the OPEC cartel in manipulating prices is easy to understand. Petroleum and natural gas are now essential to the health of industrial economies. Without them, transportation and industry would

TABLE 4-4. *Energy Self-Sufficiency in Industrial Countries*

	1965*	1975*	1975 Per Capita†
Denmark	.04	.01	5268
Finland	.10	.07	4766
Japan	.35	.09	3622
Belgium	.43	.15	5584
Italy	.22	.16	3012
Sweden	.17	.17	6178
Switzerland	.19	.21	3642
France	.48	.23	3944
Austria	.57	.39	3700
West Germany	.74	.50	5347
Great Britain	.69	.62	5265
Hungary	.76	.62	3624
East Germany	.84	.70	6835
United States	.91	.87	10999
Romania	1.18	1.00	3808
Poland	1.15	1.13	5007
Soviet Union	1.12	1.17	5546
Canada	.89	1.19	9880
Australia	.74	1.27	6485
Norway	.49	1.28	4607
Netherlands	.40	1.42	5784

*Production/Consumption.
†Measured in kilograms of coal equivalent per capita.
SOURCE: Derived from Statistical Yearbook of the United Nations, *1976*

come to a standstill. While there are alternative sources of energy, they are expensive and require extensive investment in a new energy infrastructure. The majority of industrial countries have negligible reserves, are dependent upon only a handful of petroleum exporters, and get a very small percentage of their energy from nuclear power. Thus, in late 1973 and early 1974, petroleum offered an ideal opportunity to test some of the ideas inherent in demands for a new international economic order.

The most obvious political impact of the original petroleum embargo and related price increases, precipitated by the Arab-Israeli war of 1973, was a massive shift in international political power. Leaders of OPEC countries, largely ignored in international political circles previously, suddenly found themselves courted by most major industrial nations. The immediate economic impact of the price increases was to shift a tremendous quantity of capital from oil-importing to oil-exporting countries. It has been estimated that during the first three years of higher prices the importing nations paid an additional $225 billion to OPEC for oil and, through recession, lost $600 billion worth of economic production.[31] The OPEC countries were unable to "recycle" these petrodollars rapidly enough through trade to keep the world economy from dropping into a deep recession, the gravest effects of which were felt in 1974 and 1975. Economic growth rates in industrial countries fell from a pre–price-increase average of 5.4 percent in real GNP to -1.4 percent in 1975. The developing countries experienced a decline from a 6.6 percent increase in real GNP to 1.9 percent. The least developed countries taken as a whole, however, did not experience much change in real GNP, although their plans for future economic growth based on cheap fossil fuels were severely shaken.[32]

It is estimated that by 1980 these increased oil prices will have cut 3.3 percent from the United States' real GNP, 4.5 percent from Western Europe's real GNP, and 4.7 percent from Japan's figures. This means that over the 1974–1980 period the cumulative economic loss to these areas will be the equivalent of fighting a small war.[33] It is also estimated that OPEC's financial assets will peak in the early 1980s at somewhere between $250 and $300 billion (1974 dollars).[34] And a future tight petroleum market in the 1980s will guarantee that the price of oil will continue to increase at least at a rate that will keep up with global inflation.

The impact of the OPEC cartel on the distribution of political power is not so easy to document. But as long as the cartel remains cohesive, this impact will be substantial. US support of Israel, for example, has been much more guarded than it might have been in the absence of the petroleum embargo. Japan and selected Western European countries have also moved their foreign policies in a pro-Arab direction in comparison with the late 1960s and early 1970s. OPEC countries have also purchased substantial quantities of modern arms, and their military forces now must be taken more seriously. Energy politics is creating other, more subtle, shifts in the international political economy. Differences in dependence on imported fuels have proven to be an irritant in relations among Western industrial countries, particularly as they try to frame common policies for dealing with future embargoes. And at the same time, the modest export position of the Soviet Union has taken on new significance, while the vulnerabilities of the United States have been emphasized.

The Industrial Coalitions

The energy crisis has created some serious differences among industrial countries that were not sources of friction in their relations prior to 1974. The great differences in energy self-sufficiency among the industrial powers lie at the center of these potential disputes. It has been suggested, for example, that United States policy makers actually encouraged the price increases of 1973–1974, or at least did not discourage them. The rationale is that the United States had a competitive advantage over its allies in world trade both because of its relatively high level of energy self-sufficiency and its good ties with Arab nations.[35] And there *is* evidence that the US made out much better than many other industrial countries, at least in the short run. By 1975, for example, the United States was running a balance of payments surplus of $11 billion. But this surplus was in large part due to extensive shipments of grain to the Soviet Union and other customers. By 1976, this positive balance disappeared, and the 1977 deficit was nearly $27 billion! In addition, the differing levels of energy self-sufficiency have an impact on nuclear power disputes. Countries without domestic sources of fuels, such as France and Japan, want to push forward with breeder reactors, while the United States, faced with less pressing needs, has argued for a "go slow" policy.

Coalition formation, leadership, and persistence are determined largely by what organizers and members can offer to each other to enhance materially the coalition's capabilities. In the three decades since World War II, the cement binding the members of NATO and the Warsaw Pact has been fear of military adventures by the other coalition. The coalition organizers, the United States and the Soviet Union, have been clearly predominant in both the military and economic spheres. But now the United States is increasingly seen among NATO allies as a competitor for fossil fuels. And the NATO allies are more sensitive to the threat of a new oil embargo than they are to a potential Warsaw Pact military invasion. At the same time, the natural gas and petroleum reserves in the Soviet Union have enhanced Soviet control within the Warsaw Pact. Should the Soviet Union decide not to honor petroleum and natural gas commitments to Eastern European countries, Eastern Europe would be forced to enter the hard-currency oil market, a prospect that no Eastern European leader would like to face given present shortages of foreign exchange.

The United States has historically been one of the world's largest producers of petroleum and natural gas. Unfortunately, the US has also been one of the world's largest consumers of energy and, with the exception of the Alaskan discoveries in 1970, reserves of both petroleum and natural gas have been on the decline since the mid-1960s.[36] The dependence of the United States on foreign imports of crude oil and refined products has continued to increase in the face of declining domestic production. Imports of crude oil jumped from 3.5 million barrels per day in 1974 to 4.1 million barrels per day in 1975, an increase of 18 percent. In early 1976, crude oil imports reached 5.6 million barrels per day plus 2.2 million barrels of refined products. This amount represented almost one-half of weekly supplies. In 1975, imports of crude oil and refined products amounted to 38 percent of total domestic consumption, while in 1976 this figure rose to 42 percent of consumption, largely as a result of the economic recovery.[37] The percentage of oil imported continued to rise in 1977.

It is difficult to determine the origin of all refined products that enter the United States, but sources of crude oil can be easily traced (see table 4–5). The primary US source has been Saudi Arabia, followed closely by Nigeria. Indonesia has also steadily increased as an oil supplier. Canada and Venezuela combine to supply only one-tenth of the United States' needs, and Canada has been rapidly declining as a source of crude petroleum. Canadian officials have announced plans to cease all exports of petroleum to the United States by 1981.[38] Crude petroleum statistics can be a bit misleading, however, since Venezuela did supply the US with 645,000 barrels of refined petroleum products on a daily basis in 1976.[39]

The Soviet Union's energy situation stands in stark contrast to that of the United States. In 1976, the USSR was the world's leading producer of petroleum, with an average production of 10.4 million barrels of oil per day. This production represented a 6 percent increase over that of 1975. Natural gas production increased by 11 percent over the same period. The Soviet production target for 1980 is 12.8 million barrels per day.[40] Technological problems, however, have forced the USSR to cut increases in exports to Eastern Europe in order to increase exports to hard-currency countries. In 1976, exports to hard-currency countries increased by 14 percent over 1975, while exports to Eastern Europe increased by only 7 percent.[41]

Nearly one-third of Russian petroleum now comes from western Siberia, an increase from only 9 percent in 1970, while production in the more established Volga/Ural region has been on a steady decline over the same period. Ninety percent of Soviet reserves lie east of the Ural Mountains, while four-fifths of Soviet industry lies to the west of the mountains, in the European portion of the country. Since three-fourths

TABLE 4–5. Sources of US Imports of Crude Petroleum*

	1973	1974	1975	1976	1977†
Saudi Arabia	462	338	655	1215	1449
Nigeria	448	655	729	964	1215
Indonesia	201	275	375	535	547
Algeria	120	203	280	438	506
Libya	133	5	179	423	708
Canada	1001	865	610	395	279
Iran	216	535	264	322	524
United Arab Emirates	71	80	138	222	332
Venezuela	345	302	302	214	233
Other	247	242	564	480	902
Total	3244	3500	4096	5208	6695

*Thousands of barrels per day.
†First six months.

SOURCES: World Oil (February 15, 1976), Oil and Gas Journal, (January 31, 1977), Office of Economic Research, Central Intelligence Agency, "International Oil Developments" September 9, 1976, and World Oil, February 15, 1978.

of Soviet fuel consumption takes place west of the Urals, long pipelines are being constructed from Siberia at a very high cost. By 1980, it is estimated that, on the average, natural gas will be transported 1400 miles from well to user. A similar situation will exist in the petroleum industry.[42]

The Soviet energy problem is thus quite different from that faced by the United States. Reserves of petroleum and natural gas are more than adequate to spur economic growth for quite some time. The problem lies with technology-related delays in drilling for and transporting natural gas and petroleum from Siberia to the western part of the Soviet Union. The industrial areas where natural gas and petroleum are consumed are far from the wellhead, and the cost of transportation is great. Thus, the Soviet energy problem can be solved by technology and capital, while the United States is faced with depletion of reserves.

The leaders of the two major industrial coalitions would thus seem to have very different energy futures, and these differences will continue to reshape relations with other coalition members. In the case of the Western coalition, the United States is a net energy importer and unable to help coalition members to meet energy needs. Since United States reserves are declining, the US is increasingly seen by other coalition members as a competitor for Middle Eastern petroleum. Furthermore, in order to balance international payments, the US is also involved in competition with France and West Germany in the sale of high-technology products, including nuclear reactors. The US is also attempting to limit development of the breeder reactor, which some other coalition members favor. As ecopolitical concerns become increasingly important in international affairs and as fear of a conventional East-West war subsides, the ability of the United States to dominate coalition decision making will certainly be lessened because of its natural resource vulnerability and related trade and currency problems.

The Soviet Union, in contrast, occupies a much different position within the Warsaw Pact. The present Soviet dominance within the alliance is congruent with the uneven distribution of fuels and other minerals within the bloc countries. The USSR continues to supply considerable amounts of petroleum and natural gas to Czechoslovakia, East Germany, Hungary, and Bulgaria. Only Romania is even close to petroleum self-sufficiency and, therefore, not dependent upon Soviet petroleum exports. The implications of this situation for the future of Soviet bloc relations are obvious. As natural resources, particularly fuels, become more important in determining foreign policies, Eastern Europe will be very vulnerable to Soviet demands. Although increased prices for Soviet fuels, designed to bring Soviet prices closer to world prices, may be a minor irritant in Warsaw Pact relations, Eastern European countries cannot afford to obtain much of their energy from high-priced oil from the Middle East. The flow of petroleum, natural gas, and even alternative energy technologies from the Soviet Union to Eastern

Europe guarantees the integrity of the coalition and the domination of the USSR for many decades to come.[43]

In summary, increased world energy prices and the development of a scarcity perspective in petroleum and natural gas markets have had a very different impact on the two major coalitions. The common interests holding the NATO countries together are no longer as apparent as they once were because of a diminution of the perceived threat from the Soviet Union and because of increased dependence of all coalition members on external sources of fuels. The United States is unable to exert strong coalition leadership on energy matters because of the diverse interests of NATO members. France, Italy, and Germany can hardly take a militant position in relation to OPEC because of their dependence on these countries for petroleum. The United States, however, could exploit alternative sources of energy, such as oil shale, should that become necessary, and would be much less crippled by another petroleum boycott. Such divergent interests on energy matters have precluded the development of any meaningful common energy policies among Western industrial countries. Indeed, competition to export arms and nuclear technology to OPEC nations has become strong among NATO members and several Western European countries now import natural gas directly from the Soviet Union via pipeline.

On the other side of the fence, energy- and mineral-deficient members of the Warsaw Pact find themselves drawn closer to their resource-rich coalition leader. The leadership position of the Soviet Union has been strengthened by increased fuel prices. Fragile Eastern European economies are already seriously burdened by hard-currency debts and could not withstand the economic shock involved in switching to Middle Eastern petroleum.

Petroleum and Less Developed Countries

During the period immediately following the large increase in petroleum prices and the rapid accumulation of new wealth in OPEC hands, the rest of the Third World and members of OPEC professed great solidarity. A major redistribution of the world's wealth was expected to be part of the creation of a new international economic order. OPEC was envisioned by many Third World leaders as an international Robin Hood, a cartel taking money from the hands of the industrial rich and putting it into the hands of the agrarian poor. The industrial world was collectively viewed as an enemy to be forced to pay higher costs for petroleum while the less developed world, collectively, would reap many benefits. Subsequent events have shown these expectations to be erroneous.

There are several reasons why the scenario that leaders of non–oil-exporting less developed countries had in mind has not occurred. First, there is only a very thin identity of interests between the major oil exporters, which might be called "nouveau riche" countries, and the large number of less developed countries that have nothing to export to accumulate wealth. The major oil exporters feel no more of a moral obligation to aid the world's less developed countries than do those countries that are already industrialized.[44] The oil-importing less developed countries have been forced to pay the same higher oil costs as the industrial world because OPEC has been unwilling to create a two-tiered pricing structure. And OPEC countries have not passed on much of their increased profits to less developed countries. In fact, OPEC foreign aid has been modest, certainly not nearly enough to make up for the losses suffered by the less developed world because of higher petroleum prices.

There are several basic weaknesses in the economies of less developed countries that make them especially vulnerable to increased petroleum prices. Foremost among these is the fundamental problem of their competitive trade position: the industrial countries, which export high-technology products, are in a much better trade position than are many less developed countries, which export agricultural commodities. As the price of petroleum rises, the industrial countries are able to "pass through" added costs by increasing the prices of their exports. As fuel prices rise, so do the prices of industrial goods. But the less developed countries are in no position to increase their prices as rapidly. Thus, by 1977, the industrial economies had adjusted to the higher petroleum prices by increasing exports and export prices. But the large number of non–oil-exporting less developed countries had to cope with an increasing debt burden incurred to pay for petroleum imports, as well as increased prices for imported industrial goods.

The worldwide economic recession triggered by the petroleum price increases was another factor that was not taken into consideration in the period of Third World euphoria immediately following the OPEC success. The less developed countries, mineral exporters and non-exporters alike, are very dependent on the economic health of the industrial countries for their own economic growth. Slowed economic growth in industrial countries depresses raw materials markets, worsening economic conditions in those countries dependent upon the export of raw materials to gain foreign exchange. An extended period of economic recovery was necessary in industrial countries before raw material inventories were reduced. Prices on nonfuel minerals and agricultural commodities remained depressed for several years, creating a serious gap between high-priced petroleum imports and cheapened exports in many less developed countries.

Finally, there are differences among countries in the extent to which petroleum is an essential component of growth. The early stages of industrial growth are energy intensive. In the non–fuel-exporting less developed countries with per capita incomes below $200, petroleum accounted for more than 8 percent of all 1972 imports. Given the combination of quadrupled petroleum prices and depressed economies of the less developed countries, petroleum accounted for nearly one-quarter of all imports in these countries after the price increases. In those non–petroleum-exporting developing countries with per capita incomes of $375 and above, petroleum accounted for only 5 percent of total imports. This figure has now increased to about 15 percent.[45] The world's less industrialized countries have a great need for additional petroleum imports and little potential for cutting back consumption through conservation measures. In many industrial countries, however, petroleum imports are a much smaller portion of all imports. And where they aren't, the industrial countries can compensate with a wider range of exports.

Prospects for the less developed countries offsetting increased petroleum costs with foreign aid from OPEC countries are not good. It appears that the windfall gains in real purchasing power experienced by OPEC members in the 1973–1975 period will never be repeated. By 1976, most of the members of OPEC had increased their spending to a level that exhausted the additional revenues. Iran, for example, was borrowing additional capital in the international banking community as early as 1975. Only small quantities of aid were provided to less developed countries by OPEC when the treasuries were full, and it is unlikely that more will be provided when the treasuries are depleted. Furthermore, it is illogical to expect OPEC to act as a banker for any future cartel-like withholding actions by other Third World countries. Such actions by exporters of other basic commodities would certainly not be in the interest of OPEC, since higher prices for other basic commodities would have an impact on OPEC countries and further cripple growth in the industrial world, the market for OPEC petroleum.

These results of the petroleum price hike were inadequately anticipated by most of the non-oil-exporting Third World countries, and they are linked to the emergence of a "Fourth World," which is composed of about one-fifth of all existing countries. It is now widely accepted that the quadrupled petroleum prices combined with growing debt burdens may have created a "never-to-be-developed" world, countries that have no prospects for growth within the established fossil fuel–dependent paradigm. It is estimated, for example, that these less developed countries were forced to borrow $62 billion in 1976–1977, largely to finance their bills for petroleum imports.[46] Thus, the Robin Hood expectations held by leaders of many of these countries at the time of the petroleum price increases have not been met, and it is future generations in these less developed countries that have probably suffered the most damage because of the price increases.

There are several variables that will shape the long-term future of energy politics. The ultimate constraint is the size of available reserves of petroleum in relation to demand. In the late 1970s, there was a short-term glut of crude petroleum sparked by a combination of global recession, conservation measures in consumer countries, and the efforts of small petroleum-producing countries to market newly developed reserves. This glut is not expected to continue into the 1980s. In the medium and long terms, the finite nature of petroleum and natural gas reserves juxtaposed with exponentially increasing demand means that severe market dislocations are likely. In the medium term, it is expected that demand will begin to exceed production capacity in the mid-1980s, partially because of the unwillingness of some countries to expand production.[47] And as the year 2000 approaches, depletion accompanied by skyrocketing prices will become a reality.

A second set of variables will come into play long before depletion becomes a significant factor. These variables include changes in political and economic conditions within the significant oil exporting and importing countries, the success of conservation efforts in industrial countries, and the willingness of OPEC countries to expand production.

A third set of important variables includes new national actors and new technologies in the petroleum marketplace. Included here are the use of gasified coal, oil shale, or other fossil fuel substitutes for petroleum and natural gas, and new fission or fusion technologies that might make the fossil fuels obsolete. It is impossible to speak with certainty about any of these developments. But recent history indicates little likelihood of a major breakthrough in these areas, and all alternative energy sources are expensive. There are some potential new national actors in the petroleum marketplace, including China and Mexico, but only small increases in exports can be expected in the near future. As recently as 1975, China was touted as a new Saudi Arabia, but these optimistic forecasts have mellowed over time. Virtually nothing happened between 1975 and 1977, when China was once again reported to be buying drilling equipment.[48] Mexico now has some oil and natural gas for export, but its reserves are estimated at about one-fifth and one-twentieth, respectively, those of the United States.

But the most important factor shaping the future of the international energy market is the cohesion of the Organization of Petroleum Exporting Countries. If OPEC remains effective, continued price increases can be expected. Should OPEC collapse, however, lower prices and completely different patterns of petroleum consumption would result. The Organization of Petroleum Exporting Countries has played a pivotal role in turning empty phrases about a new international economic order into an economic and political reality in which traditional dominance and dependence relationships in petroleum markets have been reversed.

Its sudden success in 1974 obscures the fact that the early days of OPEC were filled with internal bickering and frustrations.[49] Formed in 1960, the organization included Venezuela, Saudi Arabia, Kuwait, Iraq, and Iran. It was created in reaction to a fifteen-year period (1945–1960) in which world demand for petroleum increased while prices paid to oil-exporting countries declined. (In 1948, the price of a barrel of crude oil was fixed at $2.17. The major oil companies cut this price to $1.80 in 1960.[50] Petroleum prices declined in the 1945–1960 period because of three developments in the international petroleum marketplace. First, the monopoly of the Seven Sisters* in the petroleum market was disturbed by the entry of smaller "independent" producers, such as Phillips, Sun, and Atlantic Richfield. The independents were interested in cutting into the majors' markets, which meant buying and selling petroleum and gasoline as cheaply as possible. This development forced the Seven Sisters to reassess their own price structure and resulted in lower prices paid to petroleum-exporting countries, the weakest links in the pricing chain.

The emergence of the Soviet Union as an oil exporter was the second factor that undercut the established world petroleum price structure. The Soviets both sold and bartered their petroleum at prices designed to capture the market from established exporters. This maneuver also led the majors to cut prices of gasoline and, eventually, prices paid for crude petroleum in order to meet the competition.

Finally, the previously stable price structure was shaken by the entry of Italy's Ente Nazionali Idrocarburi (ENI) as the first consumer-owned petroleum company in the international marketplace. ENI undertook to obtain oil for Italy, a country with virtually no domestic production, at the lowest possible prices. This undertaking meant bulk purchases directly from producer countries and, in the short run, increased competition among the majors for a shrinking consumer market.[51]

In its early years, OPEC had little impact where the vital interests of oil companies were concerned. The companies controlled downstream transportation, refining, and sales. Therefore, they were in a position to discipline unruly political leaders through selective buying. Furthermore, during this period new discoveries outran yearly demand, and petroleum exporters were pitted against each other in a scramble to sell as much as possible. Finally, there were many political and cultural divisions within OPEC that precluded serious cooperation in taking any political actions that entailed significant risks. At the time that OPEC

---

*Gulf, Texaco, Mobil, Standard of New Jersey, Standard of California, British Petroleum, and Royal Dutch Shell.

was formed, Arab nations were ruled by conservative leaders who were not much interested in petroleum intrigue. But Iran, Venezuela, and eventually Indonesia all had different, and much more radical, perspectives on desirable political and economic policies.[52]

The closing of the Suez Canal in 1967 marked a turning point in relations between OPEC and the oil industry. It revealed Western Europe's increasing vulnerability to the interruption of oil supplies from the Middle East. Although the closing led to the use of supertankers capable of carrying huge loads of petroleum around the tip of Africa, thus circumventing the canal, the period of adjustment was expensive, and the OPEC nations experienced a taste of petroleum power.

The second Arab-Israeli war in 1973 provided a catalyst that helped forge OPEC into an effective cartel. The hostilities with Israel did not directly result in a united OPEC policy. In fact, the subsequent petroleum embargo was sponsored only by the Organization of Arab Petroleum Exporting Countries (OAPEC), not OPEC, and aimed primarily at the United States and the Netherlands. It was, furthermore, only partially effective, because non-Arab exporters increased their shipments, which were then transshipped from nonembargoed to embargoed countries. Once having raised prices dramatically as a semieconomic, semipunitive move, however, and having felt no economic or military repercussions from the industrial countries, the leaders of oil-exporting countries became more secure in their manipulation of petroleum prices. OPEC is made up of countries with remarkably different cultural, economic, social, and political histories and prospects, and it is doubtful that the cartel could yet be functioning effectively had it not been for the powerful catalytic effect of the 1973 Middle Eastern war. Although more radical elements in OPEC had begun to force prices slightly upward in 1973, these minor increases could not have provided revenues on the scale necessary to create OPEC cohesion. Once the new price structure was established, however, OPEC unity could be maintained for obvious economic reasons.

Even the sagging petroleum market of 1975, which forced some OPEC countries to produce at less than three-quarters of capacity, did not disrupt the cartel. Some OPEC members could cut production to 50 percent of preembargo levels and the economic return within the new price structure would still be two to three times as great as it was under the old. As long as all significant members of the cartel act in a politically rational manner, there is no reason for it to collapse. There is presently enough agreement among key actors to keep prices from retreating to anything close to those of preembargo times.

There are four factors that have the potential to be continued sources of conflict within the OPEC cartel. The first is the different levels of production capacity and proved reserves, which are detailed in table 4-6. The cartel includes both petroleum giants, such as Saudi Arabia, Kuwait, and Iran, and petroleum "lightweights," such as Ecua-

TABLE 4-6. *OPEC Profile*

	1977 Population Estimate (Millions)	1976 Reserves*	1976 Production†	1975–1976 Percent Change in Production	1977 Production Capacity‡	1975 Per Capita Income (US Dollars)	1975 Oil Revenues (Billions of Dollars)
Saudi Arabia	7.6	110.2	3,054	+22.2	11,500	3,010	26.8
Kuwait	1.1	69.5	700	+4.0	3,500	11,510	7.8
Iran	34.8	48.1	2,153	+9.9	6,500	1,440	19.2
Iraq	11.8	35.2	835	+2.8	3,000	1,280	8.3
Abu Dhabi	.2	24.9	572	+11.7	2,000	10,480	6.4
Libya	2.7	24.5	707	+30.6	2,500	5,080	5.8
Venezuela	12.7	18.3	840	−2.2	2,700	2,220	8.2
Nigeria	66.6	12.2	758	+14.5	2,500	310	6.4
Indonesia	136.9	11.5	550	+15.1	1,700	180	4.3
Algeria	17.8	9.6	384	+11.2	1,000	780	3.4
Qatar	0.1	5.1	181	+7.8	700	8,320	1.6
Ecuador	7.5	1.3	69	+16.4	225	550	0.6
Gabon	.5	.5	83	+1.6	250	2,240	0.8

*Billions of barrels.
†Millions of barrels.
‡Thousands of barrels per day.

SOURCES: World Oil (August 15, 1975), Washington Post (December 18, 1976), *and* Population Reference Bureau, 1977 World Population Data Sheet (Washington, D.C., 1977).

dor and Gabon. The size of reserves shapes the time and price perspectives that different OPEC nations bring to negotiating sessions.
Saudi Arabia, for example, does not worry about extracting a few extra
dimes per barrel if to do so means a cutback in production. Venezuela,
on the other hand, is a declining exporter of petroleum and cannot sustain present plans without more oil revenue. Venezuela now possesses
high-quality reserves of only 18.3 billion barrels, which means, given an
annual production of nearly 1 billion barrels, it will run out of high-
quality petroleum in less than 20 years. The relative shortness of
Venezuelan depletion horizons means that a cutback in production in
the interest of greater income per barrel is desirable.

The second factor that leads to different perceptions of self-
interest and possible conflict among OPEC petroleum exporters is population. Kuwait has the second largest petroleum reserve within OPEC
but only about 1 million people to support with production revenues.
About half of this small population is composed of workers from other
countries—and 70 percent of the labor force is of non-Kuwait origin.[53]
These imported workers do not have full Kuwait citizenship and receive
relatively low wages. In short, there are presently less than 500,000 politically and economically relevant citizens in Kuwait to be kept sat-
isfied with oil revenues.

Pricing Kuwait's present proved reserves at an average of $15 per
barrel means there is approximately $2,085,000 worth of future petro-
leum wealth in the ground for each politically relevant citizen of
Kuwait. To put it another way, 1976 production of 700 million barrels
priced at $15 per barrel yields $21,000 per relevant citizen. Thus, there is
little rush in Kuwait rapidly to pump petroleum from present reserves.
Iran, on the other hand, is populated by 34,800,000 semirestive citizens,
most of whom expect to share in the petroleum wealth immediately. Not
only does the Shah of Iran wish to squeeze the maximum possible price
from a barrel of petroleum, he also hopes to keep production high in order that adequate revenues may be provided for ambitious development projects.

A third set of potentially divisive factors is closely related to these
population differences. Each OPEC country has a different absorptive
capacity to use increased oil revenues based upon population and levels
of industrialization. Kuwait and Saudi Arabia both possess relatively
small populations and industrial infrastructures. Their ability to apply
greater petroleum revenues to worthwhile development projects is
limited, and additional money earned is likely to be placed in foreign
bank accounts. Iran, and several lesser producers, in contrast, are engaged in intense industrialization and diversification efforts and can absorb more capital than they are now earning. In fact, in 1975, in spite of
greatly increased petroleum revenues, Iran was forced to borrow to
cover development expenses. Thus, Iran and other rapidly industrializing members of OPEC feel more pressures for immediate additional

revenue than do more conservative members of the coalition.

Finally, divisive political factors are important when discussing future prospects for OPEC unity. There are many differences in political philosophy and policy priorities between Arab and non-Arab members of OPEC. Even among the Arab members there are serious differences of opinion that remain to be resolved. The 1973 war against Israel revealed an Arab world badly divided. Egypt and Syria shouldered the brunt of the military burden, and Iraq contributed some troops. Saudi Arabia and Kuwait took some responsibility for the petroleum embargo, but assistance from other Arab countries was more symbolic than real. Indeed, different colonial heritages, different developmental situations, different attitudes toward Israel and the Palestine Liberation Organization (PLO), and different importance attached to traditional values all impede efforts at community building within OPEC.[54]

Saudi Arabia, Kuwait, and Iran are the pivotal members of OPEC. Saudi Arabia possesses more than one-quarter of proved OPEC reserves, a fact that certainly shapes a Saudi self-interest that is quite different from that of lesser producers. Saudi Arabian proved reserves total more than 110 billion barrels, nearly 20 percent of the world total. When "probable" reserves are added, the total rises to 173 billion barrels, enough to keep Saudi Arabia pumping at current rates for another sixty years.[55] Ultimate depletion of Saudi reserves doesn't enter into present policy considerations, given the time frame involved. Future softening of world petroleum markets due to higher prices would be a much greater irritant to Saudi Arabia than it would be to countries with smaller reserves. Thus, Saudi Arabia is willing to sell at a lower price per barrel if this means increased production and total revenue. This attitude often puts Saudi Arabia at odds with some less wealthy OPEC members.

Saudi Arabia's leaders are politically conservative, and the population (7.6 million) is small. Furthermore, there is only a modest industrial infrastructure, and plans for industrial development have moved forward rather cautiously. Thus, both absorption capacity and need for additional revenues are minimal, and Saudi Arabia would prefer to restrain OPEC from raising prices and lowering global consumption. In December of 1976, Saudi Arabia and the United Arab Emirates refused to go along with a 10 percent price increase proposed by eleven other OPEC members. The Saudis hoped to discipline the eleven by expanding production capacity and flooding the world market. The cold winter of 1976–1977 helped to foil the Saudi plan by increasing demand, and they never were able to reach their production target at any rate. In July of 1977, a compromise was worked out. Saudi Arabia increased prices by 5 percent and other members failed to increase their prices on schedule. In this respect, it was a minor victory for Saudi Arabia.

Kuwait and Iran are the other two key actors in OPEC. Together they possess reserves nearly equal to those of Saudi Arabia. In combination *with* Saudi reserves, they account for more than two-thirds of all OPEC petroleum. These "Big Three" oil exporters hold the key to the cartel's future. If they can continue to agree on pricing policies and production quotas, no other OPEC member now has enough excess production capacity to determine world petroleum prices.

Although the size of their reserves is reasonably similar, there are few other similarities between Kuwait and Iran. Kuwait is ruled by social and political conservatives who are not inclined to engage in economic modernization at the expense of traditional values. The politically relevant population is small, as is Kuwait's ability to absorb additional petroleum revenue. Thus, Kuwait has little interest in expanding production, and it helped to maintain the OPEC price structure by cutting back production 20 percent in 1974. This cutback was in part due to lack of customers for the heavy crude produced by Kuwait but was also partly motivated by political factors. There have been reports that some influentials in Kuwait favor cutting back production in order to keep oil in the "bank" rather than to acquire foreign currency.[56]

Iran also plays a pivotal role in OPEC politics but is in a much different developmental situation. Iran has 34.8 million people, more than sixty times the politically relevant population of Kuwait, and, as noted previously, the Shah of Iran is engaged in a massive industrialization effort. He is interested in selling as much oil as possible at the highest possible prices. Thus, he has frequently opened OPEC negotiations by suggesting price increases of 20 to 30 percent, and this has put Iran at loggerheads with Saudi Arabia. While many exporters were cutting back production in 1974 and world demand was declining, Iran actually increased production by 3 percent, drilled 64 new wells, and ordered several more drilling rigs, indications of an uncompromising pursuit of greater production and more revenue.[57]

Although it possesses only half the reserves of Kuwait, Iraq's reserves of crude are larger than those of the United States. Iraq's political leadership is radical, has ambitious expansion plans, and hopes to double production by 1980. Iraq wants to move as much petroleum at as high a price possible. Thus, it was reported to be cutting prices by at least ten cents a barrel in 1976 in order to expand production.[58] In December 1976, Iraq's oil minister castigated Saudi Arabia for not going along with the price increase and threatened a campaign of active sedition against the country.[59]

The reserves of all the remaining members of OPEC combined barely equal those of Saudi Arabia. These countries can be divided into two groups. Abu Dhabi and Qatar are similar to Kuwait, Middle Eastern producers with conservative perspectives. Abu Dhabi is the largest producer among the United Arab Emirates, which is represented as a group within OPEC. It produces modest quantities of petroleum and takes positions similar to those of Kuwait on OPEC policy matters. With a population of less than 200,000, no extensive program of technological development, and conservative politicians, Abu Dhabi is quite content to hold down production to maintain prices. Qatar produces less petroleum than Abu Dhabi but also has a much smaller population, just over 100,000 people. Politics there are conservative, and absorptive capacity for additional petroleum revenues is limited.

The second group could be labeled "industrializing exporters" and is composed of Nigeria, Venezuela, Libya, Indonesia, and Algeria. Libya and Algeria bring radical political perspectives to OPEC meetings. The radical regime of Colonel Khaddafi in Libya actually instigated petroleum price increases as early as 1970 in order to gain more revenue for development programs and radical political causes. Algeria also can absorb much more oil revenue and is interested in maximum production at highest possible prices. Nigeria, Venezuela, and Indonesia, all non-Arab members of OPEC, have a common interest in larger revenues. Both Indonesia and Nigeria possess large and impoverished populations, 137 million and 67 million, respectively. And both are anxious to expand petroleum production as rapidly as possible. In 1976, both Nigeria and Indonesia increased production by 15 percent over 1975. Venezuela would prefer to increase production but is caught in a political and economic bind. Venezuelan crude is very heavy and, therefore, less desirable at present prices. There is an abundance of tar sands, expensive sources of crude oil that may play a future role in the world energy economy. Nationalization of the oil industry has compounded sales problems, since former participating oil companies have agreed to market less crude than Venezuelan leaders would prefer. Venezuela is now producing at less than three-quarters of the levels reached in 1970. Ecuador and Gabon possess minuscule reserves, and their total production is insignificant. Neither plays a significant role in the future of OPEC politics.

The future of OPEC and, by inference, the future of the world petroleum market, will be determined by the interplay of these individual actors having different policy preferences. While the actions of the "Big Three" are the most crucial to OPEC cohesion, attention must be paid to the demands of the "Middle Five" OPEC members having great absorption capacity. United by a desire to increase production and revenues, they can act collectively as a fourth power in OPEC politics. And their power will grow in the 1980s if projections of production capacity problems on a global scale prove to be wellfounded.[60]

There are some external threats to OPEC unity, but they are minimal at present. The emergence of major petroleum exporters outside of OPEC is a possibility. But only the Soviet Union has potential reserves large enough to disrupt OPEC pricing policies. And it is neither politically nor economically inclined to do so. The Soviet Union is now producing at capacity and has no trouble finding markets for its petroleum. There is no motive for it to sell petroleum on the world market below established prices.

China and Mexico could conceivably play a role in influencing the future world market. Both are newcomers to the petroleum-exporting business. China first drew world attention during the petroleum embargo in 1974, when 20,000 barrels of petroleum daily were shipped to Japan at a price of $14.80 per barrel. China exported ten times as much petroleum in 1975 and cut the price to $12.10 per barrel, making Chinese oil cheaper than the Indonesian crude imported by Japan. In February 1978, China and Japan signed a major trade agreement centering on Chinese crude petroleum and Japanese technology. Mexico is also developing export capacity in petroleum and natural gas but has pledged not to undercut OPEC prices.

China made little effort to develop an oil industry until 1960. Since that time, however, drilling and exploratory activity have rapidly increased. Between 1960 and 1968, thirty-three commercial fields were discovered. China's proven reserves have been estimated at 18 billion barrels, but some experts think that greater exploratory efforts may eventually yield reserves three times as large, which would move China into fifth place, just behind Iran.[61] These reserves have barely been touched and, since Chinese domestic requirements for oil remain modest, the Chinese can be expected to become serious exporters in the international petroleum marketplace. The Japanese estimate that China will be producing more than 3 billion barrels annually by 1985 and hope to be able to count on significant imports from China. While that would permit Japan to diversify its sources of imports, the net effect on the world petroleum market would be negligible.

With all of these factors in mind, it is possible to hazard some estimates about the future of world petroleum prices. Without some unforeseen political calamity capable of destroying the cohesion of OPEC, such as a major war in the Middle East or a series of assassinations of political leaders, there is little reason to expect the cartel to disintegrate. And, at present, a major war in the Middle East seems less likely. The current price structure seemingly has now been accepted by both producers and consumers. The only direction to expect prices to go in the near future is slowly upward, as demand continues to grow rapidly while production grows more slowly. OPEC will continue to argue that price increases should at least keep up with world inflation so that the real purchasing power of oil revenues is maintained. Thus, global inflation will set the minimum expectations of OPEC negotiators. In the short term, Saudi Arabia can act as a dampening force on price increases, but as production capacity is reached in the 1980s, more rapidly increasing prices can be expected.

The emergence of significant new actors within OPEC—Iraq, Libya, Nigeria, Indonesia, Algeria—and of the USSR, Mexico, and China outside of OPEC places some restraints on the size of price increases but only for the next few years. These countries are all interested in immediate increases in revenue. If prices increase dramatically they know that this would at present drive down world demand and decrease total revenue. The emergence of the USSR, Mexico, and China as petroleum exporters serves as a further short-term curb against excessive price increases. But none of these countries has any political or economic motives for undercutting OPEC. All three are profiting handsomely from the higher prices, and all are committed to supporting the existing petroleum prices.

In summary, given the high profits and prices that have been established within OPEC, there is little reason to expect a collapse in the cartel at present or in the near future. It is likely that prices will move upward, being restrained only by minor price-shaving maneuvers undertaken by some of the lesser petroleum exporters in the short term. As demand increases in the face of limited capacity in the 1980s, however, it is very likely that prices will increase much more rapidly. At present, Saudi Arabia can still flood the world market and thus veto price increases. But in the 1980s it will no longer be able to do so, thus giving increased political and economic leverage to each significant petroleum exporter.

ENDNOTES

1. For more information on alternative energy technologies, see Wilson Clark, *Energy for Survival* (New York: Anchor Books, 1975).
2. 1976 world oil reserves were 550 billion barrels, and annual production was 21 billion barrels. *World Oil*, "International Outlook Issue" (August 15, 1977).
3. Donella Meadows, et al., *The Limits to Growth* (New York: Universe Books, 1972), pp. 58–59. For information on yearly additions to proved reserves, see WAES, *Energy: Global Prospects 1985–2000* (New York: McGraw-Hill, 1977), pp. 119–124.
4. The most detailed estimates of future world energy supplies are found in WAES, *Energy: Global Prospects 1985–2000.*
5. GATT, International Trade 1975/76 (Geneva: General Agreement on Tariffs and Trade, 1976).
6. "Ten Year Industry Investment Must Total $955 Billion," *World Oil* (April 1976).
7. "The Money Market: Can It Handle Industry Needs?" *World Oil* (March 1976).
8. See Central Intelligence Agency, "The International Energy Situation: Outlook to 1985" (Washington, D.C., 1977).
9. The ten largest industrial companies are Exxon, General Motors, Royal Dutch Shell, Texaco, Ford Motors, Mobil, National Iranian Oil, British Petroleum, Standard Oil of California, and Unilever. *Fortune* (August 1976).
10. A readable discussion of the laws of thermodynamics is presented in Barry Commoner, *The Poverty of Power* (New York: Alfred A. Knopf, 1976), chap. 2.

11. WAES, *Energy: Global Prospects 1985–2000*, pp. 170–171.
12. For more detailed information, see Earl Cook, *Man, Energy, Society* (San Francisco: W. H. Freeman, 1976), pp. 75–87.
13. M. King Hubbert, "Energy Resources," in National Academy of Sciences, *Resources and Man* (San Francisco: W. H. Freeman, 1969).
14. *World Oil* (August 15, 1977).
15. These estimates are discussed in detail in WAES, *Energy: Global Prospects 1985–2000*, pp. 115–116.
16. Ibid., pp. 119–122.
17. Ibid., pp. 149–151.
18. Ibid. Chap. 4 has more details.
19. See "U.S. Reserves: All Downhill from Here," *World Oil* (February 15, 1976), and "U.S. Production: No Help Until 1977," *World Oil* (February 15, 1976).
20. British Petroleum, "LNG in the Next Ten Years" (London, 1976).
21. See "The Hottest Item on the Shelf," *Fortune* (April 1973), and "A Flood of Foreign LNG for U.S. Factories," *Business Week* (October 13, 1975).
22. See "U.S. Reserves: All Downhill From Here," *World Oil*.
23. Cook, *Man, Energy, Society*, pp. 236–237.
24. See Lee Schipper and Allan Lichtenberg, "Efficient Energy Use and Well-Being: The Swedish Example," *Science* (December 3, 1976).
25. Glenn Hueckel, "A Historical Approach to Future Economic Growth," *Science* (March 14, 1975).
26. See Richard Gordon, *The Evolution of Energy Policy in Western Europe* (New York: Praeger, 1970). Contemporary data are from the Organization for Economic Cooperation and Development, *World Energy Outlook* (Paris, 1977), p. 91.
27. See Central Intelligence Agency, Office of Economic Research, "International Oil Developments" (September 9, 1976).
28. Figures reported in *Business Week* (October 17, 1977): 52; Murray Seeger, "Search for New Energy May Alter Soviet–East Europe Ties," *Washington Post* (September 18, 1977); Danilo Rigassi, "The USSR: West Siberia Is Where the Reserves Are," *World Oil* (August 15, 1977). See also Iain Elliot, *The Soviet Energy Balance* (New York: Praeger, 1974).
29. Executive Office of the President, *The National Energy Plan* (Washington, D.C., 1977), p. 14.
30. See William Drozdiak, "The Dutch Gas Bubble," *The Washington Post* (June 20, 1977).
31. Reported in *Business Week* (December 20, 1976): 45.
32. See Davis Bobrow, Robert Kudrle, and Dennis Pirages, "Contrived Scarcity: The Short-Term Consequences of Expensive Oil," *International Studies Quarterly* (December 1977).
33. See Edward Fried and Charles Schultze, eds., *Higher Oil Prices and the World Economy* (Washington, D.C.: Brookings Institution, 1975). pp. 46–48.
34. See Hollis Chenery, "Restructuring the World Economy," *Foreign Affairs* (January 1975), and Thomas Enders, "OPEC and the Industrial Countries: The Next Ten Years," *Foreign Affairs* (July 1975).
35. William Greider and J. P. Smith, "A Proposition: High Oil Prices Benefit U.S.," *Washington Post* (July 10, 1977).

36. See "U.S. Reserves: All Downhill From Here," *World Oil*, and "U.S. Production: No Help Until 1977," *World Oil*.
37. "Economic Recovery Spurs Oil Demand Rise," *World Oil* (February 15, 1976).
38. Reported in *World Oil* (February 15, 1976).
39. *World Oil* (February 15, 1977), 59.
40. Rigassi, "The USSR."
41. Seeger, "Search for New Energy May Alter Soviet–East Europe Ties."
42. See Donald Kelley, ed., *The Energy Crisis and the Environment* (New York: Praeger, 1977), chap. 3.
43. See George Klein, "Eastern Europe: Czechoslovakia, Romania, and Yugoslavia," in Kelley, ed., *The Energy Crisis and the Environment*. For more information on Eastern European hard-currency debts, see Richard Portes, "East Europe's Debt to the West: Interdependence Is a Two-Way Street," *Foreign Affairs* (July 1977).
44. See John Lewis, "Oil, Other Scarcities, and the Poor Countries," *World Politics* (October 1974).
45. Wouter Tims, "The Developing Countries," in Fried and Schultze, eds., *Higher Oil Prices and the World Economy*, p. 177.
46. David Beim, "Rescuing the LDCs," *Foreign Affairs* (July 1977).
47. See Central Intelligence Agency, "The International Energy Situation."
48. For the optimistic predictions, see "China's Production May Jump Six-fold by 1985," *World Oil* (October 1975). See also Ross Munro, "Chinese Oil Boom in Taching Slows," *Washington Post* (December 19, 1976), and Jay Mathews, "China Resumes U.S. Drilling Equipment Purchases," *Washington Post* (July 5, 1977).
49. For a discussion of early OPEC quarrels, see Michael Tanzer, *The Political Economy of International Oil and the Underdeveloped Countries* (Boston: Beacon Press, 1969), pp. 70–77.
50. Jahangir Amuzegar, "The Oil Story: Facts, Fiction and Fair Play," *Foreign Affairs* (July 1973).
51. See Cook, *Man, Energy, Society*, pp. 250–257.
52. See Tanzer, *The Political Economy*, pp. 71–73.
53. For more information on these differences, see Nazli Choucri, *International Politics of Energy Interdependence* (Lexington, Mass.: D. C. Heath, Lexington Books, 1976), pp. 100–108.
54. Ibid., pp. 101–112. See also Russell Stone, ed., *OPEC and the Middle East* (New York: Praeger, 1977).
55. Figures are taken from *World Oil* (August 15, 1977).
56. Reported in *World Oil* (August 15, 1975).
57. Ibid.
58. Reported in *Business Week* (January 26, 1976): 91.
59. See Flora Lewis, "Iraqi Aide Condemns Saudis on Oil Price," *New York Times* (December 19, 1976).
60. Statistics on reserves and production for the lesser OPEC producers are taken from *World Oil* (August 15, 1975). The projections of production shortages are found in WAES, *Energy: Global Prospects 1985–2000*, chap. 3.
61. For an optimistic view of China's potential, see *World Oil* (August 15, 1975): 145–154. For a more sober view, see *World Oil* (August 15, 1977): 173–174.

SUGGESTED READINGS

1. Nazli Choucri. *International Politics of Energy Interdependence.* Lexington, Mass.: D.C. Heath, Lexington Books, 1976.
2. Chu-yuan Cheng. *China's Petroleum Industry.* New York: Praeger, 1976.
3. Wilson Clark. *Energy for Survival.* New York: Anchor Books, 1975.
4. Barry Commoner. *The Poverty of Power.* New York: Alfred A. Knopf, 1976.
5. Earl Cook. *Man, Energy, Society.* San Francisco: W. H. Freeman, 1976.
6. Fred Cottrell. *Energy and Society: The Relation Between Energy, Social Change and Economic Development.* New York: McGraw-Hill, 1955.
7. Iain Elliot. *The Soviet Energy Balance.* New York: Praeger, 1974.
8. Edward Fried and Charles Schultze, eds. *Higher Oil Prices and the World Economy.* Washington, D.C.: Brookings Institution, 1975.
9. Selig Harrison. *China, Oil, and Asia: Conflict Ahead?* New York: Columbia University Press, 1977.
10. Neil Jacoby. *Multinational Oil.* New York: Macmillan, 1974.
11. Arthur Klinghoffer. *The Soviet Union and International Oil Politics.* New York: Columbia University Press, 1977.
12. Donald Kelley, ed. *The Energy Crisis and the Environment.* New York: Praeger, 1977.
13. Leon Lindberg. *The Energy Syndrome.* Lexington, Mass.: D.C. Heath, Lexington Books, 1977.
14. Arjun Makhijani. *Energy and Agriculture in the Third World.* Cambridge, Mass.: Ballinger, 1975.
15. Russell Stone, ed. *OPEC and the Middle East.* New York: Praeger, 1977.
16. Raymond Vernon, ed. *The Oil Crisis.* New York: W. W. Norton, 1976.
17. Mason Willrich. *Energy and World Politics.* New York: The Free Press, 1975.
18. Workshop on Alternative Energy Sources. *Energy: Global Prospects 1985–2000.* New York: McGraw-Hill, 1977.
19. Joseph Yager and Eleanor Steinberg. *Energy and U.S. Foreign Policy.* Cambridge, Mass.: Ballinger, 1974.

5

Nonfuel Minerals: The New Cartels?

The OPEC cartel and the related politics of energy have been largely responsible for the development of ecopolitics. But industrial societies do not survive on energy alone. They also require large quantities of nonfuel minerals, such as iron, copper, bauxite, and lead. And these minerals could also play an important role in the ecopolitics of the future.

Prior to the large increase in petroleum prices, nonfuel minerals made up a significant portion of the value of world commodity trade. The value of world fuel exports stood at $43 billion in 1972, trade in all ores and minerals stood at $11 billion, and total world trade in primary products at $136 billion. Thus, fuels were valued at only four times the value of nonfuel minerals in world trade. By 1975, however, fuels accounted for $170 billion of value, which amounted to more than eight times the value of all nonfuel minerals.[1] The value of each traded nonfuel mineral is now slight in relation to petroleum, and the implications of this fact are not lost on exporters of these minerals, who would like to redress this balance by forming their own cartels and increasing export prices just as have the fuel exporters.

In the mid-1970s, the average citizen of the United States required more than 8000 pounds of petroleum, 5000 pounds of coal, 5000 pounds of natural gas, and one ounce of uranium to provide needed energy. At the same time, this statistical person consumed 9000 pounds of sand and gravel, 8500 pounds of stone, 1200 pounds of iron and steel, 50 pounds of aluminum, and 25 pounds of copper—all used to produce homes, buildings, transportation networks, and vehicles.[2] Just as each nation needs more energy to sustain traditional types of economic growth, greater quantities of nonfuel minerals are also needed. As industrial societies have grown and become more complex and technologically sophisticated, the variety and quantity of nonfuel minerals required has increased on a per capita basis in much the same manner as energy consumption. And demand for these minerals, many of which are not available domestically in industrial countries, has led to lateral pressures that, in turn, have resulted in complex interdependence relationships among contemporary mineral exporters, importers, and multinational corporations.

Many industrial nations now import considerable quantities of nonfuel minerals. Taken as a whole, for example, OECD Europe imports more than three-quarters of its yearly consumption of chromium, copper, lead, manganese, nickel, phosphate, tin, and tungsten. Japan imports *all* of its yearly consumption of bauxite, chromium, nickel, phosphate rock, and tungsten and very large percentages of other minerals. The United States has similar vulnerabilities but is in a better position than its OECD allies (see table 5-1).[3]

There is a link between the world energy problem and potential shortages of nonfuel minerals. Given an ample and cheap supply of energy, there is little reason to expect shortages of many nonfuel minerals. Mines can be dug deeper, less rich grades of ore can be processed, and substitutes for scarce minerals can be created from those that are more abundant. But cheap and abundant energy is very unlikely to be available in the short and medium terms, and this will place limits on the availability and price of nonfuel minerals. Since many of these minerals now are perceived to be in relatively short supply at present prices, relevant actors in industrial countries have been engaged in a scramble to insure access to future supplies.

In a peculiar way, then, OPEC and higher energy prices have helped to create the physical and political base for other potential cartels. And the possibility of new cartels forming in nonfuel mineral markets has created a feeling of urgency in some industrial countries. Task forces have been set up to evaluate mineral self-sufficiency, bilateral and multilateral mineral agreements have been struck between importers and exporters, price agreements for basic commodities have been one of the main points of contention in North-South negotiations, and considerable stock-piling of minerals has taken place.

ARTEL FORMATION

The focus in this chapter is on the potential impact of nonfuel minerals on ecopolitics. An attempt is made to sort out the differences and similarities between the successfully cartelized international petroleum market and the markets for various nonfuel minerals. There are a number of unanswered questions implicit in this sorting operation. There are wide differences of opinion, for example, on the extent to which the OPEC success can be emulated by any other cartel of mineral exporters. There are many factors operating in international politics and economics that could lead to the conclusion that OPEC will be the forerunner of a new international economic order featuring a variety of cartels and international agreements.[4] But there are also forces operating that have historically broken up cartel arrangements, and they could lead to skepticism about possiblities for less developed countries cooperating for a substantial period in any cartel-type operations.[5]

There are two sets of factors that will determine the success or failure of future cartels composed of exporting nations. The first concerns the political and economic conditions that seem essential to cartel formation and success. These conditions include variables such as the

TABLE 5-1. *Comparative Import Dependence, 1972*

	United States		OECD Europe		Japan	
	Import Volume (Thousands of Tons)	Imports as a Percentage of Consumption	Import Volume (Thousands of Tons)	Imports as a Percentage of Consumption	Import Volume (Thousands of Tons)	Imports as a Percentage of Consumption
Bauxite and Alumina	13389	88	3726	51	4996	100
Copper and Copper Ore	383	17	2439	93	2511	90
Iron Ore	36334	32	75307	37	111519	94
Lead and Lead Ore	314	19	789	75	204	76
Nickel and Nickel Ore	140	90	240	89	3179	100
Zinc and Zinc Ore	715	55	1863	61	1123	80
Tin and Tin Ores	56	100	116	96	32	97
Tungsten Ore	3	42	22	100	2	100
Manganese Ore	733	95	3696	98	2921	90
Chromium Ore	408	100	970	100	875	100

SOURCE: *Council on International Economic Policy, Special Report: Critical Imported Materials (December 1974).*

number of large producers involved, their political and economic perspectives, their share of the total market, the cost of market entry, supply and demand elasticities, and so on. The second set of factors concerns the properties of each nonfuel mineral. Included here are such things as relative importance, geographical distribution, possible substitutions, world consumption patterns, and consumer vulnerability to supply interruption.

The emphasis in this chapter is on potential for cartel formation in nonfuel minerals. This emphasis deliberately neglects the agricultural raw materials that are the source of export earnings for many of the less developed countries. The most important reason for this decision is that agricultural markets are clearly less suited to OPEC-type cartel formation. The value of international trade in all foods is much less than fuels, the variety of foods is great, the number of producers is enormous, there are extensive possibilities for substitution, and the demand for many agricultural commodities is very elastic. Furthermore, there is great difficulty in controlling production and export of agricultural commodities because of year-to-year fluctuations in weather. Excess production of crops must be physically stored if kept off markets, and spoilage is an important factor. Finally, the chief exporters of agricultural commodities are often industrial countries, and they sell mainly to other industrial countries. Thus, there is very little potential for ecoconflict in agricultural markets and little reason to subject them to detailed analysis here.[6]

Political Factors

A cartel is a combination of commercial enterprises formed in order to restrict competition. The aim of commercial cartels is to control production so as to maximize collective profits. One of the problems in evaluating the prospects for future cartel formation in mineral markets is that agreements among exporting nations are much different in nature than agreements among competing commercial firms. In the case of firms, a model of rational economic man seeking to maximize profits often suffices as a starting point for analysis. In the case of nations, however, assumptions about economic rationality often must be called into question, and political factors become more important. OPEC is one example of the importance of politics. In the absence of the political conflict in the Middle East in late 1973, which led to the OAPEC boycott, OPEC probably would have continued to exist only as a weak cartel boasting of modest gains for at least another decade.

There are significant differences between commercial enterprises and nation-states that are not usually emphasized in the literature dealing with cartels.[7] The most important of these is the one previously mentioned: that political considerations and ideologies can be much more important in motivating nation-state behavior than is simple profit maximization. In addition, decisions in regard to sharing production and the added revenue gained through collusion can be much more difficult in the case of political entities than in the case of established firms controlling known shares in a well-understood market. In the case of commercial firms seeking to maximize profits, collusion most often takes place among established firms familiar with and having nearly perfect information about competitors who join in these illegal activities. Predictability of the behavior of others is essential in calculating the risks involved. If there is little confidence that other firms will abide by agreements, it is nearly impossible to initiate market-sharing arrangements. There are only limited possibilities for "trial" arrangements permitting conspirators to get to know each other better.

A key political requisite for cartel formation involving mineral-exporting nations is mutual understanding and unity of purpose. This unity can be provided by shared historical experiences, a common enemy, or by a rapid and unusual set of events. In the absence of trust and shared experiences, a catalyst may be required that is powerful enough to overcome the political bickering and inertia characteristics of most potential exporting cartels. Once an economically beneficial agreement has been struck, however, less energy is necessary to maintain a cartel than must go into its creation when the benefits of membership are much less clear.

Israel provided the catalyst necessary for the Organization of Petroleum Exporting Countries to overcome internal mistrust. Petroleum was first withheld from selected industrial countries for political rather than economic reasons. The crisis atmosphere, the divisions and weaknesses the embargo exposed in the industrial world, and the implicit territorial guarantees on the part of the Soviet Union resulted in the rapid implementation of a new price structure in the world petroleum market that would have been impossible without years of protracted bargaining among cartel members and their customers.[8] Once a new structure of prices was established and the economic payoffs became clear to all participants, it proved difficult to destroy cartel solidarity.

The sequence of events or the common enemy that might catalyze cartel formation in nonfuel mineral markets remains a matter of speculation. At present, the level of trust among potential members of such cartels is not very high.[9] But given the rapid transformation of the international system that has taken place in the three decades since World War II, such a sequence of events is not impossible. And the widening North-South gap between industrial and less developed countries could lead to "enemy creation," the industrial world being collectively viewed as an enemy by less developed countries.

A second political factor related to future cartel success is the degree of ideological homogeneity among major cartel members. Unlike commercial firms, where profits are more important than politics, considerable ideological homogeneity and shared goals among potential cartel members are helpful in making agreements on prices and on principles of market allocation. Attempts by ideologically diverse nations to form exporter cartels are likely to fail if there is a lack of shared political perspectives.[10] In the case of OPEC, political diversity and lack of shared perspectives was a serious problem that inhibited effective cooperation for the first decade of the organization's existence. Indonesia, Venezuela, Iran, Kuwait, and Saudi Arabia share few political values and perspectives in common, and there are still internal disputes over market shares based upon lack of trust and agreement among them.

Ideological homogeneity among potential participants in nonfuel mineral cartels is even less likely. Copper, for example, is produced in large quantities by the United States, Canada, Chile, Zambia, Zaire, and Peru. A more disparate collection of political regimes would be hard to imagine. While the International Council of Copper Exporting Countries (CIPEC), the nascent cartel in the copper market, meets regularly to talk about copper prices, there is little likelihood of a cooperative effort among Chile, Peru, Zambia, and Zaire to raise them. In fact, the council has been most effective in conducting studies and disseminating information, not in increasing prices.[11]

Recognition of mutual self-interest among producers is a third political factor that facilitates cartel formation. Feelings of covariance, the belief that economic and political fortunes rise and fall together, are essential.[12] A decision to restrict output or to raise prices represents commitment to a potentially dangerous course of action that leaves all cartel members in an exposed position. If a member of such a cartel breaks rank, it can maximize short-run gain and make long-term arrangements at the expense of other participants. It is difficult for nations without perceived common interests to take such risks. This is especially true for countries at different levels of industrial development, which may very well perceive their interests to be mutually antagonistic.

A fourth political factor in cartel formation is the relationship between politics and economics within producer nations and within consumer markets. Often, nations are characterized as importers or exporters of commodities, and it is assumed that political leaders control the flow of commodities across their borders. In reality, the extent to which the flow of commodities is subject to control by political elites varies among nations. Transnational economic actors (multinational corporations) are responsible for many decisions in both exporting and importing nations, and they can effectively inhibit or aid exporter cartel formation.[13] In the world petroleum market, for example, national actors now exert considerable control over petroleum exports, although the purchasing patterns of large multinational oil companies are also important. These multinational companies play a much larger role in import markets. Indeed, it could be argued that in many cases they dictate national energy policy.[14] The world aluminum market is similarly con-

TABLE 5–2. *World Mineral Reserves*

	Percentage of World Reserves		Percentage of World Reserves
Bauxite		*Lead*	
Australia	26	United States	36
Guinea	26	Canada	12
Brazil	15	USSR	11
		Australia	11
Chromite		*Manganese*	
South Africa	62	South Africa	45
Rhodesia	33	USSR	38
		Australia	8
Cobalt		*Molybdenum*	
Zaire	28	United States	49
Oceania	27	USSR	15
Zambia	14	Canada	14
Cuba	14	Chile	14
USSR	8		
Copper		*Nickel*	
United States	20	New Caledonia	44
Chile	20	Canada	16
Canada	9	USSR	10
USSR	9	Australia	9
		Indonesia	8
Iron Ore		*Tin*	
USSR	31	China	24
Brazil	17	Thailand	15
Canada	12	Malaysia	12
Australia	10	Bolivia	10
		Indonesia	8
Zinc		*Tungsten*	
Canada	23	China	54
United States	20	Canada	12
Australia	12	USSR	9
USSR	8		

SOURCE: *Bureau of Mines*, Mineral Facts and Problems, 1975 ed. (Washington, D.C.: Government Printing Office, 1976).

trolled by only six corporations, and they represent a powerful force in shaping domestic import patterns.[15]

Each mineral market is characterized by a greater or lesser dominance of nonnational actors, and each nation is characterized by a different degree of government intervention in trade. This variety results in a complex matrix of semiindependent national actors and semiindependent multinational corporations that crisscrosses the world mineral marketplace. Cartels are most likely to develop in markets where national actors control exports and where the private sector controls most imports.

Economic Factors

In discussing cartel formation among firms or nations, there is more general agreement on the list of economic factors that are likely to be closely related to the success of a cartel than there is on political factors. In a free and unorganized market, there are many buyers and sellers, and the costs of organizing a cartel may be prohibitive. But most mineral markets are not examples of free markets and they are usually highly organized. So the economic potential for cartel formation is present.

The number of significant exporters that must be involved in an attempt to form a cartel and control a market is the most crucial economic variable in determining cartel potential. Where there is a large number of significant exporters, the costs and risks of organizing a cartel are very high. A large number of significant exporters means that all of the political and economic factors that can impede cartel formation are exaggerated. Large numbers of participants mean more risk of price cutting, less likelihood of political agreement, more arguments about prices and markets, and so on. When there are only a very few significant exporters, however, the market is more amenable to cartelization, and organization costs and risks are much lower.

On this basis alone, the petroleum market would not seem to have been a good candidate for cartel formation, since there are several large and many small petroleum exporters. But when known reserves, production capacity, world demand, and domestic consumption requirements are figured into the analysis, there are really only four or five countries that could be considered large-scale exporters. One of these is the USSR, but Russia will certainly consume much of its future production domestically. China could possibly develop an oil industry but at present is bogged down with technological problems. The other exporters are the core members of OPEC: Kuwait, Saudi Arabia, and Iran. Tin, copper, and a number of minerals of lesser importance would seem to be at least as amenable to cartel formation from this perspective. Malaysia alone accounts for 40 percent of world tin production, and there are only a handful of other major producers. While the copper market is dominated by six big producers, two of them, the United States and Canada, consume most of what they produce domestically and cannot be considered exporters.

Elasticity of supply and demand for a mineral is a second economic factor of critical importance in cartel formation. Elasticity of demand refers to the relationship between the price charged for a commodity and the quantity demanded. Demand for a commodity is considered to be elastic when a decrease in price leads to greater total revenue because of a larger demand in response to the lower price. Similarly, an increase in price in an elastic situation leads to diminished total revenue because of a resulting decreased demand. In an inelastic demand situation, however, an increase in price leads to an increase in revenue or a decrease in price to a decrease in revenue, because demand does not fall off or increase rapidly enough to offset the changed price.

If consumers can and want to curb purchases quickly when prices increase, there might be no jump in total revenue from price increases. So a cartel can be effective only if demand for a commodity is relatively inelastic. This occurs when a price increase does not send so many customers from the marketplace that the additional revenue from higher prices is negated by lost sales. Similar rules apply to sellers. If small increases in price bring many more exporters into the market to sell commodities, cartels are very unlikely because the influx of new exports will drive prices back down. Markets in which additional production does not materialize in response to large price increases are inelastic and are more amenable to cartelization.

There are many factors that shape the elasticity of supply and demand for any commodity. On the demand side, there is wide variation in the intrinsic importance of each commodity to the importer. Fossil fuels, the most prominent examples, have become absolutely essential to the economic health of industrial societies in the short and medium term; there are no readily available alternatives, and industrial economies collapse without them. When substitution can easily be made or consumers can do without a mineral, however, substantial price increases as a result of cartel action might not be feasible.[16] On the supply side, cartel members must be certain that higher prices cannot call forth additional production and exports from noncartel members, or they must be willing to take these new producers into membership. Thus, collusion is less likely when there are no serious economic or technological barriers to the entry of new supplies into a market. When rising prices call forth additional supplies from outside a cartel, the total return to each cartel member may drop below what it would be if there were no cartel.[17]

There is a third set of economic factors that is best viewed from an ecological perspective. In competition among species, time and diversity are considered to be critical resources.[18] Species that are more diverse genetically or that can subsist for long periods without essential nutrients overcome those with lesser diversity or endurance. Similarly, in economic relations among nations, time and diversity are critical variables. They are essential in determining the outcome of any attempt to restrict supply and exact higher prices within a cartel. Increased prices are certain to encounter at least short-term consumer resistance based upon utilization of existing stocks of raw materials, switches to substitutes, or conservation efforts. The length of time that each exporting country can survive within the constraints of a reduced total market and reduced revenue is a function of that country's foreign exchange reserves, import needs, and the diversity of its economic production and exports. The length of time required to force importers to accept new prices and to reenter the market is, in turn, related to factors that shape the elasticity of demand for any particular commodity. Exporting countries with stronger reserve positions and related longer time horizons can much more effectively wait out those exporters that are not similarly blessed. And importing nations can, in many cases, do without commodities for periods of time exceeding exporter "waiting capacity."

Most oil-exporting countries are "one crop" economies and are more than 90 percent dependent upon petroleum for export revenue. But foreign exchange reserves have not been a pressing problem for OPEC because the politically motivated price increases have been almost instantaneous. In addition, the petroleum market is characterized by short time horizons for importers because of very inelastic demand for petroleum and inability to store great quantities at low cost. When the oil embargo went into effect in late 1973, Western Europe had less than a sixty-day supply of petroleum on hand.[19] The world copper market and CIPEC are much different than OPEC. Three of the largest exporters, Zambia, Chile, and Zaire, earn more than half of their export revenue in normal years from the export of copper. Zambia earns more than 90 percent of its foreign exchange from copper ore exports. These countries have chronic economic difficulties related to market fluctuations and very small foreign exchange reserves. They are in no position to go for long periods of time without exporting considerable quantities of copper. Their plight is shared by other less developed exporters of mineral commodities. The industrial countries are much more economically diverse and often can use time as an ally in "waiting out" boycotts or price increases in markets dominated by exports from less developed countries.

The Minerals

There is a final group of variables related to the intrinsic nature of minerals traded that is important in determining prospects for exporter collusion. The different qualities of the minerals that enter into international markets must be understood to complete an assessment of the potential for any particular exporter cartel; in other words, cement or gravel exports are much different from iron ore or uranium. The foremost factors to consider about a basic commodity are its scarcity, its distribution, and the proportion that actually enters into world trade.

Many mineral commodities rarely enter the international marketplace. Some, such as clays, salts, or cement are very abundant and produced in almost all consuming countries. There is little reason for extensive international commerce in them. Others are produced in very few countries and much needed in others. Some minerals are imported because foreign sources are cheaper than domestic ones. Others are imported because they are found in only a very few areas of the world. The significance of a commodity in international trade could be called its volatility. The higher the percentage of world production of a basic commodity entering into international trade, the higher the volatility of the market and the greater the likelihood that collusion could have a serious impact.

Comparative difficulties of transport and storage represent another category of differences among minerals. Petroleum and natural gas, for example, are difficult to transport and store. Tankers and pipelines are costly, and they can be easily disrupted—pipelines can be severed, and tankers are vulnerable at sea. It is difficult to store enough petroleum and natural gas for long-term emergencies, since consumption is large and storage tanks are very costly to build. During normal times, there is little economic incentive to spend billions of dollars to create these facilities. Nonfuel minerals vary considerably in storability. Some metals, such as iron and copper, which are used in large quantity, can be stockpiled only at significant expense. Other metals, such as cobalt and molybdenum, are used in such minute quantities that several years' consumption in industrial countries can be stored at minimum cost. And transportation is much the same. Those minerals used in small quantities can be easily transported, while bulky minerals can be transported only at significant cost.

Finally, the nature of the geological processes by which minerals have been formed are important in determining potential for collusion in mineral markets. Some minerals, such as iron and aluminum, are abundant throughout the earth's crust in gradually decreasing richness. Others, like copper, have been geologically deposited in fairly well-defined areas and are not found in continuously less rich grades in most geographical regions of the world. Still other minerals, such as cobalt or chromium, are produced in quantity in only one or two countries. And minerals also vary considerably in the quantity that remains to be exploited in relation to yearly demand for them. Obviously, then, the characteristics of different minerals are important in determining potential for exporter collusion. The more widespread world distribution, the less likely is collusion among mineral exporters.

WORLD MINERAL MARKETS

It is also important to understand the structure of existing world mineral markets in order to assess the likely future of cartel formation in any particular case. It is pointless to speculate about the future possibility of cartels in mineral markets without knowing something about the nature of each mineral: its physical properties, the processes by which it was formed, and the extent and location of the world's reserves, both known and potential. It is also important to understand the economics of exploitation in each case, including the role that it plays in industrial production, the cost of extracting and processing ores, and the possibility and cost of substitutes for the mineral. Finally, a series of political factors is also important. These include things such as the geographic location of world reserves, different national costs of extraction, and comparative import dependencies of major importers.

The data used to analyze world mineral markets can be misleading. Dependency statistics derived from mineral trade figures vary from year to year depending on the current economic conditions and so should always be read in the context of previous data. In years of industrial growth and heavy demand, corporations build inventories in anticipation of future needs. This inventory building is often accompanied by hoarding and speculation, which exaggerates import figures and dependency statistics. This occurred during 1973 and early 1974, when fear of shortages, both short term and long term, doubled and even tripled mineral prices.[20] During recessions, in contrast, corporations work from inventories and cut back on their purchases of raw materials. Thus, during periods of economic prosperity, many factors combine to indicate excessive dependence of certain mineral-deficient industrial countries on foreign imports. In times of recession, such dependency statistics may indicate more self-sufficiency than is the actual case.

For a related reason, mineral trade figures for the US can be less than accurate or even inconsistent. Government actions taken to build or reduce stockpiles of critical minerals make an accurate year-by-year profile of US sensitivity and vulnerability difficult to construct. When stockpiles are being built, excessive dependency on imports can be indicated. Similarly, when stockpiles are reduced by government sales, the sales are treated as supplies from domestic sources. This can lead to much lower apparent levels of dependence on foreign supplies.

Also, minerals are imported into the United States and other industrial countries in various stages of processing. In the aluminum industry, for example, considerable amounts of bauxite ore are imported. But an intermediate product, alumina, is also imported. Then there is direct importation of aluminum metal itself. Finally, a substantial quantity of aluminum is imported in finished and semifinished industrial imports ranging from kitchen utensils to Volkswagons. The original mineral content of all of these products is difficult to figure, and there is no set of statistics available that gives a comprehensive picture of the total importation of minerals in all forms for any industrial country.

Finally, it is important to be aware of the significant problem of transshipment when examining comparative dependency figures and sources of imported raw materials. Minerals are not always imported directly from the country of origin. In 1976, for example, Ireland supplied 44 percent of the industrial diamonds purchased by US companies, but Ireland has no domestic source of diamonds. Most of them came from South Africa. If such facts are not taken into account, transshipment figures can yield a distorted picture of the international flow of raw materials. Exports and imports of recycled scrap add another difficult dimension to an already complicated picture.

While petroleum is now by far the most politically crucial and economically prominent commodity in international trade, many of the nonfuel minerals are crucial to industrial processes and extremely vital to importing countries. Choucri has identified thirty-seven such minerals and gathered dependency data for each of them.[21] The Council on International Economic Policy has singled out nineteen such minerals for special attention. Six fuels and minerals—petroleum, natural gas, coal, iron, aluminum, and copper—account for two-thirds of world consumption by value. Much of the remaining one-third of world consumption is accounted for by sand, gravel, and stone—minerals that are superabundant and therefore not important by value in international trade.[22] In the sections that follow, each of the important minerals and families of minerals is analyzed, and the structure of global trade in minerals is outlined in greater detail.

Iron

Iron was used in weapons and utensils long before 1000 B.C. But it was not until the invention of the blast furnace at the beginning of the eighteenth century that iron—and eventually steel—could be produced in quantities significant enough to make it the backbone of industrial societies. In the blast furnace, iron ore is smelted into pig iron, which, in turn, is transformed into cast iron, wrought iron, or steel. Cast iron is used to make machine parts and has many industrial applications. Wrought iron is softer and corrosion resistant, so it is often used in water pipes and for ornamentation. Steel, which is iron combined, or "alloyed," with various metals to yield different materials with desired properties, is the most important derivative of iron ore. The principal alloys used in making steel are manganese, chromium, nickel, tungsten, vanadium, and molybdenum. The most valued attribute of steel is its strength. It is essential in the construction of buildings and is used to reinforce concrete, in the holds of ships, and in railroad tracks and engines, as well as in automobiles. Additional thousands of items are produced from the many alloys of steel.

Because it is so central to transportation, defense, heavy construction, and industrial production, it is impossible to conceive of an adequate substitute for iron. Aluminum is not nearly as strong and cannot replace steel used as reinforcing material. But there is little reason to worry about the need for substitutes from either a political or geological point of view, since iron is one of the most abundant elements in the earth's crust. In fact, the present cutoff grade (richness of ore that is being economically mined) is only 3.4 times the average crustal abundance.[23] Scarcity is not a serious problem in the iron market, since it is predicted that, at present levels of demand, proven world reserves of iron ore will last two hundred years, while in the United States proven reserves are adequate to meet domestic demand for thirty years.[24] In the last twenty years, known world reserves of iron have increased by 1000 percent.[25] Yet, world demand for steel is expected to grow at only about 4 percent annually over the next decade, while demand in the United States is expected to grow at between 2 and 3 percent per year. In addition, nearly one-third of the iron consumed around the world now comes from recycled scrap.

Commercial deposits of iron ore are found throughout the world, and there are several major producers. The Soviet Union produces nearly one-quarter of all iron ore, the United States about 12 percent, and Australia 10 percent. Several minor producers—Brazil, France, India, Sweden, Canada, and China—all produce between 5 and 10 percent of the world total.[26]

The United States now meets 70 percent of its consumption requirements from its domestic mines. In addition, many American corporations own significant shares in secure foreign mines, and this ore, counted as imported ore, distorts the true level of self-sufficiency. In 1973, Canada accounted for half of United States imports and Venezuela for one-third. Western Europe now imports slightly over one-third of its iron consumption. Nearly three-quarters of the imports come from African and Latin American countries. Japan, by contrast, is very vulnerable to foreign suppliers, importing 94 percent of its iron ore. Nearly half comes from sources in the industrial world, such as Canada, Australia, New Zealand, Rhodesia, and South Africa, 21 percent comes from Latin America and the Caribbean, and 19 percent comes from Asia.[27]

Attempts have been made to form an iron ore–exporting association. In 1975, eleven countries signed an agreement giving birth to the Association of Iron Ore Exporting Countries (AIOEC). The signatories to the agreement were Algeria, Australia, Brazil, Chile, India, Mauritania, Peru, Sierre Leone, Sweden, Tunisia, and Venezuela. But the agreement does not give the association any withholding or price-fixing power, and the politically diverse participants are bound merely to consult and mutually aid each other.[28] Thus, there is little reason to fear the impact of an iron ore cartel in the near future.

Copper

Copper is another building block of industrial civilization. Like iron, it has a long and noble history but its useful characteristics are much different. It is valued for its ductility, conductivity, resistance to corrosion, and high melting point, a combination of properties not found in most other metals. Sixty percent of mined copper in the U.S. is used in the electronics industry, and a similar situation exists in other industrial countries. About half of the remaining copper is consumed by the related communications industry. Copper is used extensively in home wiring, in electrical power transmission, and in communication systems. It is also used in electric motors, where its high conductivity and high melting point make it an ideal material.[29]

Because copper has such a unique set of important properties, there are few good possibilities for substitution. Aluminum or iron is being substituted in high-power transmission lines but neither material is as effective as copper. Aluminum has been substituted for copper in home wiring, but corrosion and a rash of wiring fires have led to a ban on aluminum wiring in homes in many areas. There are few practical substitutes for copper in electric motors, where heat is an important limiting factor.

At current rates of consumption, known world reserves of copper will last between thirty and forty years.[30] Given a projected rate of growth in world copper consumption of 4.6 percent annually, these known reserves will last only twenty years.[31] In this respect, copper is in shorter supply than petroleum or natural gas. But there are indications that new discoveries and new recovery techniques will postpone any real shortages until well into the twenty-first century.

Because of the high demand for this critical mineral and the relatively tight supply situation, the price of copper has been subject to dramatic fluctuations. During the period of economic expansion in 1972–1974, it soared to over $1.40 per pound, three times its 1971 price, due to high demand, speculation, and hoarding. In the subsequent global recession of 1974–1975, the price fell as low as $.63 per pound.

Unlike iron ore, copper is not found abundantly throughout the earth's crust. The United States is the world's leading producer of copper, mining nearly one-quarter of the world's total. Other significant producers are Chile, Zambia, Canada, Zaire, Peru, and the USSR, each producing about 10 percent of the world's total.[32] Since the United States consumes much of the copper it produces domestically, the world export market is mostly shared by four countries—Chile, Peru, Zambia, and Zaire. These four countries account for more than one-third of non-Communist mine capacity and two-thirds of world primary copper exports. They formally banded together in 1967, well before the OPEC successes, to form CIPEC, the Council of Copper Exporting Countries. So far, CIPEC has been ineffective in increasing copper prices. This ineffectiveness is mostly due to the fact that copper accounts for such a large share of the export earnings for these countries (90 percent in Zambia, 70 percent in Chile, and 50 percent in Zaire) that they cannot afford to withhold production long enough to outlast importing countries. In addition, the potential threat of a price increase has already spurred exploratory efforts in other countries, such as Australia, the Philippines, and Puerto Rico, and interest has risen in mining copper in the seabed.[33]

In 1974, CIPEC members agreed to cut back their exports by an initial 10 percent to be followed by an additional 5 percent reduction in 1975. Their objective of sustaining the prevailing prices failed, largely due to the worldwide depressed demand for metals that accompanied the global recession. There has been no accumulation of a buffer stock of copper, which could be used to iron out fluctuations in copper prices, because CIPEC countries have been unable to obtain the necessary funding. The International Monetary Fund finances a tin buffer stock because the tin organization includes exporters and importers, but CIPEC is excluded from funding because it does not include importing countries. The World Bank has also proved to be nonresponsive to pleas for assistance in building stockpiles.[34]

The United States meets only a small percentage of its domestic needs through imports. Most of this copper comes from Canada and only very small portions come from CIPEC countries—3 percent from Chile and 4 percent from Peru. Western Europe and Japan are in a much more serious position, importing 81 percent and 92 percent of copper consumption, respectively. Furthermore, Western Europe imports half of its copper from CIPEC countries, making it extremely vulnerable to any future CIPEC price increase or embargo. Japan imports nearly one-third of its copper from these same countries but also imports from Canada and the Philippines in significant quantities.[35] Thus, the potential for effective cartel action is much greater in the copper market than it is for iron, but economic problems in the exporting countries limit their freedom of action.

Aluminum

Aluminum is the third building block of industrial nations, second only to iron in quantity consumed. It is used extensively in the construction industry in applications where the rigidity of steel is not necessary. Aluminum is light and bends easily. It can replace steel where great weight does not need to be supported. Its other applications include the aircraft industry, where it is desired because it is a light but durable metal especially suited to airplane construction, and the automobile industry, particularly given the recent push for lighter, energy-efficient vehicles. In recent years, about 25 percent of aluminum consumption in the United States has gone into the construction industry, 19 percent into transportation equipment, 16 percent into cans (aluminum is used as a substitute for tin), and 13 percent into the electrical industry.[36]

Aluminum is used as a substitute for other metals, such as iron and copper, so it is hardly reasonable to discuss substitutions for it. Should aluminum for some reason become unavailable, it would simply mean a retreat to more conventional metals.

Aluminum ore is much like iron ore in that it is spread abundantly in the earth's crust and is found in many different clays and oxides. Bauxite is the aluminum ore that is most widely mined. It is estimated that proven world reserves are adequate to last over a hundred years at present rates of consumption. The present cutoff grade for ore is only about 2.2 times the average crustal abundance.[37] Further, new reserves of aluminum ore are constantly being found, and proven reserves have increased over 300 percent in the last twenty years.[38] This rate is more than double that at which new copper is being found. And there is an abundance of ore-bearing clays that would become exploitable reserves should the price of bauxite double.

World bauxite-aluminum production is tightly controlled by six large multinational firms. Accurate ore production figures are not freely available, since all transactions are semisecret and take place within these vertically integrated companies. Bauxite and aluminum are not even traded on commodity exchanges, and only finished aluminum has a price quoted by manufacturers. The selling price of this finished aluminum is not closely related to the price of bauxite ore, since ore makes up only about 7 percent of the final bill to consumers. The production of aluminum requires much energy, and final prices are determined more by the cost of electricity at smelters than by the cost of the ore.

Seven bauxite producers—Australia, Guinea, Guyana, Jamaica, Sierre Leone, Surinam, and Yugoslavia—established the International Bauxite Association in 1974. These seven countries account for about 65 percent of world bauxite production and 80 percent of world trade.[39] Since then, four new members, Ghana, Haiti, the Dominican Republic, and Indonesia, have joined. Given the disparate political orientations of member governments, the tight control of the industry by six companies, and the abundance of aluminum-bearing ores worldwide, withholding actions are unlikely to be successful, and only limited price increases can be expected.

The exception to this generalization is Jamaica, which nearly doubled its bauxite prices in 1975. Jamaican bauxite ore is particularly rich and Jamaica's main customer is the United States. Over the short term, American industry has chosen to pay higher prices rather than retool in order to shift from the rich Jamaican ore to other alternatives. But in the long run, less rich ores could become competitive if additional price increases are demanded.

The United States now imports about between 85 and 90 percent of the bauxite that is consumed domestically. Jamaica supplies over half, although this amount could diminish if there are further large price increases. Surinam and Guyana are the other major suppliers. Large quantities of alumina, refined bauxite ore, are also imported from Australia and Jamaica. Despite the high percentage of importation, the United States could not now be considered extremely vulnerable to Third World bauxite politics for several reasons. First, aluminum is a metal used in many applications by preference rather than necessity. Second, there is a large group of exporters and aspiring exporters that would like to compete for the American market. In fact, the Council on International Economic Policy concluded in 1974 that a real glut of bauxite is a long-term possibility given continued softening of demand.[40] Third, since the six big aluminum producers control the energy-intensive downstream processing facilities, they will continue to have considerable leverage over price, and even doubling the price of bauxite would add only 10 percent to final costs. Finally, there is a significant strategic stockpile of aluminum (almost one year's consumption) and a wide variety of less rich domestic aluminum-bearing ores in the United States. These ores would become competitive with bauxite under emergency conditions at a cost of from 2 to 3 billion 1973 dollars and would enable the US to reach self-sufficiency within ten to fifteen years.[41]

As in the case of other essential minerals, Japan is more dependent on foreign sources than is the United States. Japan imports all of its bauxite and aluminum from abroad: 38 percent of Japanese bauxite comes from Asia, and the rest comes from industrial countries. Western Europe, by contrast, imports only half of its ores from outside of the European region; aluminum is one of the few minerals in which Western Europe is more self-sufficient than the United States. Nonetheless, Western Europe imports nearly one-third of its requirements from Third World African and South American countries.[42]

Other Minerals

The remaining important nonfuel minerals can be divided into three categories: the ferroalloys, the precious metals, and the nonferrous metals. Ferroalloys are the metals that are alloyed with iron to produce specialty steels. Often they are added to steel in only very small amounts, sometimes as low as 1 percent, to yield desired properties, such as hardness, luster, durability, or resistance to high temperatures. The main ferroalloy elements are chromium, nickel, manganese, cobalt, molybdenum, niobium, and tungsten. There are a wide variety of ferroalloy elements and countless numbers of combinations in which they are employed. Substitution for some of these alloys may be accomplished by varying quantities of other alloys employed in steel-making processes. Vanadium, molybdenum, and manganese, for example, all increase the tensile strength of steel. Even though many industrial countries import very high percentages of their consumption of each of these minerals, this potential vulnerability is mitigated by their ability to switch to different combinations of alloys as well as to do without some of the alloy products. But this vulnerability would increase should exporters withhold combinations of ferroalloys simultaneously.

Chromium is one of the most important of the ferroalloys. Presently, more than three dozen types of stainless steel containing chromium are produced in the United States. Three-quarters of the chromium consumed there is used to produce highly specialized steels for the aircraft industry, so chromite ore is a mineral of great political significance, especially since the Western Hemisphere presently produces no significant amounts. About one-third of world production takes place in the Soviet Union, one-quarter in South Africa, and smaller quantities are produced in Turkey, Rhodesia, and the Philippines. South Africa and Rhodesia together possess nearly 99 percent of the non-Communist world's chromium reserves. Since the political situation in both countries is shaky, these supplies cannot be considered secure. The white minority regime in Rhodesia, for example, was once the target of a United Nations mineral embargo. The United States respected this embargo between 1968 and 1971. But it forced the United States to buy more chromium from the Soviet Union, leading to higher Soviet prices. In 1971, Congress decided not to respect the embargo, and between 1971 and 1977 US policy was hotly debated. The Carter administration, with its emphasis on human rights, pressed a renewal of the embargo through Congress in 1977.

The United States, Western Europe, and Japan all meet close to 100 percent of their chromium needs through imports. Japan gets a significant portion of its imports from the Philippines as well as Rhodesia and South Africa. Western Europe meets about half of its needs through Soviet imports. The United States imports nearly one-third of its chromium from the USSR, one-third from the Union of South Africa, and about 20 percent from Turkey and the Philippines. None of these countries can be considered a secure source of supply. The Soviet source is dependent upon continued relaxation of East-West tensions; US relations with Turkey have been strained because of Cyprus; and South Africa is less than a desirable source because of the human rights problems. Thus, chromium is one of the weakest links in the United States' mineral picture, a weakness that is shared by Western Europe and Japan. Indeed, a special committee was set up in 1975 by the National Materials Advisory Board of the National Research Council and charged with the responsibility of reducing US consumption of chromium.

It is not likely that any cartel composed of less developed countries would profit from a price increase or withholding actions in the international chromium market. Rather, chromium is a negotiating chip. It is not at all inconceivable that an under-the-table "unholy" alliance among Rhodesia, South Africa, and the Soviet Union could dramatically influence world prices of chromium. To guard against the adverse affects of such a possibility, the United States presently stockpiles a three-year supply of chromium and chromite ores.

Nickel is the most costly ferroalloy import for the US, which imports about three-quarters of yearly consumption.[43] The largest percentage of nickel consumption is used for stainless steels. Canada produces nearly half the world's nickel, and the Soviet Union produces about one-fifth. The price of nickel has nearly doubled over the last ten years, and this has led to new nickel discoveries in Australia, the Philippines, and possibly Colombia and Guatemala. If the price of nickel continues to rise, harvesting nickel-bearing manganese nodules from the deep seabed becomes a distinct possibility. In addition, there are possibilities for developing expensive substitutes for almost all known uses of nickel.[44]

The other ferroalloys are less important to industrial economies. Cobalt, the most critical of the other alloys, is mixed with iron to make permanent magnets, essential components of communications equipment. No good substitutes for cobalt now exist. Most of the world's reserves are in Zaire and Zambia. It is possible that these two countries could artificially increase cobalt prices, but such an action would represent a nuisance rather than an economic hardship because of the small role played by cobalt in total imports. The United States now imports about 95 percent of cobalt consumed and stockpiles about a three-year supply.

Manganese is also used in steel-making processes. The Soviet Union provided much of the world's supply prior to World War II but cut off the supply in the immediate postwar period, which spurred a worldwide search for other sources. The search was fruitful, and there is presently a worldwide abundance of manganese and a large, politically diverse group of exporters.

Tungsten and tungsten carbide are used in making drill bits and other heavy-duty mining equipment. Tungsten is also alloyed with iron to make high-temperature steel. It is found in a large number of countries. During the Korean War, there was fear of a tungsten shortage, and premium prices were paid to build a stockpile. During the late 1950s and early 1960s, however, a depression hit the industry, and many mines were closed. Some have never been reopened, but they could be if tungsten prices continue to rise.

The precious metals are well known and require little description. Gold and silver are desired for their luster and are used largely in jewelry and as backing for currency. The monetary value of gold is mostly psychological, and it is used as a hedge against inflation. Silver is being increasingly used in industry, particularly in the electronics industry as well as in photography. Silver and gold are found in many areas of the world, although South Africa and the USSR possess by far the largest portion of world reserves.

The platinum group of metals is used not only for fine jewelry but also as a catalyst in the chemical and petroleum industries. Platinum is also sometimes used in catalytic converters in automobiles. South Africa, with 60 percent of production, and the USSR, with 32 percent, dominate the platinum market. There are less efficient substitutes for platinum, and spiraling platinum prices could be dampened by the possibility of substitution.

Copper is the principal nonferrous metal in international trade, but tin and zinc are two others worthy of attention. Tin is used to manufacture pewter, bronze, and other metal alloys. It is also used as a solder and a coating for steel in tin cans, which contain very little tin and a large amount of steel. US tin consumption has risen rapidly in recent years, mostly because a large amount of tin solder is used in miniature calculators and computers. Seven countries produce the vast majority of the world's tin. They include Malaysia, which produces 40 percent of the world total, Australia, Bolivia, Indonesia, Nigeria, Thailand, and Zaire.

The world tin market is controlled by a series of five international tin agreements that predate the OPEC cartel by nearly twenty years and that may be prototypes for future commodity agreements. Unlike the OPEC agreement, the international tin agreements embrace both producers and consumers of tin. They establish an International Tin Council (ITC) to supervise and administer the agreements. The council uses three main policy instruments to stabilize the world tin market. The first is a buffer stock of tin that is used to control price fluctuations through open-market buying and selling. The second is use of member export controls for short periods, and the third is the setting of optimal price ranges by the council if the buffer stock should fail. The United States refused membership in the ITC for a long period, preferring instead to protect itself with its own strategic stockpile.[45] But US policy changed in late 1976, and the US formally ratified the fifth tin agreement.

Heavy world tin demand combined with an inadequate buffer stock has often caused the price of tin to rise above the agreed ceiling level, but it has never dropped below the supported floor. But since tin is not critical to industrial economies and since the industry is well organized within the framework of the international tin agreements, there is little reason to fear future dramatic actions from tin producers. Known reserves of tin are equal to a forty-five year supply at present rates of consumption.

World supplies of lead are adequate to meet projected demands, and supplies are found in many countries. In addition, the low melting point of lead means that it can be easily recycled. But zinc, which is used in galvanizing and diecasting processes as well as in photography and automobiles, is another matter. According to many experts, zinc may soon disappear as a widely used metal. The new reserves that have been found are in very remote areas, and this zinc will be costly to exploit and transport. No high-grade deposits of zinc have been discovered in the United States in decades, and recent estimates of world reserves indicate that they will last only between twenty and twenty-five more years.[46]

Two-thirds of the zinc used in the United States and Western Europe is imported. Japan imports more than 80 percent of its consumption. There are several major producers of zinc, including Canada, the United States, and the Soviet Union, and it is unlikely that any less developed country will benefit substantially from the developing shortage.

Table 5–3 reveals that US dependence on foreign sources is much greater for these minerals used in smaller quantities than it is for iron

TABLE 5-3. *Net US Imports of Selected Minerals as a Percent of Consumption*

Mineral	1950	1960	1970	1975	Major Foreign Source (1972–1975)
Columbium	100	100	100	100	Brazil, Thailand, Nigeria
Mica (sheet)	98	94	100	100	India, Brazil, Malagasy
Strontium	100	100	100	100	Mexico, Great Britain, Spain
Cobalt	90	66	98	98	Zaire, Belgium-Luxembourg, Finland, Norway
Manganese	77	89	95	98	Brazil, Gabon, Australia, South Africa
Titanium (rutile)	W	75	100	95	Australia, India
Chromium	95	85	89	90	USSR, South Africa, Philippines, Turkey
Aluminum	58	68	83	84	Jamaica, Australia, Surinam, Canada
Asbestos	94	94	83	84	Canada, South Africa
Tin	82	82	81	84	Malaysia, Thailand, Bolivia
Platinum group	74	82	78	83	Great Britain, USSR, South Africa
Tantalum	99	94	96	81	Thailand, Canada, Australia, Brazil
Nickel	90	72	71	72	Canada, Norway, New Caledonia
Mercury	87	25	41	69	Canada, Algeria, Mexico, Spain
Zinc	41	46	54	61	Canada, Mexico, Australia, Peru, Honduras
Tungsten	80	32	50	55	Canada, Bolivia, Peru, Thailand
Gold	25	56	59	52	Canada, Switzerland, USSR
Antimony	33	43	40	49	South Africa, China, Bolivia, Mexico
Cadmium	17	13	7	41	Canada, Mexico, Australia, Belgium-Luxembourg
Silver	66	43	26	35	Canada, Mexico, Peru
Iron	4	15	21	29	Canada, Venezuela, Japan, Common Market (EEC)
Lead	40	33	22	11	Canada, Peru, Australia, Mexico
Copper	31	E	E	E	Canada, Peru, Chile, South Africa

Note: E = Exports; W = Withheld.

SOURCE: *US Department of the Interior*, Mining & Mineral Policy, 1977 *Annual Report of the Secretary of the Interior* (January 1977), p. 24.

and copper. While considerable harm could be done to the US economy if supplies of these minerals were interrupted, the damage would be limited to a few industries. Dramatic price increases could cause similar localized turmoil but would not have nearly the same effect on the economy that the oil price increase had.

SCARCITY, CARTELS, AND INDUSTRIAL COUNTRY VULNERABILITY

The previous analysis of mineral markets and nascent cartels indicates that the probability a cartel composed of less developed exporters of any important nonfuel mineral could effectively withhold exports and increase prices is small. While producer associations exist in most important mineral markets, there are serious political and economic barriers that prevent them from acting effectively. Even if one or two of these associations could engage in cartel behavior, the impact on most industrial countries would be small. Doubling or tripling the price of a nonfuel mineral would certainly benefit the few exporting countries involved, but for most importing countries the dollar impact of these increases would be very small. And for most nonfuel minerals, doubling prices would lead to the development of substitutes or use of less rich grades of ore by industrial countries.

Thus, in terms of cartel potential, fuels are unique. Highly dependent importers simply cannot do without fuels for extended periods, for they are central to industrial activity. Substitutes for them are extremely expensive or do not exist. But most important, the OPEC cartel was activated by the use of petroleum as a political weapon. The economic aspects were added later. Until the political dimension became important, OPEC was just another example of an ineffective exporter organization.

Even if several of these nascent organizations could function as viable cartels, it would not solve many Third World problems. There is no neat division between the problems of an industrially developed world, on the one hand, and those of a less developed world on the other. In 1974, for example, the less developed world accounted for only one-third of the value of world nonfuel mineral exports.[47] In addition, the less developed world possesses no more than 45 percent of the world's known reserves of nonfuel minerals.[48] In most cases, selected industrial countries would benefit as much or more from price increases in nonfuel minerals than would the less developed countries.

Table 5–4 summarizes the share of world exports of various minerals that are accounted for by exports from less developed countries as well as relative vulnerabilities of industrial countries. There are only a few mineral markets that are dominated by less developed countries. These include petroleum, bauxite, tin, and manganese ores. The greatest share of other nonfuel minerals is exported by the industrial countries.

TABLE 5-4. *World Trade in Selected Raw Minerals*

	Number of Significant LDC Exporters*	LDC Share of Exports†	1973 US Imports as a Percent of Consumption	1973 Japanese Imports as a Percent of Consumption	1973 OECD Imports as a Percent of Consumption	Average 1972–1974 Value in World Trade (millions of dollars)
Petroleum	6	77	—	—	—	$86,658
Copper	4	59	17	90	93	6581
Iron	4	37	32	94	37	3508
Zinc	1	18	55	80	61	1187
Tin	4	84	100	97	96	1056
Silver	2	31	NA	NA	NA	697
Lead	1	28	19	76	75	605
Bauxite	3	65	88	100	51	424
Manganese	3	59	95	90	98	234

*More than 5 percent of world total.
†Data in percentages averaged for 1972–1974.

SOURCES: *World Bank, Commodity Trade and Price Trends 1976, and Council on International Economic Policy, Special Report: Critical Imported Minerals (Washington, D.C., 1974).*

There are significant differences among industrial countries in ability to adjust to or profit from contrived scarcities in nonfuel mineral markets. These differences in vulnerability usually parallel the vulnerabilities that exist in the petroleum market. Japan is in the least secure position and is vulnerable to the actions of other countries in almost all mineral markets. The Japanese are presently attempting to reduce this vulnerability by diversifying their sources of supply, trading with China, creating a Japanese sphere of influence in the Far East, and altering foreign policy, when possible, so as not to needlessly antagonize resource suppliers. Western European countries are also vulnerable in many categories, although less so than Japan. The United States is now vulnerable only in selected areas but will become more so over time (see table 5–5). For the present, its strategic stockpile and substantial industrial reserves of most minerals diminish the economic damage that could be caused by exporter cartels in the short run.[49] The Soviet Union, by contrast, is almost completely self-sufficient, with a natural resource base that permits independence from foreign suppliers. It is estimated that the Soviet Union is self-sufficient in twenty-six of the thirty-six minerals essential to industrial society, while the United States is self-sufficient in only seven.[50]

United States vulnerability is greatest in the iron alloys, where the total economic impact of price increases would be the least because of the small quantities involved. While disruption of supplies of these minerals would have some economic repercussions, particularly in the important specialty steel industry, the strategic stockpile now acts as a buffer, and substitutions are real possibilities. The United States imports all of its tin consumption, but aluminum and steel have been substituted in many commercial applications. Manganese is important because of its crucial role in the production of steel, but the political diversity of world manganese exporters makes interdiction of US supplies an unlikely event. The economic cost of imported nickel exceeds the cost of imported iron ore, but Canada, seemingly a reliable ally, supplies most import needs. Furthermore, the price of nickel has doubled over the last decade and has reached the point where various substitutes in steel-making are already under development.

There are also important differences among less developed nations on the exporter side of mineral markets. Not all less developed nations have been equally favored with abundant natural resources. The majority have extremely small or nonexistent mineral-extracting sectors. It is estimated that 61 out of 103 less developed nations have no serious mineral prospects. About 90 percent of developing nation exports of fuels and minerals are accounted for by countries containing less than one-fourth of the population of the less developed world.[51] Thus, the fortunes of less developed countries do not vary uniformly with increasing or decreasing nonfuel mineral prices. Most of them have little or no role as exporters in mineral markets.

TABLE 5–5. *United States Requirements and Reserves of Selected Minerals*

Commodity	Probable Cumulative Primary Mineral Demand 1971–2000*	Reserves at 1971 Prices*	Units†
Aluminum	370	13	Million S.T.
Antimony	822	110	Thousand S.T.
Cadmium	560	264	Million lb.
Chromium	19	——	Million S.T.
Cobalt	540	56	Million lb.
Columbium	288	——	Million lb.
Copper	93	81	Million S.T.
Iron	3	2	Billion S.T.
Lead	34	17	Million S.T.
Manganese	50	——	Million S.T.
Molybdenum	3	6	Billion lb.
Natural Gas	1,098	279	Trillion cu. ft.
Nickel	14	——	Billion lb.
Petroleum	276	38	Billion bbls.
Thorium	21	2	Thousand S.T.
Titanium	32	33	Million S.T.
Tungsten	1,000	175	Million lb.
Uranium	1,240	130	Thousand S.T.
Vanadium	471	115	Thousand S.T.
Zinc	62	30	Million S.T.

*As estimated by US Bureau of Mines, 1973.
†Notes and definitions:
  S.T. = short tons
  L.T. = long tons
  lb. = pounds
  bbls. = 42 gallons

SOURCE: *National Commission on Materials Policy,* Material Needs and the Environment Today and Tomorrow *(Washington, D.C., 1973).*

The Third World is actually composed of three groups of countries having different mineral interests and prospects. The top tier of nouveau riche oil-exporting countries is interested mainly in maintaining and increasing petroleum prices. But whether they are financially willing to support price-increasing cartels in nonfuel mineral markets remains unclear, since very few petroleum exporters also export nonfuel minerals in significant quantities. The second tier of less developed countries, composed of a small number of nonfuel mineral exporters, favors dramatic increases in prices for their exports. But such increases would be of no benefit to oil-exporting countries or to the agrarian less developed countries that make up the bulk of the Third World. Any increases in the price of nonfuel minerals would also benefit many industrial exporters, and those who are not exporters would pass increased costs through in the form of higher prices for industrial goods. For the bottom layer of less developed countries, the so-called "Fourth" or "never-to-be-developed" world, increases in any mineral prices would be another serious economic setback.

Mineral commodity agreements between industrial and developing nations establishing floor prices for commodities are now seen as measures to advance the less developed world. But they also have drawbacks. Since most of these less developed countries are net importers of minerals, the establishment of floor prices for mineral commodities would result in higher import bills for them as well as others.[52] Further, any monopolistic raising of prices implies that the supply reaching the market must be curtailed, which means that the entry of potential producers or appreciable expansion of established production must be restricted. The burden on those less developed countries whose entry is inhibited or expansion prevented could be both severe and arbitrary.[53]

Copper is a particularly good case in point. Peru, Chile, Zaire, and Zambia are the major copper exporters. There are several other less developed nations that now produce only a small amount of copper but that would like to expand production in the future—countries such as Mexico, the Philippines, Iran, Brazil, and Panama. Any scheme regulating or restricting prices or sales would tend to cement the dominant positions of the major copper exporters at the expense of those with few exports but good potential. Given this fact, a uniform, long-term commodity policy evolving within the Third World is an unlikely prospect.

A final set of questions is related to the limits to growth debate. It is clear that the question of real resource scarcity and its impact on future economic growth is very important and complex. The global trend in all fuels and minerals is for the industrial world, with the notable exception of the Soviet Union, to increase consumption and become more dependent on external supplies as domestic ores and fuels become depleted. But this global trend toward increasing industrial dependence on mineral imports is tempered by the extent to which new technologies permit utilization of less rich grades of ore or the development of substitutes.

There are three kinds of limits on the exploitation of any nonrenewable resource. The first is the limit of comparative utility. A mineral resource remains a resource only so long as it performs a function for human beings more cheaply than any other substance. When mineral exporters consider cartel action, they must assess the potential for substitution—both the use of other minerals for similar purposes and the cost of new technologies that would make mining less rich grades of ore practical. There is a real ceiling, for example, on the maximum tax that Jamaica can effectively put on bauxite since, at high prices, kaolin clays in the United States become competitive sources of aluminum. This is also why another quadrupling of petroleum prices is very unlikely, given the range of energy alternatives that become practical at that price.

A second limit to resource exploitation is one of preference. All extraction of natural resources has physical and psychological costs and benefits. Extraction will take place only when relevant public opinion finds the benefits of extraction to exceed these costs or when it is felt that the level of living or quality of life would be enhanced by such extractions. For example, although the United States possesses enough coal to permit energy self-sufficiency for at least the next century, the scars left by strip mining are heavy environmental costs and dangers to miners are heavy social costs that now prevent a rush to increased coal consumption. Although Norway could reap great economic benefits from recent discoveries of offshore petroleum, government policy is to exploit these resources very slowly so as not to destroy the fabric of Norwegian society. The preference limitation, which is closely related to perceptions of quality of life, is becoming an important constraint as the goal of greater industrial growth *at any cost* is increasingly called into question in all countries.

The ultimate limit to resource exploitation occurs when the net energy or work required to find, recover, process, and transport minerals exceeds the amount of energy or work equivalent produced by these minerals, and when the amount of energy or work that must go into finding and exploiting minerals places a perceived drain on the availability of other needed goods and services. In the long run, the increasing energy and related economic costs of extracting and processing a mineral will represent an effective barrier to its continued use as a resource. This explains why approximately one-third of the world's petroleum reserves will never be pumped. It simply will be too costly in energy terms to pump and transport this petroleum.[54]

Future prices and availability of nonfuel minerals will be determined by very complex calculations that include demand, new technologies that can be applied to extraction and processing, the average crustal abundance of minerals, present cutoff grades, and the physical properties of mineral ores. There is only a very general relationship between crustal abundance and price. Gold and silver have a very low crustal abundance and their high price makes them "precious" metals. Iron and aluminum, on the other hand, are abundant and relatively cheap on a per pound basis. But the cutoff grades that can now be profitably mined are also an important factor in determining costs. Cutoff grades are very high for iron and aluminum but so is crustal abundance. It is the relationship between the two that is important. Obviously, the cutoff grade for a mineral will never reach crustal abundance, since machinery would then be literally chewing up mountains and breaking down seawater.

Predicting when any particular mineral will become so difficult to obtain that it can no longer be considered a resource is an extremely difficult undertaking because of all of these interrelated factors. The most likely mineral future is one of multiple and connected mineral scarcities related to higher energy prices, and this situation will give mineral exporters more room to maneuver. As these scarcities become cumulative, major technological breakthroughs will be required to maintain present patterns of economic growth. Technology is the strong suit held by the industrially developed countries, and they possess the sophistication required to increase resources in mineral-exporting countries. Less developed countries, in contrast, need markets to earn foreign exchange essential for economic growth. Open mineral warfare between exporters and importers is therefore extremely unlikely. Since traditional forms of economic growth are desired by all parties, future compromises will be essential.

Despite the unlikelihood of nonfuel mineral cartels forming, there is little reason for the many vulnerable industrial importers to be encouraged by the preceding analysis. Within the next two decades, preference and economic aspects of scarcity will operate to change the structure and psychology of nonfuel mineral markets. Tremendous capital investments will be required for exploration, extraction, and refining if all needs are to be met while preserving environmental integrity. The necessity of drilling deeper and mining less rich grades of ore will mean greater costs and will tend to increase the role of imports from less developed countries. An increasingly significant portion of gross national product will have to be exported from industrial countries to less developed countries both for imports and to support mining activities.

The costs of developing and using substitutes for those minerals in shortest supply will also be considerable. Aluminum, for example, is touted as a metal to replace copper, which is in shorter supply. But more than twice as much energy is required to mine and smelt aluminum than for any equivalent amount of copper. Thus, a major shift to aluminum will require more energy. The long-term problem for industrial countries is one of a multiple and interrelated set of shortages of both raw materials and refining capacity as well as steadily increasing vulnerability to Third World initiatives.

Even though a new set of effective cartels is not just around the corner, there are many things that Third World countries could do in the short run that would have a negative impact on economic prosperity in industrial countries. They could collectively use their mineral-exporting power to embargo particular industrial countries for political reasons. If these countries also threatened to embargo countries that transship to a target country, an embargo could be an effective weapon. Third World countries could also exert pressure on industrial country investments in their territory through taxation or confiscation. Another possibility for some countries is simply to repudiate their massive debts to industrial countries, which might throw the international economy into turmoil. Finally, some Third World countries could use their cheap labor deliberately to cut prices on manufactured exports, thereby denying markets to foreign exchange–starved industrial countries.[55] Any or all of these, taken in combination with cartel actions in selected mineral markets, could seriously damage economic growth in the industrial world. Thus, the absence of many cartel possibilities for Third World countries does not preclude ecopolitical initiatives that would be destructive to industrial economies.

Finally, it is important to keep international political factors and human rights concerns in mind when analyzing possible future scarcities. This is particularly critical because of the large role to be played by presently politically sensitive countries in southern Africa in meeting future world nonfuel mineral needs. The copper belt in Zaire and Zambia is one of the richest in the world and important to future world economic health. Two-thirds of world cobalt is also produced by these two countries. South Africa possesses more than three-quarters of world chromium reserves, two-thirds of platinum reserves, half of the world's gold, and one-fifth of the world's uranium.[56] The political future of all these countries is of vital importance to the presently industrialized countries of the world, and political events there must be watched by the industrial world with keen interest.

ENDNOTES

1. General Agreement on Tariffs and Trade, *International Trade 1975/76* (Geneva, 1976), table 5.
2. Figures are from the Department of the Interior, *Mining and Minerals Policy 1973* (Washington, D. C., 1974).
3. See Council on International Economic Policy, *Special Report: Critical Imported Minerals* (Washington, D.C., 1974), p. 43.
4. See C. Fred Bergsten, "The Threat from the Third World," *Foreign Policy* (Summer 1973), and Zuhayr Mikdashi, "Collusion Could Work," *Foreign Policy* (Spring 1974).
5. See Stephen Krasner, "Oil Is the Exception," *Foreign Policy* (Spring 1974).
6. For a treatment of agricultural markets, see Cheryl Payer, ed., *Commodity Trade of the Third World* (New York: John Wiley & Sons, 1975).
7. For an analysis of general cartel theory and its applicability to cartels composed of national actors, see Davis Bobrow and Robert Kudrle, "Theory, Policy and Resource Cartels: The Case of OPEC," *Journal of Conflict Resolution* (March 1976).
8. See Michael Tanzer, *The Political Economy of International Oil and the Underdeveloped Countries* (Boston: Beacon Press, 1969), pp. 70–75. For a readable general account of the early oil politics of the Middle East, see Leonard Mosely, *Power Play* (Baltimore: Penguin Books, 1973).
9. See H. Jon Rosenbaum and William Tyler, "South-South Relations: The Economic and Political Content of Interactions Among Developing Countries," *International Organization* (Winter 1975).
10. Membership in fledgling cartels is detailed in Zuhayr Mikdashi, *The Inter-*

national *Politics of Natural Resources* (Ithaca, N.Y.: Cornell University Press, 1976), chap. 3.

11. Mikdashi, *International Politics*, p. 88.
12. See Karl Deutsch, "Communication Theory and Political Integration," in Philip Jacob and James Toscano, eds., *The Integration of Political Communication* (Philadelphia: J. B. Lippincott, 1964).
13. See Theodore Moran, "New Deal or Raw Deal in Raw Materials?" *Foreign Policy* (Winter 1972).
14. Anthony Sampson, *The Seven Sisters* (New York: Viking, 1975), chap. 15.
15. Council on International Economic Policy, *Special Report: Critical Imported Minerals*, p. A–2.
16. For a discussion of these points, see Krasner, "Oil Is the Exception."
17. Ibid., pp. 73–74.
18. See Kenneth Watt, *Principles of Environmental Science* (New York: McGraw-Hill, 1973), pp. 81–87.
19. Walter Levy, "Oil Power," *Foreign Affairs* (July 1971): p. 736.
20. An in-depth look at several key mineral markets during this period is offered in National Commission on Supplies and Shortages, *The Commodity Shortages of 1973-74: Case Studies* (Washington, D. C., 1976).
21. Nazli Choucri, "Population, Resources, Technology: Political Implications of the Environmental Crisis," *International Organization* (Spring 1972): 31.
22. Philip Connelly and Robert Perlman, *The Politics of Scarcity* (London: Oxford University Press, 1975), p. 53.
23. Earl Cook, "Limits to Exploitation of Non-Renewable Resources," *Science* (February 20, 1976).
24. Council on International Economic Policy, *Special Report: Critical Imported Minerals*, p. A–18.
25. Ibid., pp. A–18 – A–19.
26. See Charles Park, Jr., *Earthbound* (San Francisco: Freeman, Cooper, 1975), chap. 3. Detailed analyses of all important minerals and US supplies are found in Donald Brobst and Walden Pratt, eds., *Professional Paper 820— United States Mineral Resources* (Washington, D. C.: U.S. Department of Interior, 1973).
27. Council on International Economic Policy, *Special Report: Critical Imported Minerals*, part III.
28. Mikdashi, *International Politics*, pp. 97–102.
29. See Park, *Earthbound*, pp. 99–103.
30. Council on International Economic Policy, *Special Report: Critical Imported Minerals*, pp. A–57 – A–59, part III.
31. Donella Meadows, et al., *The Limits to Growth* (New York: Universe Books, 1972), pp. 56–57.
32. Park, *Earthbound*, pp. 99–103.
33. For a more detailed analysis of the world copper market, see Ann Seidman, ed., *Natural Resources and National Welfare* (New York: Praeger, 1975).
34. See Mikdashi, *International Politics*, pp. 81–89.
35. Council on International Economic Policy, *Special Report: Critical Imported Minerals*, pp. A–57 – A–59, part III.
36. Ibid., p. A–1.
37. Cook, "Limits to Exploitation."

38. Council on International Economic Policy, *Special Report: Critical Imported Minerals*, p. 13.
39. Park, *Earthbound*, pp. 110–113.
40. Council on International Economic Policy, *Special Report: Critical Imported Minerals*, p. A–6.
41. Ibid., pp. 27–28.
42. Ibid., p. 43.
43. Secretary of the Interior, *Mining and Minerals Policy* (Washington, D.C., 1977), p. 55.
44. For more information on minerals discussed in this section, see relevant portions of Park, *Earthbound*, and Brobst and Pratt, eds., *Professional Paper 820—United States Mineral Resources.*
45. Mikdashi, *International Politics*, pp. 118–128.
46. See Edmund Faltermayer, "Homely Metals Are Becoming Precious Again," *Fortune* (May 1976).
47. General Agreement on Tariffs and Trade, *International Trade 1975/76*, pp. 22–23.
48. Bension Varon and Kenji Takeuchi, "Developing Countries and Non-Fuel Minerals," *Foreign Affairs* (April 1974): 508.
49. United States reserve figures and goals are outlined in Secretary of the Interior, *Mining and Minerals Policy*, pp. 28–29. See also National Commission on Supplies and Shortages, *Government and the Nation's Resources* (Washington, D. C., 1976).
50. Raymond Ewell, "U.S. Will Lag USSR in Raw Materials," *Chemical and Engineering News* (August 24, 1970).
51. Andrew Freyman, "Mineral Resources and Economic Growth," *Finance and Development* (March 1974): 21.
52. See David McNichol, *Commodity Agreements and the New International Economic Order* (Pasadena: California Institute of Technology, Social Science Working Paper No. 144, 1976).
53. Kenji Takeuchi and Bension Varon, "Commodity Shortages and Changes in World Trade," *The Annals* (July 1975).
54. See Cook, "Limits to Exploitation," for a more extensive discussion.
55. See Bergsten, "The Threat from the Third World."
56. See Secretary of the Interior, *Mining and Minerals Policy*, pp. 149–151.

SUGGESTED READINGS

1. American Association for the Advancement of Science. *Materials*, Special Edition of *Science*. February 20, 1976.
2. Rex Bosson and Bension Varon. *The Mining Industry and the Developing Countries*. New York: Oxford University Press, 1977.
3. Donald Brobst and Walden Pratt, eds. *Professional Paper 820—United States Mineral Resources*. Washington, D. C.: Department of the Interior, 1973.
4. Philip Connelly and Robert Perlman. *The Politics of Scarcity*. London: Oxford University Press, 1975.

5. Council on International Economic Policy. *Special Report: Critical Imported Minerals*. Washington, D. C., 1974.
6. Gerald Garvey and Lou Ann Garvey. *International Resource Flows*. Lexington, Mass.: D. C. Heath, Lexington Books, 1977.
7. International Economic Studies Institute. *Raw Materials and Foreign Policy*. Boulder, Col.: Westview Press, 1976.
8. Zuhayr Mikdashi. *The International Politics of Natural Resources*. Ithaca, N.Y.: Cornell University Press, 1976.
9. National Commission on Supplies and Shortages. *Government and the Nation's Resources*. Washington, D. C., 1976.
10. David Novick. *A World of Scarcities: Critical Issues in Public Policy*. New York: John Wiley & Sons, 1976.
11. Charles Park. *Earthbound*. San Francisco: Freeman, Cooper, 1975.
12. Cheryl Payer, ed. *Commodity Trade of the Third World*. New York: John Wiley & Sons, 1975.
13. Ann Seidman, ed. *Natural Resources and National Welfare: The Case of Copper*. New York: Praeger, 1975.

6

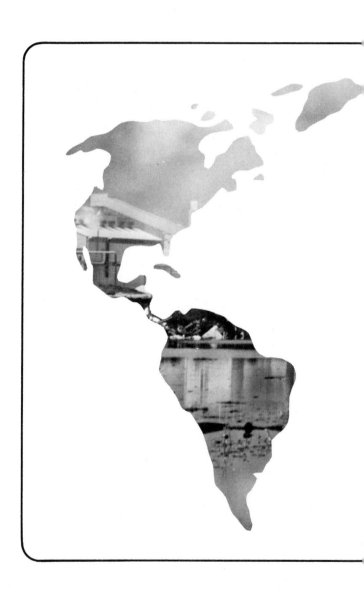

Technology and Ecopolitics

Scientific and technological discoveries linked to energy from fossil fuels provided a foundation for the Industrial Revolution and an impetus for the development of commerce and political relations among nations. Industrialization fostered improvements in transportation, communications, and industrial productivity, which in turn led to international politics and world trade. Growth, expansion, and conquest on a global scale characterized the change in the scope of relations among countries accompanying the great transformation of agrarian societies into industrial ones. But these scientific and technological innovations that have changed global and national carrying capacities have not been randomly distributed. Almost all significant technological innovations related to fossil fuel–based industrialization have taken place in only a small number of countries and then have been slowly transferred from these countries to the less industrialized world. The scientific and technological revolution has permitted the countries in which these innovations have taken place to use existing resources more effectively and to gain access to a larger resource base through trade and conquest. In ecological terms, science and technology have increased the resources available to a small group of national populations and enabled them to increase their rates of energy conversion and thus to grow in an exponential manner.

In relations among nations, rates of energy conversion can serve as an index of power relationships. Indeed, power can be defined as the rate of flow of useful energy.[1] Since all human activity and growth, like that of other species, is related to energy forms and flows, power is the control that one actor exercises "over some set of energy forms and flows that constitute part of the meaningful environment of another actor."[2] Put more simply, all individual and, in the aggregate, national activities require resources and energy. The technologies of the Industrial Revolution have enhanced differentially the flow of energy and resources under the control of different national populations. Those nations that are now more technologically sophisticated control greater flows of energy and exercise power over those that are less technologically sophisticated. Scientific knowledge and technological innovation have thus resulted in increased control of some actors by others and an international power hierarchy based upon differential control and conversion of fossil fuels and other natural resources.

The outward expansion of Western Europe that accompanied the Industrial Revolution brought greater flows of energy and resources under Western European control. The transformation of these resources into useful artifacts enhanced the capabilities of Western European powers and created the vast empires that, in turn, helped to advance the Industrial Revolution. The power hierarchy characteristic of the present economic and political paradigm was thus created and sustained by European technological preeminence. Within this hierarchy, the highly industrialized nations have been able to sustain large populations at very high standards of living. This feat has been accomplished by using indigenous natural resources more effectively and by importing increasing quantities of resources from areas of the world within their spheres of influence. During much of the course of Western European industrial development, needed raw materials were simply expropriated from colonial possessions as a result of the exercise of naked force. More recently, most technologically advanced countries have kept themselves afloat by virtue of favorable terms for their high-technology trade with the newly independent less developed countries, selling industrial products dearly and buying raw materials cheaply. But that era may be quickly coming to an end.

Demands for a new international economic (and political) order are aimed at destroying this hierarchy created by the different levels of national technological sophistication and stemming the rapid growth in natural resource consumption on the part of industrial countries. While industrial countries still possess this important technological edge, they are increasingly forced to import fuels and other natural resources from technologically less developed countries. The tables are now turning, and the suppliers of these resources are exerting their own power by making them more expensive, or even periodically denying them, to technologically sophisticated countries.

The rest of this chapter focuses on global ecopolitics from the perspective of the industrially developed countries. These countries seek to use their technological sophistication to preserve the established international hierarchy created by the Industrial Revolution. While they still possess a great technological edge over the less developed countries, their vulnerabilities to the initiatives of natural resource exporters are growing. Furthermore, as the old paradigm that has governed relations among nations begins to change, the ethics of technological imperialism are coming under increasing fire. Since the bulk of the world's population lives in the less developed countries and since many fossil fuel–based technological innovations have little relevance to their developmental situation, a search for new, more "appropriate" technologies is now under way.

The industrial countries, faced with increasingly unfavorable balances of payments, are forced to compete with each other and sell more sophisticated and dangerous new technologies to trade partners who are increasingly skeptical about the long-term benefits to be gained from them. The hope in technologically developed countries is that new methods of producing energy and processing natural resources will free them from increasing vulnerability to less developed countries and will maintain the existing international power hierarchy. Energy from nuclear fission and eventually fusion are important components of this strategy. It remains to be seen if these costly and potentially dangerous technologies can gain acceptability quickly enough to stem a transfer of power to energy and mineral exporters in the less developed world.

TECHNOLOGY AND SOCIOECONOMIC TRAPS

Biologist Garrett Hardin has suggested a metaphor that aptly describes one of the impacts of technology on relations among nations.[3] His image is one of a tragedy that unfolds on a medieval "commons," an area open to all herdsmen to pasture their livestock. The tragedy that develops on the commons is related to the fact that there is only limited "opportunity" or carrying capacity for herdsmen to use it. In the absence of accepted institutionalized regulations governing the use of the commons, each herdsman will attempt to put as many animals as possible on it because it seems to be in his own self-interest to do so. Within the industrial paradigm of capitalist societies, which emphasizes minimal government interference in economic matters, there is great resistance to rules limiting individual initiative in using such commons. Given a limited commons and increased population pressures, a tragedy unfolds as the commons is decimated by excessive grazing. The herds on it collapse due to starvation. Each individual actor is locked into a system that encourages the relatively unbridled pursuit of self-interest on a free, but finite, commons. Within the ethical system that is at the core of the expansionist industrial paradigm, freedom on a commons thus brings ruin to all.[4]

The tragedy of the commons is rooted in the fact that human beings are ill-equipped psychologically to link their short-term actions with long-term consequences. In some cases, this inability is simply due to individual selfishness. In the absence of strong ethical principles to the contrary, selfish individuals on a commons may not care that it will ultimately collapse because they may have plans to market their herds early and invest the proceeds in other pursuits. In other cases, such apparently shortsighted behavior may be due to lack of appropriate information. Each herdsman may not realize that others are acting similarly or that the commons has limited capacity. There are still others who are willingly ignorant of the future impact of their actions. Proponents of this "eat, drink, and make merry" philosophy may not care that there won't be a commons for future generations.[5]

The tragedy of the commons is one variation of a larger set of dilemmas that could be called problems of coordination.[6] If the world were a perfectly rational place run by perfectly rational individuals possessing perfect information, tragedies of this nature would not take place. Appropriate ethics and laws would govern the use of such commons in the interest of the welfare of present and future generations. Unfortunately, when confronting these issues the world is far from rational at present. In international affairs, there are no commonly accepted policies governing commons in the interest of all humanity. Even if there were such policies, it is very unlikely that the actions of individual "sovereign" countries could be coordinated to bring about a desired future. Each nation in the international system usually attempts to maximize its own self-interest, disregarding any common interest of all humanity.

Robert Goodin defines a coordination problem as existing whenever it is "rational" for all agents involved to prefer joint to independent decision making. There are two necessary conditions for the existence of a coordination problem: actors must be mutually involved, and there must be danger of disagreeable outcomes for everyone if all individuals act independently.[7] In the case of Hardin's commons, the tragedy unfolds because all actors are mutually dependent upon one piece of real estate and do not act collectively to avert the collapse of the herds. In international relations, it is becoming more obvious that the delicate nature of the ecosphere and the relatively limited quantities of some critical natural resources make all nations much more mutually dependent. And if nations continue to act in their perceived short-run self-interest in these matters, as they have throughout most of the Industrial Revolution, their actions will lead to a disagreeable outcome for the collective.

John Platt has used the term "social trap" to refer to situations where individual actors, organizations, or whole societies get themselves involved in a course of action or set of relationships that later prove to be unpleasant or lethal.[8] He has analyzed a series of situations in which all actors collectively suffer because of individuals who act in what they perceive to be their own self-interest while the situation changes. The essence of such traps is that the self-interested behavior that gathers momentum in one set of circumstances cannot be rapidly changed to conform to a new set of circumstances.

In times when dominant social paradigms are in transition, of course, the number of social, political, and economic traps that people find themselves in increases very dramatically.[9] Tragedies of the commons, problems of coordination, and social traps are therefore abundant in ecopolitics. Many of them have been triggered by the rapid and unequal growth of technology. The most obvious category of such ecopolitical problems is directly parallel to Hardin's medieval tragedy and is based upon cutthroat competition among individual national actors for limited natural resources. Technological development and industrial growth, for example, have created an international social trap in energy markets. The industrial countries remain locked in a growth paradigm that makes them increasingly vulnerable to the machinations of less developed petroleum exporters. To escape this vulnerability, industrial countries are turning to alternative fuels, a process that could lead to a global tragedy through environmental pollution or through a major nuclear reactor accident. In addition, the global scramble for fossil fuels threatens environmental destruction because of strip-mining, offshore drilling, and spills from petroleum tankers. The only way to break out of this trap is to reevaluate fundamentally the core assumptions inherent in the growth paradigm.

Food is another category of resource problems that illustrates a contemporary tragedy of the commons. Growing populations and increasing individual consumption of food put pressure on available land and oceanic fisheries. In many countries, for example, intense cultivation of land is leading to long-term decreases in per acre productivity. Irrigated land becomes useless after several years of production because the soil becomes too saline as a result of minerals left behind by the irrigation water. The world's fisheries are another example of an international food tragedy. Desperate for protein, the Japanese are using a larger, more technologically sophisticated fleet to increase their harvest of the world's fish; as a result, the Japanese (and other fishing nations) have now harvested the oceans to the point where there is serious doubt about the ability of the world's fish to reproduce rapidly enough to sustain the world fish catch at its present level.

The use of nitrogen fertilizer to increase world crop yields may ultimately represent a more serious social trap. The use of nitrogen fertilizer on a global basis is about 40 million tons a year. This is about one-third of the total natural fixation of nitrogen on land. By the year 2000, fertilizer use will have quadrupled. This increase means that artificial fixation of nitrogen will be double the natural rate at that time. Nitrous oxide rises in the atmosphere from fertilized soils and is believed to be affecting the earth's ozone layer. If the ozone layer becomes depleted, dangerous ultraviolet radiation will pass through and increase the human cancer rate. It is estimated that over the next fifty years this source of ozone depletion alone could reduce the earth's supply by 1.6 to 9 percent.[10] But each nation, seeking to expand food production through increased use of fertilizer, will continue to contribute to this tragedy that will slowly unfold over time.

There are two sets of coordination problems or traps that are of particular importance to the future welfare of industrial nations and all humanity. The first involves an ecopolitical tragedy of the oceanic commons, where the self-interested behavior of individual actors is now leading to less than optimal solutions for the whole. The quest for food and minerals on the part of technologically sophisticated states is leading to this tragedy. The most obvious cause is the introduction of technologically sophisticated fishing equipment into oceanic fisheries.

Sonar, fine-mesh nets, and mechanized processing equipment have all combined to make fishing the oceanic commons a much more efficient process; so efficient, in fact, that there is real concern that self-interested actors are decimating whale and fish populations. The ocean floor is also under attack by industrial countries in search of petroleum and natural gas in offshore areas as well as manganese nodules at greater depths. These resource-deficient countries seek to reap the wealth of the deep as rapidly as new technologies make it possible without considering long-term ecological, economic, and ethical implications for humanity as a whole.

The second set of coordination problems or traps that affects the future of the whole human race centers around conflict over export earnings from high-technology trade. It is in the self-interest of each industrial country to capture as great a share of the world high-technology export market as possible. While the resulting intense competition seems to be a short-run imperative for both private and public actors in these countries, this competition leads high-technology exporters to take risky actions that may not be in the interest of less developed countries or in their own long-term self-interest. Exports of weapons, fossil fuel–intensive industries, and private automobiles fall into the former category, and exports of nuclear reactors and reprocessing technologies fall into the latter. This coordination problem has become more pronounced since the quadrupled oil prices have drained each of the industrial countries of tens of billions of petrodollars. Each industrial country, acting out of self-interest, now plays a beggar-thy-neighbor trade strategy that can increase friction among industrial countries, cause conflict and energy problems in less developed countries, and lead to nuclear weapons proliferation and the possible destruction of a significant portion of the human population.

During the transition from an industrial to a postindustrial paradigm that is now under way, some industrial countries will get caught in socioeconomic traps and be affected by tragedies of the commons much more than others. The relative vulnerability of industrial countries to these changes and the origins of some of these future coordination problems are discussed in the following sections.

INDUSTRIAL COUNTRIES: SENSITIVITY TO VULNERABILITY

Many industrially developed countries have nearly exhausted the deposits of natural resources found within their territorial limits. Some smaller countries never had an extensive domestic natural resource base with which to industrialize. Whatever the reason, many of these countries have moved beyond mere sensitivity to the natural resource policies of less developed countries and now must be considered vulnerable to their initiatives.

Japan is the most extreme case of an industrial country living well beyond reasonable limits of self-sufficiency. The pressures that lead to tragedies of the commons, both concrete and abstract, are very obvious in the case of the Japanese economy. Japan, with 3 percent of the world's population, has one of the world's largest fishing fleets and is a principal actor in the tragedy of the oceanic commons. Japan also imports tremendous quantities of food and minerals; in 1972, for example, the country's overall rate of food self-sufficiency was only 73 percent, compared with 82 percent in 1963.[11] But Japan is also a principal actor in an international competition for the limited high-technology export market. Since Japan must import such a large proportion of its resource consumption, Japanese industry must maintain or increase its share of the high-technology low-energy-intensity export market or the Japanese economy will be in serious trouble.

In 1976, Japanese oil imports cost $23 billion. Twelve billion dollars' worth of industrial exports were shipped to oil-exporting countries, leaving a trade deficit with these countries of $11 billion. An additional trade deficit of $4 billion was run with Canada and Australia, chiefly because of imports of coal and several minerals, mainly iron and copper ore, from these countries.[12] To make up for these deficits, Japan enjoyed a $5.4 billion surplus in trade with the United States and a $4.2 billion surplus in trade with Western Europe. Since Japan produces almost the same portfolio of high-technology products as the United States and Western Europe, Japanese officials fear a possible trade war, particularly as rising natural resource prices intensify internal pressures for more Japanese export activity in order to maintain a reasonable trade balance.[13]

Rising energy prices already have forced an end to domestic production of aluminum in Japan, and the petrochemical industry is threatened. Former Japanese Vice Minister of the Ministry of Internal Trade and Industry (MITI) Eme Yamasita has projected Japanese imports of oil at 500 million metric tons per year by 1985. He figures that Japan "can hardly physically obtain that amount of oil and it is doubtful that [Japan] can export enough industrial goods to get the foreign exchange to pay for it."[14] Thus, the structure and future growth of Japanese industry is clouded by uncertainty over supplies of natural resources.

Future Japanese industrial development is also severely limited by lack of coastal sites suitable for heavy industries, the current very high levels of pollution, and rising wages, which take away the comparative advantage of cheap Japanese labor. So, Japan is moving in the direction of high-technology knowledge industries, such as computers, communications equipment, and systems engineering. The important Japanese steel industry, responsible for 16 percent of Japan's exports in 1975, is projected to provide only 6 percent of all exports in 1985. Shipbuilding is projected to fall from 10 percent of exports in 1975 to only 6 percent in 1985. Metal products, which made up 23 percent of Japanese exports in 1975, will fall to 9 percent of all exports by 1985. Exports of electrical machinery, on the other hand, are expected to rise from 15 percent of all exports in 1975 to 21 percent in 1985.[15]

Japan is admittedly the extreme case along the industrial sensitivity-vulnerability spectrum. Other industrial countries vary in the degree to which they have become dependent on others as a source of raw materials. The data in table 6–1 reveal some of these differences. In 1975, Japan ran up a net deficit of $44 billion in trade in primary products. This deficit contrasts sharply with what occurred in Canada, which, in the same category, managed a trade surplus of $7 billion. Western European countries taken collectively are nearly as dependent upon foreign suppliers as Japan, although the $71 billion Western European trade deficit is smaller on a per capita basis than is the Japanese deficit.

Table 6–2 contains trade data for OECD industrial countries for the decade 1965–1975. It shows that most of these countries have been running a chronic trade deficit that, in many cases, has been growing over time. Of these countries, only Australia, Belgium, Canada, West Germany, Sweden, and the United States exhibit a reasonably balanced trade profile. Some, such as Great Britain and Spain, have been plagued with very heavy trade deficits over the entire decade.

Figures 6–1 and 6–2 illustrate shifts in import patterns over time in the five most important free market industrial countries. In all these countries, the percentage of total imports accounted for by food and raw materials has declined over the last quarter century. But in Japan, West Germany, and Great Britain, the quantity of these materials imported has risen substantially. This apparent paradox is due to the expansion of

TABLE 6–1. Trade in Basic Commodities*

		Food	Fuels	Raw Materials	Minerals	Total Primary Products
Canada	1972	1.11	.65	1.84	1.41	5.02
	1975	1.58	1.24	2.44	2.03	7.31
United States	1972	1.14	−3.24	.02	−.46	−2.55
	1975	10.35	−21.94	1.42	−.15	−10.32
EEC Europe†	1972	−9.72	−11.86	−5.83	−3.14	−30.55
	1975	−13.94	−42.35	−8.09	−6.33	−70.71
Japan	1972	−3.66	−5.65	−3.20	−2.76	−15.27
	1975	−9.54	−25.43	−4.37	−4.92	−44.27

*Billions of dollars. Minus signs indicate net deficit.
†European Economic Community.

SOURCE: *General Agreement on Tariffs and Trade, International Trade 1975/76 (Geneva, 1976).*

TABLE 6–2. *Trade Balances in Industrial Countries (Exports-Imports)**

	1965	1970	1972	1973	1975
Australia	N.A.	N.A.	1923.60	2691.84	1913.64
Austria	−500.28	−692.04	−1320.60	−1749.24	−1874.28
Belgium-Luxembourg	8.16	242.64	495.96	471.48	−1897.80
Canada	121.32	2826.96	1256.28	1890.36	−1653.24
Denmark	−537.95	−1095.00	−713.64	−1585.44	−1619.04
Finland	N.A.	−330.96	−251.52	−504.24	−2114.52
France	−288.72	−1179.24	−824.40	−1431.72	−2029.92
Federal Republic of Germany	420.12	4374.60	6444.36	12,941.28	15,813.60
Greece	−805.92	−1315.90	−1474.92	−2019.00	−3024.48
Iceland	−8.04	−10.80	−41.52	−66.60	−179.52
Ireland	−413.52	−534.00	−490.20	−660.60	−596.40
Italy	−159.24	−1751.40	−733.44	−5576.52	−3533.88
Japan	282.72	436.56	5120.52	−1382.88	−2110.20
Netherlands	−1070.76	−1626.48	−735.12	−409.68	−704.40
Norway	−763.08	−1242.12	−1091.40	−1539.12	−2479.08
Portugal	−326.64	−609.84	−898.92	−1114.20	−1892.28
Spain	−2052.36	−2360.28	−2911.32	−4449.60	−8577.60
Sweden	−405.36	−223.44	677.64	1529.04	−642.24
Switzerland	−708.24	−1330.32	−1617.84	−2095.80	−345.24
Turkey	−117.84	−297.36	−619.44	−779.64	−3239.76
United Kingdom	−2427.48	−2372.88	−3511.08	−8297.16	−9495.84
United States	5721.48	3263.16	−5879.52	2192.76	10,711.20
Yugoslavia	−197.40	−1195.08	−990.36	−1753.08	−3624.36

*Millions of dollars.

SOURCE: *Organization for Economic Cooperation and Development,* Statistics of Foreign Trade Monthly Bulletin *(Paris, 1974, 1976).*

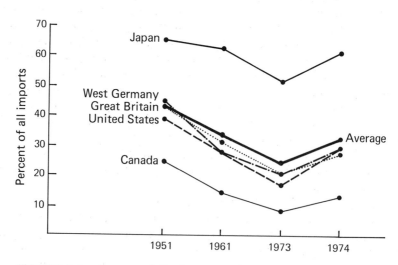

FIGURE 6–1. *Imports of Crude Materials and Minerals* [SOURCE: Data derived from *United Nations Annual* (New York, 1951–1975).]

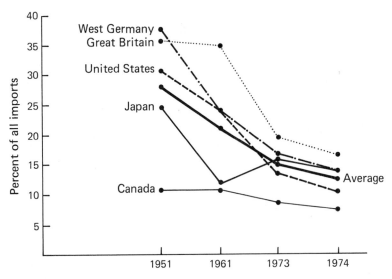

FIGURE 6-2. *Agricultural Imports* [SOURCE: Data derived from *United Nations Annual* (New York, 1951–1975).]

high-technology trade among the industrialized countries, which masks the increasing significance of raw material imports. The vulnerability of Japan shows up clearly in these data. Crude materials and minerals made up 63 percent of Japan's imports, while they totaled an average of only 27 percent for these other industrial countries over this period. Japanese raw material imports and food, taken together, totaled 77 percent of the import bill in 1974, as opposed to a 39 percent average for other Western industrial countries. Canada, by contrast, is well below the average, with only 23 percent of its imports falling into these combined raw material and food categories.

The data in these tables illustrate how increased imports of primary commodities can trigger the dynamics of the tragedy of a trade commons. The greater the overextension of any country, the more intense the internal pressure to capture high-technology export markets to pay for increasingly expensive natural resource imports. Thus, Japan has become an aggressive exporter of high-technology products, flooding the world market with television sets, automobiles, cameras, electronic equipment, and a wide variety of other such products. Industry and government work hand in hand to facilitate this trade, since Japan's economic survival depends upon running a trade surplus in high-technology products. In 1977, Nashiro Amaya, an official of MITI, admitted that Japanese prosperity depends upon the United States accepting a regular deficit in trade with Japan. He claimed that if the United States ever rejects this imbalance, it will throw Japan into economic chaos.[16] With persistent unemployment and trade balance problems of its own, it is difficult to see the United States continuing to accept a regular deficit in trade with Japan. Both the United States and Western Europe must worry about their own serious unemployment and balance of payments problems, and they informed the Japanese of this in trade negotiations in 1977 and 1978.

Figure 6–3 reveals export patterns for these key industrial countries since 1951. During this period, Great Britain, Japan, and West Germany were heavily dependent upon the export of high-technology manufactured products. The United States and Canada also steadily increased their high-technology exports throughout the period, but both countries remained diversified exporters at the end of the period.

FIGURE 6–3.   *Export Activity*
Part A: Exports of manufactured goods as percent of all exports
Part B: Exports as percent of GNP in 1974 [SOURCE: Data derived from United Nations, *World Trade Annual* (New York, 1951–1975); World Bank, *World Bank Atlas, 1975* (Washington, D.C., 1976); and Organization for Economic Cooperation and Development, *Statistics of Foreign Trade Monthly Bulletin* (November 1975).]

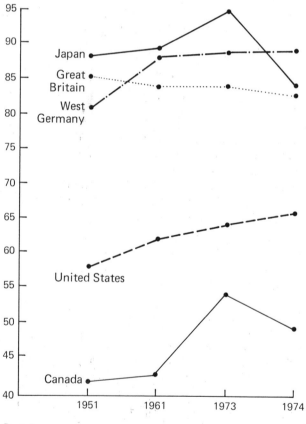

Part A:

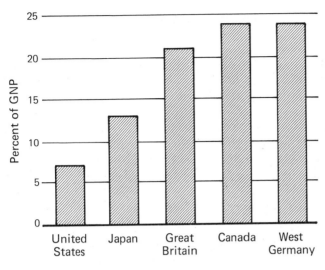

Part B:

Differences in the role that total exports play in each country's economy are also significant. When exports are compared to gross national product, the United States stands out because of its relatively minor involvement with the international economy. Even the Japanese economy is not as heavily involved in international trade as some more mature industrial ones. Great Britain, Canada, and West Germany are all much more closely tied to the international economy. Other industrial countries are even more "global" in their economic activity. In the Netherlands, for example, exports are 49 percent of gross national product, and in Belgium they are 53 percent.

These differences, when combined with figures on the composition of trade in each country, illustrate the distinction between sensitivity and vulnerability.[17] By virtue of their heavy involvement in international trade, most Western European industrial countries are sensitive to the actions of many trade partners. But this heavy involvement does not mean vulnerability in all cases. Japan, on the other hand, does not exhibit the same high level of total trade involvement, but the nature of its modest involvement makes Japan vulnerable to the manipulations of raw material exporters.

In summary, the industrial countries differ in the extent to which they have developed vulnerabilities in raw materials. Some industrial countries are net exporters of energy, but this case is not usual. Most are moving in the direction of Japan, a country that produces only a small percentage of natural resources consumed. Because natural resources are essential for economic growth, it would appear that these countries will become more vulnerable to exporters of these resources over time, since zero growth in consumption is not a viable policy option.

Is the United States Becoming More Vulnerable?

The United States is the most important national actor in the global economy. The 6 percent of the world's population living there consumes approximately 30 percent of the world's annual production of fuels and nonfuel minerals. This same 6 percent is responsible for one-quarter of the gross world product. Exports from the US amount to approximately 12 percent of the world total.[18] Obviously, economic conditions in the United States are important to countries that rely upon it as a trade partner. The United States does not rely heavily upon international trade, at least in relation to the size of gross national product, but the impact of its international economic activity on the rest of the world is great because of the sheer volume of that activity.

The size and scope of its economic activity make the US a logical target for radical critics of the old international economic order. By virtue of being the largest of the world's economies and headquarters for a large number of multinational corporations, the United States is forced to bear the brunt of attacks by Third World political leaders who are dissatisfied with the present international distribution of wealth and income. And, by virtue of its high consumption of resources, the US is vulnerable to charges of profligate use.

Industry in the US developed in an atmosphere of both global and domestic natural resource abundance. As late as 1951, minerals, crude materials, and agricultural commodities composed 40 percent of US export earnings. The United States has historically supported industrial growth with domestic natural resources while many other industrial nations became dependent on external suppliers very early in their industrialization efforts. More recent trends, however, indicate that the United States will not likely continue to be nearly as self-sufficient in the future. Thus, the US is likely to become more vulnerable to natural resource exporters and a competitor with other industrial countries for remaining resources.

Over the last decade, fuels have made up the bulk of the value of US imports. In 1970, net imports of fuels accounted for only 4 percent of all imports; this figure spiraled to around 23 percent in 1976.[19] In 1974, 3.5 million barrels of crude oil were imported into the United States on a daily basis. This figure jumped to 4.1 million barrels per day in 1975 and reached 5.6 million barrels of crude petroleum per day plus 2.2 million barrels of refined products in 1976.[20] Other imports have remained fairly stable over time. Imported food now accounts for about 10 percent of the United States' total import bill, although the US is a large net exporter of food. Manufactured goods make up about 15 percent, and machinery and transport equipment about 25 percent of all imports.[21]

The bulk of US trade takes place in high-technology items. It is difficult to define and measure the exact extent of this trade because definitions are somewhat arbitrary. There are at least three commonly used definitions in the United States, one created by the National Science Foundation and two by the Department of Commerce. Depending upon the definition chosen, technology-intensive items account for between 40 and 75 percent of all US exports of manufactured goods and between 20 and 50 percent of all imports of manufactured goods. Thus, the United States maintains an export surplus in the high-technology category that is counterbalanced by deficits in mineral and fuel trade.[22] But concern has recently been expressed that research and development have been lagging in the United States and that its strong role in high-technology trade will erode, leaving it in an increasingly precarious trade position.[23]

The bulk of US export earnings (about 43 percent) comes from sales of machinery and transport equipment. Automobiles and aircraft make up over one-third of this total. The United States is atypical of industrial countries, since exports of agricultural commodities make up about 21 percent of all exports. Since 1960, the United States has exported considerably more food than is imported, and this ratio has been steadily climbing as external demand for food grows.[24] In 1976, food imports were estimated at $12.5 billion and exports at $23.5 billion. The US also exports considerable quantities of crude materials.

The United States imports in large quantities from four industrial countries—Canada, Japan, West Germany, and Great Britain. In 1975, these four countries accounted for nearly one-half of all imports. Italy, France, and Mexico accounted for smaller quantities of imports. Three members of OPEC, Venezuela, Nigeria, and Saudi Arabia, round out the top ten sources of US imports because of the petroleum trade. Nigeria and Saudi Arabia were not major trade partners with the United States in 1972, but by 1975 these countries accounted for 6 percent of all US imports. In 1975, Nigeria, Venezuela, and Saudi Arabia accounted for almost half of US petroleum imports.[25]

The economy of the US is most sensitive to the Japanese and Canadian economies, and actions taken by individual lesser trade partners would not inconvenience the US to any great extent. From the reverse perspective, however, the United States is the principal market for exports from a large number of trading partners. Table 6–3 lists "client-states" that depend upon the US for one-third or more of all export activity. In most cases, the US is also their main source of imports. In these countries, economic and political fortunes are tied to the US economy. While these countries could exercise few economic sanctions over the United States, the US could severely disrupt their vulnerable economies through trade embargoes or similar economic actions.

Sixteen countries derive more than one-third of export earnings from markets in the United States. They can be classified as diverse or specialized traders. Canada, Mexico, and Korea have developed a broad trade profile with the United States. Trade with these countries is not based upon one or only a handful of products. The specialized coun-

TABLE 6-3.   Source of United States Imports*

	1972	Percent†	1974	Percent†	1975	Percent†
Canada	14907	27	22282	22	22170	23
Japan	9068	16	12455	12	11425	12
West Germany	4250	8	6427	6	5409	6
Great Britain	2987	5	4021	4	3773	4
Venezuela	1297	2	4679	5	3625	4
Nigeria	271	—	3286	3	3281	3
Mexico	1632	3	3386	3	3066	3
Saudi Arabia	194	—	1672	2	2623	3
Italy	1757	3	2593	3	2457	2
France	1369	2	2305	2	2164	2
Iran	199	—	2132	2	1398	1
Total Imports	55555		100972		96940	

*Millions of dollars.
†Percent of all imports.
SOURCES: US Department of Commerce, United States General Exports: World Areas by Commodity Groupings 1975 (Washington, D.C.: Bureau of the Census, 1976) and United Nations, World Trade Annual (New York, 1973–1975).

tries, on the other hand, gain most of their export revenue from only one or two basic commodity exports to the US, and they are very vulnerable to fluctuations in US demand. Foremost among these specialized traders are the so-called "banana republics," Honduras, Panama, Costa Rica, and Ecuador. Nicaragua, the Dominican Republic, and the Philippines also deal mainly in basic agricultural exports. The remaining five specialized US trade partners export fuels and nonfuel minerals. Venezuela exports both crude petroleum and refined products, and Trinidad makes its export earnings from refined petroleum products. Haiti and Jamaica are large exporters of bauxite, while Peru depends on metallic ores and anchovies in its dealings with the United States.

In summary, Canada, Japan, and possibly Mexico are diverse traders that are economically sensitive to political and economic initiatives from the United States because of the volume of trade with the US. The specialized traders that are most vulnerable to US actions are Haiti, Jamaica, Peru, Trinidad, and Venezuela, all countries that supply either fuels or nonfuel minerals to US industry, and the rest of the specialized traders, which export mainly agricultural commodities (see table 6–4).

On the other side of the coin, since most specialized traders export mainly agricultural products to the United States, there are very few countries that can significantly affect economic growth in the US through their economic activities. The major exception is the small group of petroleum exporters. But Saudi Arabia is the only significant Arab exporter of petroleum to the United States. Nigeria and Indonesia desperately need export revenue for development, and Venezuela

TABLE 6–4.   Vulnerable US Trade Partners

Year		Percent of Exports to US	Percent of Imports from US	Major Exports
1973	Mexico	69	63	Diverse basic commodities
1974	Canada	67	67	Diverse industrial products and raw materials
1972	Haiti	66	44	Coffee, bauxite
1971	Dominican Republic	64	47	Sugar, coffee, tobacco
1972	Honduras	56	44	Bananas
1973	Panama	45	35	Bananas
1971	Surinam	45	34	Bauxite
1972	Trinidad	45	19	Fuels
1974	Philippines	42	24	Lumber, sugar, copper
1973	Jamaica	41	39	Bauxite
1972	Venezuela	40	45	Petroleum
1972	Ecuador	38	30	Bananas, coffee, cocoa
1974	Korea	34	25	Various manufactured goods
1972	Peru	33	30	Fish meal, metal ores
1973	Nicaragua	33	34	Coffee, cotton, meat
1973	Costa Rica	33	35	Bananas, coffee

SOURCES: United Nations, Yearbook of Trade Statistics 1974 (New York, 1975) and United Nations, World Trade Annual (New York, 1975).

would also like to increase its exports. The United States is vulnerable to actions taken by OPEC as a whole at present, but individual members or small factions could not severely affect its economic growth. As the gap between oil production and consumption narrows in the future, however, this situation could rapidly change.

The United States is not particularly vulnerable to either price increases or embargoes on nonfuel minerals because, although it imports almost all of its consumption of several minerals, such as nickel, cobalt, manganese, tin and bauxite, present stockpiles are adequate for more than two years' normal consumption. Furthermore, in 1976, the US trade deficit in nonfuel minerals and metals trade was a relatively modest $4 billion, an increase of only $2 billion over the 1970 figure.[26] All US nonfuel mineral dependence is thus mitigated by the stockpile, an ability to absorb higher prices since each mineral makes up only a small portion of US trade, and the possibility of developing substitutes. Recent increases in Jamaican bauxite prices, for example, have been easily absorbed by the US economy. An increase in price or an embargo on any of the other nonfuel minerals, an unlikely event, would be more a nuisance than a long-term threat to the economy. Furthermore, there is no single country that has a monopoly on the export of any mineral to the United States. Short of the formation of a "macrocartel" covering a large number of nonfuel minerals, an event that is not possible within the next decade, there is little that nonfuel mineral exporters or exporters of farm products can do to affect economic growth in the United States adversely. In this respect, the United States is much less vulnerable than Japan or several other OECD countries.

Thus, in the competition among technologically developed industrial countries, the United States is presently much less vulnerable to trading partners than are its allies. And this difference means that the US and its industrial allies may disagree on international trade and resource politics. In fact, the US is now in a position to damage the economies of several less developed countries should it choose to do so. But in the long term, economic growth in the US will likely chip away at self-sufficiency as more resources will be imported in the future.

TECHNOLOGY AND THE OCEANIC COMMONS

The most striking analogy to Hardin's medieval tragedy of the commons in contemporary international affairs is the problem of managing the oceans. They have historically been open to all nations, and those that have been most pressed for food have turned to them as a source of protein. But other natural resources in the oceans are now attracting the attention of technologically developed countries. The tragedy of the oceanic commons has only recently become a major issue in international politics, for prior to the 1960s, there was little evidence that need for fish, mineral resource demands, and pollution were large enough in relation to the vastness of the oceans to make much difference. Now, however, pressures are growing for wholesale exploitation of the vast storehouse of natural resources found in this oceanic treasury.

In traditional international law, freedom of the seas was guaranteed to all nations outside a zone extending three miles from shore (the distance that cannon balls could be shot by hostile powers). Use of the oceanic commons was relatively unrestricted as long as ships using the oceans respected the rights of others. The debate over the right to exploit this commons, however, began with the discovery of oil in the offshore areas of the United States in the early 1940s. This discovery started a chain of events that culminated in the first United Nations Conference on the Law of the Sea in 1958. In 1945, President Harry Truman proclaimed the right of the US to exploit the mineral resources on the continental shelf beyond the territorial sea. Other nations followed with declarations of their own, most notably Chile, Ecuador, and Peru, which stated that their national jurisdiction extended 200 miles into the oceans. This declaration ultimately lead to confrontations between Peruvian authorities and the United States tuna fleet, which have continued over the last two decades.

At the 1958 conference, four conventions were adopted. The first set a twelve-mile maximum for national territorial seas. A second specified a series of rights shared by all nations on the high seas. A third provided for nations to regulate fisheries in their coastal waters beyond the twelve-mile limit. The fourth, and ultimately most important convention, gave nations rights to explore for mineral resources outside of the territorial sea to a depth of 200 meters or until the waters no longer permit the exploitation of the natural resources of these areas. This fourth convention led to a series of unilateral territorial claims well beyond 200 miles from coastlines.[27]

In 1967, Arvid Pardo, the ambassador to the UN from Malta, startled the diplomatic community by suggesting that the ocean floor, beyond the limits of national jurisdiction, be treated as the common heritage of mankind. An international organization should be created, according to him, to oversee ocean resources and to use revenue derived from the exploitation of those resources for development in the poor countries. Since his speech, there have been several attempts to reach agreement on use of the seabed, most notably the Third United Nations Conference on the Law of the Sea, which began in 1973 and continued through 1978. Between Pardo's speech in 1967 and 1973, however, the "common heritage" of mankind shrank from 65 percent of all ocean space to only 35 percent by means of unilateral declarations by coastal states.

Population pressures accompanied by new technological developments are responsible for the unfolding of this tragedy of the oceanic commons. The same lateral pressures that Choucri and North claim lead one state occasionally to move against another also drive those nations that are well beyond self-sufficiency in food and minerals to the sea for fish and natural resources. There are three categories of marine resources that attract the efforts of these nations: fish, petroleum and natural gas, and manganese nodules.

About one-fifth of all protein consumed by human beings comes from the oceans. Fishing has always been carried out on the high seas, but it has only been recently that technologically developed nations have begun to decimate fisheries with the aid of modern equipment. Today, ships from the Soviet Union and Japan travel the oceanic commons searching for fish with the aid of sonar. Fine-mesh nets catch ever-smaller specimens, and factory ships follow closely behind to process and freeze them. The intensity with which the oceans are fished has grown substantially, and the world fish catch, which had systematically increased in the 1960s, suddenly peaked and then dropped in the 1970s.

Potential finds of petroleum and natural gas provide greater pressures for "ocean grabs" on the part of coastal powers. Because of the geological processes that formed these reserves, the largest portion of offshore oil and gas is found on the continental shelf in less than 200 meters of water. Almost all coastal nations have some potential for recovery of fossil fuels from coastal waters, and for this reason there is heavy pressure to maintain a 200-mile resource zone.

Manganese nodules are a deep seabed resource that are formed by processes not yet well understood. These objects, which look much like a baked potato, are composed of copper, nickel, cobalt, manganese, and other minerals. The most profitable concentrations are found in deep sea areas not yet within the national jurisdiction of any coastal powers. But it is the industrially developed countries that are developing equipment to do deep seabed mining, and the United States and Japan may well act unilaterally to get these resources if a binding international agreement is not reached very shortly.

Thus, Ambassador Pardo's dreams of a seabed authority to control the oceans for the benefit of all mankind and especially for a Third World Development fund have been shattered by technology and the dynamics behind lateral pressures. It now appears that the principle of a resource zone of 200 miles for coastal states will remain generally accepted. This means that, instead of an international organization controlling oceanic resources, nearly one hundred individual nations will continue to nibble away at the resource treasury without regard for the needs of others. Although this "privatization" of the oceanic commons may help to save some fish stocks because of the interest of some coastal powers in keeping others out, the utopian ideas of Ambassador Pardo have been trampled under by the dozens of individual actors who don't see it to be in their self-interest to control the oceanic commons with an international ocean regime.[28]

NUCLEAR POWER: PANACEA OR SOCIAL TRAP?

Energy from fission and fusion seemingly offers technologically advanced countries a means by which they can use their sophistication to decrease dependence on imported petroleum and natural gas. These new energy technologies are perceived to be vital to the economic welfare of industrial countries because they represent ways to overturn the balance of payments deficits associated with imported fossil fuels and to overcome the long-term depletion problem. And these technologies can further improve trade balances for industrial countries by enlarging the international market for nuclear reactors, enriched uranium, and reprocessing equipment. In this respect, fission, and eventually fusion, represent potential ecopolitical instruments for freeing the industrial world from its vulnerabilities to the less developed exporters of petroleum and natural gas and maintaining the existing international power hierarchy.

Fission and fusion, however, will not cheaply and rapidly solve world energy problems. Fission is proving to be an expensive way to generate electricity, is potentially dangerous, and is running into stiff resistance. It will be decades before fusion power will be commercially on-line—and there are serious questions about it ever being feasible. While scientists understand the principles behind the fusion of light atoms, the process that created the hydrogen bomb, much work remains before a scaled-down fusion reaction can be contained for the required length of time in a laboratory setting, let alone in a commercial one. Fusion requires confinement of light atoms in very high density at temperatures of 100 million degrees centigrade. Since no known materials can confine this high-temperature reaction, magnetic fields or laser implosion techniques must be used. Both of these require tremendous amounts of electricity and, once such a technique is developed in a laboratory setting, it must then be demonstrated that more electricity will be produced by it than is consumed in a commercial setting.[29] There will be no commercial fusion power plants on-line before the year 2000, and the commercial applications of fusion, if they ever become a reality, will not make a significant impact on energy production until decades after the turn of the next century.

Electric power from fission is created by processes that are similar to those that occur in a nuclear weapon explosion. In both cases, uranium or plutonium atoms "fission"—or split—when struck by a neutron. The fission process produces a chain reaction that results in each atom producing two or more neutrons, other fission products, gamma rays, and heat. In the chain reaction, neutrons strike other uranium or plutonium atoms, thereby sustaining the reaction, while the released heat produces steam and eventually electric power. The main difference between a nuclear reactor and a nuclear explosion is the rate at which the chain reaction proceeds. In an atomic bomb, the entire fission chain reaction occurs almost instantaneously. In a nuclear reactor, the chain reaction is very carefully controlled to produce only the amount of heat needed to generate electricity effectively. While most nuclear reactors now use low-enriched uranium, future reactors are likely to use high-enriched uranium or plutonium, both of which can be used to make nuclear weapons.

Naturally occurring uranium is a mixture of two isotopes, 99.3 percent uranium-238 and about .7 percent uranium-235. Uranium-238 fissions at a slow rate, which makes it ineffective at sustaining the chain reactions required in both nuclear reactors and atomic bombs. Uranium-235, in contrast, fissions much faster and is thus the preferred fuel. The U-235 in naturally occurring uranium is too dilute to be of much use either in a reactor or in nuclear weapons, so naturally occurring uranium must be enriched to between 2 percent and 4 percent concentration of U-235 for light water reactors (LWR) and up to 90 percent concentration for high-temperature gas-cooled reactors before it can be used.[30]

There are two commercially established methods of enriching or concentrating U-235: gaseous diffusion and gas centrifuge. Gaseous diffusion is the method most frequently used at the present time. It requires a great deal of electricity—enough power is used by each plant to meet the needs of a medium to large city—and enrichment facilities are very expensive, now costing billions of dollars.

Despite the expense and technological problems involved, electricity from fission is now a commercial reality. Technology optimists hope that it will fill the gap between the depletion of reserves of petroleum and natural gas and the time that power from fusion may become available. For many reasons, however, nuclear power is at best a Faustian bargain, and the momentum behind it has created a dangerous social trap. It has the potential to provide needed energy in the medium term, but the economic and social costs involved make it a very controversial bargain. Nuclear power plants represent a serious risk because there is no margin for error in building and maintaining them. Faulty construction of a conventional power plant might lead to an explosion and fire, even to a few deaths. But similar faulty construction in a nuclear reactor could lead to hundreds of thousands of deaths through the release of radioactive gases and particles into the atmosphere. It is not possible to predict exactly when a fatal error will be made, but one major nuclear reactor accident will be one accident too many.

Contrary to popular belief, an accident at a reactor would not result in a nuclear explosion. Rather, the most serious nuclear accident is one in which a reactor overheats, melts down the core, and drops more than one hundred tons of molten radioactive material through the floor of the containment vessel. This type of incident, known as the China syndrome, could be triggered by the loss of core cooling in a reactor. Without this cooling, the radioactive material in the core reaches an extremely high temperature, which leads to core disintegration. Once the reactor containment vessel is breached, the steam and gases rising from the China-bound mass make their way to the surface, forming a deadly, airborne radioactive cloud.[31] There have as yet been no serious accidents of this magnitude, but there have been several close calls. As the number of reactors increases and as vigilance over them decreases, there is greater likelihood of such a serious accident taking place.

In addition to the physical dangers inherent in nuclear power plants, the capital costs of these facilities are rising rapidly. Between 1970 and 1976, the cost of building nuclear power plants in the US doubled.[32] A typical nuclear power plant generating 1000 megawatts of electricity now costs around $1 billion. The average nuclear power plant produces electricity only between 50 and 60 percent of the time, the rest of the time being devoted to repairs and maintenance.[33] Thus, nuclear power plants are an expensive and dangerous item that very few countries can afford to build in large numbers. Nuclear power is a type of technology developed by and for wealthy industrial countries, and it is unclear that it will ever be of much value to the less developed countries, where capital and expertise are in limited supply.

In spite of the perceived need for nuclear power, its negative aspects have considerably slowed the pace of plant construction in the United States, Japan, and Western Europe. In a 1975 forecast, the Organization for Economic Cooperation and Development projected a total nuclear power capability of 513 gigawatts (the equivalent of power produced by 740 million tons of oil) in OECD member countries by 1985. Only two years later, it revised its projection downward to 325 gigawatts, representing an energy equivalent of 464 million tons of oil. The difference was due to slippage in plant construction timetables and increasing public disenchantment with nuclear power.[34] In 1974, the same group projected Japanese nuclear power production in 1985 at 14.4 percent of total energy consumption. In 1975, the figure was revised downward to 9.6 percent of total energy production, and in 1977 it was again revised down to 7.8 percent of the total. It is clear that the nuclear panacea has run into more problems and resistance than originally anticipated.

In 1976, there were forty-six countries using or planning to use nuclear reactors to generate power. Two hundred and twenty-nine reactors were either operating or under construction worldwide outside of the US, and 136 were operational or under construction in the US. Nuclear power was responsible for generating 18 percent of all electricity in Switzerland, 15 percent in West Germany, and 9 percent in the US.[35]

There are several different types of reactors now on-line or under development. The first generation of nuclear power plants is equipped with light water reactors (LWRs). These reactors use water as a coolant and moderator to slow down neutrons and make them more efficient in fission processes. Light water reactors use low-enriched uranium as a fuel. Almost all nuclear power is at present produced by these light water reactors.

In the 1980s, two additional types of reactors will begin to play a significant role in power production: the high-temperature gas-cooled reactor (HTGR) and the liquid metal fast breeder reactor (LMFBR). The HTGR differs from the light water reactor in its use of high-enriched uranium and thorium as fuels and helium as a coolant. The attractiveness of the HTGR is its higher efficiency in producing electricity. The LMFBR is the nuclear hope for the future and could become the workhorse of the nuclear power industry by the turn of the century. The advantage of the LMFBR is that it produces nuclear fuel while making electricity. The LMFBR is fueled by plutonium. Quantities of relatively abundant uranium-238 are packed in close proximity to the reactor core. During the chain reaction, some uranium-238 captures a neutron and becomes plutonium-239. This process obviates the need for enrichment of naturally occurring uranium-238 and extends the useful life of world uranium reserves considerably.[36]

The data in table 6–5 indicate that the breeder reactor might be-

TABLE 6-5. Reasonably Assured Uranium Reserves, 1975*

	$15†	$15–$30†
United States	320	134
Australia	243	No estimate made
South Africa	186	90
Canada	144	22‡
Niger	40	10
Algeria	28	⎯
France	37	18
Gabon	20	⎯
Brazil	10	1
Argentina	9	11
India	3	26
Spain	10	94
Sweden	⎯	300
Other	30	24
Total	1080	730

*Data in 1000 tons of uranium; centrally planned economy data not available.
†Price per pound of uranium oxide.
‡Very conservative estimate.

SOURCE: Organization for Economic Cooperation and Development, Uranium: Resources, Production and Demand (Paris, December 1975), p. 22.

come a necessity because of limited world uranium reserves. Uranium, like the fossil fuels, is found in concentration in only a limited number of places on the earth's surface. Extremely large quantities of the abundant U-238 must be used to produce reactor fuels containing a high percentage of the relatively rare U-235. The breeder reactor, then, represents a method of extending the usefulness of world reserves of U-238 by using it as a raw material to create plutonium.

The price of uranium has been increasing, reflecting uncertainty about its future availability. As recently as 1972, a pound of uranium oxide sold for about $6. At present, the same pound sells for more than $40. Present reserves of uranium total about one million tons yet cumulative uranium demand could be four million tons by 2025. While there is little doubt that exploration of more remote areas and rising prices will yield new uranium reserves, prices will be high, and uranium-exporting countries stand to profit handsomely.[37]

The Nuclear Tragedy of the Commons

Nuclear technology can lead to an international tragedy of the economic commons that bears only faint resemblance to the pastoral variety of the Middle Ages. The international market for nuclear technology is now limited. The countries capable of exporting nuclear reactors and related technologies are scrambling to capture a larger share of this export market and to expand it. In the process of seeking their own economic interest, in this case by vying for reactor contracts, competitors take steps that result in short-term gain but possibly in long-term destruction. As one way of undercutting their competition, exporters in the reactor market sell reactors, uranium enrichment, and reprocessing technologies that could be used to fabricate nuclear weapons in politically unstable less developed countries.

Highly enriched uranium is not only useful in nuclear reactors, it is also a material from which nuclear weapons can be easily made. Naturally occurring uranium does not have nearly enough U-235 content to make it useful for bomb production. But uranium can be used in weapons construction when it is enriched beyond a 10 percent concentration of U-235. The higher the concentration of U-235, the smaller the quantity needed to make up a critical mass, the minimum amount of material needed to sustain a chain reaction in a bomb. Various neutron-reflecting materials can be placed around enriched uranium to enhance the chances of a nuclear explosion. In combination with a good neutron reflector, about 1000 kilograms of uranium enriched to 10 percent concentration of U-235 is required for critical mass. But only 20 kilograms of fully enriched uranium are required to get the same results.[38]

To understand better the nuclear tragedy of the commons, it is necessary to understand the economics and to know the actors involved. The United States has dominated the history of nuclear reactor development. Using the expertise gained in the World War II weapons program, the US nuclear energy effort grew very rapidly in the two decades following the war. The US government has spent more than $100 million in and directly related to nuclear development. This investment has paid handsome returns as, prior to 1975, the US had built 70 percent of the world's reactors and nailed down two-thirds of all export orders. But in 1975, it became clear that the US was losing its traditional predominance in nuclear markets. In that year, only eighteen reactors were ordered outside of the United States, and American companies got only four of those contracts.[39]

Prior to 1975, the Soviet Union and the United States monopolized the uranium enrichment business. United States government-owned plants in Oak Ridge, Tennessee; Paducah, Kentucky; and Portsmouth, Ohio, provided enriched uranium for nearly all the reactors in the non-Communist world. This monopoly in uranium enrichment, although somewhat of a barrier to nuclear weapons proliferation, became an irritant to those countries dependent upon the United States for nuclear reactor fuel. Many potential foreign purchasers were left in the dark about their future supplies as US enrichment plant expansion plans were hampered by disagreements over whether new plants should be built by government or private enterprise.

In order to free themselves of this dependence on US sources and to avoid the harsh consequences of overbooking of US facilities in the early 1980s, a consortium of five countries, France, Spain, Italy, Belgium, and Iran, known as Eurodif, began construction of an enrichment facility in 1975, with a capacity close to the collective capacity of those in the United States. In 1976, the same five countries proposed plans for a second facility of similar size to be operational by 1985. This second plant is to use the gaseous centrifuge technique, which is also being pressed forward in other countries.

In addition to the Eurodif facilities, there are several small experimental enrichment plants in operation in other countries, and larger ones are on the drawing boards. Great Britain, West Germany, and the Netherlands plan to build a large centrifuge plant in the near future. Canada wants to build its own gaseous diffusion plant in order to increase its take from the world uranium market. Australia and South Africa hope to construct large enrichment plants in the 1980s for similar reasons. And Japan, now forced to import enriched uranium as well as other fuels, hopes to buy into an enrichment facility and to operate its own reprocessing facility in the near future.[40]

The implications of this international spread of enrichment facilities for the proliferation of nuclear weapons are obvious. Enrichment facilities can produce the enriched uranium needed to make a nuclear weapon. With adequately enriched uranium or plutonium on hand, a small number of technical papers from the open literature, and a college-level knowledge of physics, any dedicated individual can construct a primitive weapon.[41] Criminals, terrorist groups, or less developed countries need only to obtain enriched uranium or plutonium to go into the nuclear weapons business.

Another serious environmental and weapons proliferation problem is posed by fuel reprocessing. After a reactor burns a load of fuel, the irradiated fuel elements contain some unused uranium, plutonium created during the reaction, and a series of other radioactive products. Since uranium is no longer abundant relative to projected demand, the remaining uranium and newly created plutonium can be recycled to fuel other reactors after being reprocessed. But reprocessing involves the removal of irradiated fuel elements from reactors, storage of these elements in water-filled cooling basins for several months while the heat from the decay of radioactive products dissipates, and transportation of the spent elements to plants where the usable uranium and plutonium can be chemically separated from other waste products. The reprocessed uranium and plutonium are then fabricated into new fuel elements, and the remaining products must then be permanently stored, away from contact with human beings.

There are serious technological and safety problems associated with reprocessing. Existing reprocessing facilities were originally designed to reprocess only low-exposure (low-enriched) fuels and cannot handle high-exposure reactor fuels, which emit much greater radioactivity and require better shielding and care during reprocessing. The first plant for reprocessing high-exposure fuels was opened in the mid-1960s in West Valley, New York. It never reached its designed capacity because of technical problems, and was closed for modification and expansion in 1971. It may resume operation in 1980. Other facilities in the United States and abroad have been plagued by similar problems. Serious questions are now being raised about the adequacy of storage capacity for spent fuel elements at reactor sites while decisions regarding reprocessing and waste disposal are yet to be made.[42]

Reprocessing of nuclear fuel also presents great security risks because plutonium-239 is extracted through the reprocessing procedures. Plutonium, one of the most toxic substances known to humanity, can be directly used in the construction of nuclear weapons. Plutonium can be handled fairly easily if proper precautions are taken because the alpha particles that it emits have very little penetrating power. There is thus no need for extensive shielding when working with it. If airborne plutonium particles penetrate the human body, however, they are likely to cause a slow and painful death. Even the tiniest specks of plutonium dust, when inhaled or eaten, can kill an unfortunate victim because of alpha particle radiation damage to internal organs. Hence, plutonium can be handled safely as long as it is kept inside an airtight container. If particles get loose in the atmosphere, they bring certain death to those exposed.[43]

The second unsavory characteristic of plutonium is the ease with which it can be used in making nuclear weapons. Natural uranium must be enriched before it is useful in weapons manufacture, and large quantities must be used. Plutonium, on the other hand, is already suitable for weapons use, and only about 4 kilograms inside a beryllium neutron reflector form a critical mass.[44] And a typical large power reactor produces in excess of 200 kilograms of plutonium per year. Thus, plutonium diversion into weapons production is much more simply accomplished than is diversion of uranium.[45]

Plutonium can now be extracted from existing nuclear reactors by any country seeking to join the nuclear club, given an adequate period of time to accomplish the task. In the future, they may all be able to get plutonium at reprocessing facilities much more easily. It is estimated that eighteen nations, in addition to the six existing nuclear powers, possess enough plutonium to make at least three to six nuclear weapons each. In addition, five countries will have acquired this capability by 1980.[46] Twelve nonnuclear states, among them Brazil, Argentina, Pakistan, and Iran, now have plans to develop their own reprocessing facilities. These facilities will permit large-scale stockpiling of plutonium that could easily be converted to weapons use.

The Economic Trap

The inexorable pressures of increased competition for nuclear export markets combined with increasing technological sophistication have led industrial countries into an international economic trap that has been set in motion by their willingness to trade off sales of nuclear reactors and associated technologies in the short run without squarely facing the consequences of the worldwide spread of nuclear weapons in the long run. For the industrial countries, competition for the potential hundreds of billions of dollars in future exports in the high-technology nuclear industry cannot easily be resisted. For the less developed countries, the promise of the nuclear power and possibly the nuclear weapons offered by these technologies is also difficult to resist.

The United States has been the prime mover behind reactor sales and, thus, a primary actor in this tragedy. As of 1976, the US had nuclear power cooperation agreements with twenty-two countries and potential agreements with five more. By the end of 1976, the US had earned more than $3 billion from the sale of reactors and related equipment. The cumulative total is projected to rise to $7 billion by 1980, and to $75 billion by 2000. By 1980, the United States will have garnered nearly $3.5 billion through sale of fuel-cycle–related exports and by 2000, between $46 and $65 billion will have been earned from these exports, depending upon the share of the international market captured. Much of this revenue will come from uranium enrichment. All US enrichment capacity is booked up until 1983, when enriched uranium sales will total nearly $1 billion annually. In 2000, the enrichment business will yield the US between $3.5 and $4.5 billion yearly in exports. (All of these figures are in 1974 dollars.) And reactors and fuel cycle products are increasing in price much more rapidly than the general rate of inflation. By 2000, it is estimated that between 3 and 5 percent of all US exports will be nuclear-related. The total of nuclear exports from the US by 2000, then, is expected to be between $120 and $140 billion.[47]

The United States captured the early international nuclear market by virtue of its development of economically attractive light water reactor technology, control of enrichment technology, ability to write long-term contracts for fuel delivery, and access to loans through the Export-Import Bank. But other industrial countries now would like to get a share of the future international market for themselves. Both France and West Germany have aggressively entered the nuclear marketplace and have not restricted themselves to reactor sales. In 1976, West Germany set a precedent by agreeing to provide Brazil with reprocessing technology. France followed suit by offering similar technologies and facilities to South Korea and Pakistan. Diplomatic pressure by the United States forced cancellation of the sale to South Korea, but such pressure did not work when applied to Pakistan. West Germany followed up by negotiating a reprocessing agreement with Iran.

France and West Germany see penetration of Third World markets as an imperative if they are to be competitive in the nuclear market. An official of West Germany's largest nuclear company has put it this way: "To fully exploit our nuclear power plant capacity we have to land at least three contracts a year for delivery abroad. The market here is about saturated and the United States has cornered most of the rest of Europe, so we have to concentrate on the Third World."[48] The logic, or tragedy, of this economic competition has led the French and Germans to break American dominance of the reactor market by undercutting the United States through sale of reprocessing technology that the US has refused to sell. Thus, there has been progressive weakening of control over nuclear technology as competitive pressures have forced sales to more politically marginal countries and as formerly secret reprocessing technologies have been used as bait. The relentless spread of nuclear technology has led the Stockholm International Peace Research Institute to predict that nuclear war is inevitable, as thirty-five countries will be able to make nuclear weapons by 1984.[49]

India was the first Third World country to become a nuclear power by using materials provided by industrial countries—in this case, the United States and Canada—for an underground test explosion in 1974. The reasons India made the decision to explode the bomb are not clear, although internal political pressures and the nuclear weapons program of the neighboring Chinese certainly played a role. What was made clear by the Indian bomb is that it is relatively easy for a country dedicated to making nuclear weapons to use materials from nuclear power plants to fabricate them and that there are few sanctions for doing so.

Many countries do not now have nuclear weapons only because they have not made a political decision to make them; the necessary materials and expertise, however, are widespread (see table 6–6). And there are many countries possessing nuclear reactors or having them under construction that may soon feel that their national security needs require nuclear weapons. Among the most likely candidates are countries engaged in regional rivalries, especially with countries that now possess nuclear weapons or that are thought to be likely to get them in the very near future. This list includes Pakistan, Argentina, Brazil, Peru, Cuba, Indonesia, Iran, Israel, Libya, South Africa, South Korea, Taiwan, and Thailand. None of these countries has exhibited an uninterrupted record of domestic political stability or peaceful resolution of international disputes over the last two decades.

It is becoming apparent that little can now be done to stop the spread of nuclear technology and thus halt weapons proliferation. Six countries, West Germany, the United States, France, Canada, Japan, and Sweden, are selling reactors or components on the world markets. Five countries—the United States, Great Britain, France, the Soviet Union, and China—now have commercial enrichment plants. An additional six

TABLE 6-6. *Potential Members of the Nuclear Club**

	Operating Commercial Reactors	Reactors Under Con- struction	Reactors Ordered	Status of Non- Proliferation Treaty
Israel	0	0	0	Not signed
South Africa	0	0	2	Not signed
Pakistan†	1	0	1	Not signed
Brazil†	0	3	6	Not signed
Argentina	1	1	3	Not signed
South Korea	0	1	1	Party to treaty
Japan	10	14	0	Party to treaty
Indonesia	0	0	0	Not ratified
Taiwan	0	4	2	Party to treaty
Egypt	0	0	0	Not ratified
Spain	3	7	7	Not signed
Iran†	0	4	4	Party to treaty

*As of 1976, countries capable of going nuclear by 1984 and having political reasons to do so.
†Reactor and reprocessing sales announced in 1977.
SOURCES: *Carl Walske, "Nuclear Electric Power and the Proliferation of Nuclear Weapon States,"* International Security *(Winter 1976–1977); William Epstein,* The Last Chance *(New York: The Free Press, 1976), chap. 17; and United States Central Intelligence Agency,* Nuclear Energy *(Washington, D.C., 1977)*

countries are building enrichment facilities. And at least six countries have commercial reprocessing facilities.[50]

The spread of nuclear information opens up possibilities for "gray marketeering" on a global scale. There have already been commercial sales of reactors and reprocessing equipment to countries that are likely candidates for the nuclear club. But on a different level, the possibility now exists for unofficial and unsanctioned transfer of such information from technologically developed to less developed countries. There could be many motives for such activities. Individuals could sell information, blueprints, or even plutonium, for the money involved. A future nuclear power might provide such information to other countries as a political favor or simply to create chaos. Libya's Colonel Khaddafi has already tried to purchase a nuclear weapon from China. Although the Chinese refused to go through with the sale, there are many other potential nuclear powers, such as South Africa, that could have motives for completing such a sale.[51] The South Africans were apparently prepared to carry out a nuclear test in 1977, and only the joint intervention of the Soviet Union, the United States, and France forced them to change their minds.[52]

Interest in purchasing gray market information, blueprints, uranium, or plutonium is not limited to national leaders. Terrorist groups or even organized crime might use possession of a small nuclear device to pursue their own goals. The information that such a group would need to make such a bomb is not difficult to obtain once plutonium or enriched uranium is at hand. In 1975, an undergraduate chemistry student at the Massachusetts Institute of Technology was asked to demonstrate how easy it was to make such a device for a television audience. Starting from scratch, he made a device requiring five to ten kilograms of plutonium that would have yielded a small nuclear explosion. And given the weak safeguards in effect at present, obtaining plutonium or enriched uranium would not be difficult for any dedicated group. In 1968, for example, Israel hijacked a shipment of 200 tons of uranium oxide that was in transit from Antwerp, Belgium, to Genoa, Italy. This diversion of EEC uranium was kept secret for nearly ten years.[53]

There are other aspects of new technologies that make terrorism a much more worrisome problem than it has been in the past. Threat of dissemination of plutonium dust could have an effect similar to the threat of a nuclear explosion. Such dust could be hidden by terrorists in remote control bombs in large cities. If terrorist demands weren't met, the small bombs could be exploded, spreading plutonium dust throughout the city, killing tens of thousands of people over the ensuing weeks and months as the plutonium would lodge in their bodies and destroy from within. Perhaps this is the most critical aspect of the social trap. Advanced industrial countries depend upon technologies that are sophisticated and dangerous and create problems beyond the social control capabilities of these societies. As long as terrorism exists, the threat of such disasters is very real.[54]

The organization ostensibly responsible for curbing the proliferation of nuclear weapons is the International Atomic Energy Agency (IAEA), established in Vienna, under United Nations auspices, in 1957. The main instrument of use to it is the Non-Proliferation Treaty (NPT), which was initialed by the major nuclear powers in 1968. The IAEA was set up originally both to accelerate the development of peaceful applications of atomic energy and to halt the proliferation of nuclear weapons. While the IAEA was to account for nuclear materials in projects when countries requested it, it also was to offer assistance to countries wishing to experiment with nuclear power within the control of the IAEA, and these countries could thus be held accountable by the agency. In reality, the International Atomic Energy Agency has not been terribly effective. Several important countries are not members. Furthermore, the rapid proliferation of nuclear reactors and enrichment facilities has overwhelmed its small inspection staff. Any country that has a nuclear reactor, is willing to run the risk of detection, and wants to make an effort to do so can divert enriched uranium or plutonium into weapons production. Since there are many competing suppliers of reactors and nuclear fuel, the IAEA has virtually no effective sanctions against such activity.[55]

The Non-Proliferation Treaty (NPT) obliges signatory nations having nuclear weapons not to transfer weapons or related nuclear technology to nonnuclear weapons states or to assist them in any way with weapons development. Nonnuclear signatories agree not to develop nuclear weapons on their own. The treaty requires signatory states to maintain records of all of their nuclear materials, and the IAEA is charged with the responsibility of enforcing the agreement. The flaws in the treaty are similar to the problems experienced by the IAEA itself. The small inspection staff is inadequate to police the agreement. Existing nuclear powers are not subject to IAEA inspection. As of 1975, many key countries including Algeria, Argentina, Chile, China, Cuba, France, India, Israel, Pakistan, Portugal, Saudi Arabia, Spain, South Africa, Uganda, and Zambia had not become parties to the treaty.[56] Also, there are no real sanctions for not signing or for violating the agreement. When the United States had a near monopoly on nuclear technology and uranium enrichment, close cooperation between the IAEA and the US afforded a possibility for sanctions. At present, however, there are too many competing sources of fuel and technology for sanctions to be effective. And one of the nuclear reactor exporting countries, France, is not a party to the Non-Proliferation Treaty.

The international nuclear trap is now baited. Large increases in international nuclear reactor commerce, new sources of enriched uranium, a push for reprocessing facilities, and the use of plutonium combine to make international agencies and agreements ineffective in stopping the proliferation of nuclear technology and, eventually, weapons. Economic pressures within industrial nations, both international balance of payments pressures and those from domestic industries, have established momentum for vigorous nuclear export competition. Thus, the social and economic trap in the nuclear field results from the inability of exporting countries to coordinate export sales and agree on safeguards.

By 1985, the number of countries with nuclear capability will have increased dramatically. Some countries may choose to follow the Israeli strategy and not openly display nuclear weapons, but develop and stockpile them for an emergency. But given continued competition among nuclear exporters and the related proliferation of nuclear technologies, it is unlikely that all countries will refrain from developing such weapons in the absence of well-understood sanctions for doing so.

In summary, technology has created great differences among nations in capabilities. Industrially developed countries now dominate an international power hierarchy and hope to use their technological edge to maintain it. At the same time, new technologies are spawning problems that cannot be controlled by existing political institutions and social mechanisms. These new technologies are creating coordination problems, social traps, and tragedies of the commons, both within and among nations. Industrial countries are attempting to reduce their vulnerabilities to certain less developed countries by exploiting seabed resources and by irresponsibly exporting inappropriate nuclear technologies. It remains to be seen how long it will be before this baited nuclear trap is sprung.

ENDNOTES

1. See Howard Odum, *Environment, Power, and Society* (New York: Wiley-Interscience, 1971), p. 26.
2. Richard Adams, *Energy and Structure* (Austin: University of Texas Press, 1975), p. 12.
3. Hardin gives credit to William Lloyd as being an intellectual father of the concept. William Lloyd, *Two Lectures on the Checks to Population* (Oxford: Oxford University Press, 1833).
4. Garrett Hardin, "The Tragedy of the Commons," *Science* (December 13, 1968). See also Garrett Hardin, *Exploring New Ethics for Survival* (New York: Viking, 1972).
5. These themes are pursued in Garrett Hardin, *The Limits of Altruism: An Ecologist's View of Survival* (Bloomington, Ind.: University of Indiana Press, 1977); G. R. Lucas and T. W. Ogletree, eds., *Lifeboat Ethics: The Moral Dilemmas of Hunger* (New York: Harper & Row, 1976); and Garrett Hardin and J. Baden, eds., *Managing the Commons* (San Francisco: W. H. Freeman, 1977).
6. See Robert Goodin, *The Politics of Rational Man* (London: John Wiley & Sons, 1976).
7. Ibid., p. 27.
8. John Platt, "Social Traps," *American Psychologist* (August 1973).
9. See Thomas Schelling, "On the Ecology of Micromotives," *The Public Interest* (Fall 1971).
10. See Harbert Rice and Nien Dak Sze, *The Analysis of Fertilizer Impacts on the Ozone Layer* (Concord, Mass.: Environmental Research and Technology, Inc., 1976).
11. Kiyoshi Kojima, *Japan and a New World Economic Order* (Tokyo: Charles E. Tuttle Co., 1977), pp. 136–137.
12. See Saburo Okita, "Natural Resource Dependency and Japanese Foreign Policy," *Foreign Affairs* (July 1974).
13. Reported in John Saar, "Japan Pondering Future Role in Trade," *Washington Post* (February 20, 1977).
14. Ibid.
15. Kojima, *Japan and a New World Economic Order*, chap. 6.
16. Reported in Saar, "Japan Pondering Future Role in Trade."
17. Robert Keohane and Joseph Nye, *Power and Interdependence* (Boston: Little, Brown, 1977), pp. 12–16.
18. General Agreement on Tariffs and Trade, *International Trade 1975/76* (Geneva, 1976), pp. 3, 89.
19. Council on International Economic Policy, "International Economic Report of the President" (Washington, D. C., 1977), Appendix B.
20. See "Economic Recovery Spurs Oil Demand Rise," *World Oil* (February 15, 1976).

21. U.S. Department of Commerce, *U.S. General Imports: World Area by Commodity Groupings* (Washington, D. C., 1974, 1975, 1976).
22. Council on International Economic Policy, *International Economic Report of the President*, chap. 12.
23. See Robert Gilpin, "Technology, Economic Growth, and International Competitiveness" (Washington, D. C.: Joint Economic Committee, 1975).
24. Council on International Economic Policy, *International Economic Report of the President*, Appendix B.
25. "Middle East, North Africa Imports up 63% in 1975," *World Oil* (February 15, 1976).
26. Council on International Economic Policy, *International Economic Report of the President*, Appendix B.
27. See John Swing, "Who Will Own the Oceans?" *Foreign Affairs* (April 1976).
28. See Jack Barkenbus, "The Politics of Ocean Resource Exploitation," *International Studies Quarterly* (December 1977), and Barry Buzan, *Seabed Politics* (New York: Praeger, 1976).
29. See Wilson Clark, *Energy for Survival* (New York: Anchor Books, 1975), pp. 313–321.
30. See Energy Research and Development Agency, *U.S. Nuclear Power Export Activities* (Washington, D. C., 1976).
31. See The Union of Concerned Scientists, *The Nuclear Fuel Cycle* (Cambridge, Mass.: MIT Press, 1975), chap. 4.
32. See Nuclear Energy Policy Study Group, *Nuclear Power Issues and Choices* (Cambridge, Mass.: Ballinger, 1977), chap. 3.
33. Nuclear Energy Policy Study Group, *Nuclear Power Issues and Choices*, pp. 109–121.
34. Organization for Economic Cooperation and Development, *World Energy Outlook* (Paris, 1977).
35. Carl Walske, "Nuclear Electric Power and the Proliferation of Nuclear Weapon States," *International Security* (Winter 1976–1977).
36. For a complete description of reactor fuel cycles, see Mason Willrich and Theodore Taylor, *Nuclear Theft: Risks and Safeguards* (Cambridge, Mass.: Ballinger, 1974), chap. 3.
37. Organization for Economic Cooperation and Development, *Uranium: Resources, Production and Demand* (Paris, 1975), pp. 15–21.
38. Willrich and Taylor, *Nuclear Theft*, p. 17.
39. For a more detailed discussion, see Edward Wonder, "International Regimes and Regulation of Nuclear Commerce," paper presented to the annual convention of the International Studies Association, 1977.
40. Energy Research and Development Agency, *U.S. Nuclear Power Export Activities*, pp. 3–69.
41. See John McPhee, *The Curve of Binding Energy* (New York: Farrar, Straus, & Giroux, 1974).
42. Energy Research and Development Agency, "LWR Spent Fuel Disposition Capabilities: 1975–1984" (Washington, D. C., 1975).
43. Willrich and Taylor, *Nuclear Theft*, p. 13.
44. The Union of Concerned Scientists, *The Nuclear Fuel Cycle*, p. 121.
45. Willrich and Taylor, *Nuclear Theft*, p. 13.
46. Thomas B. Cochran and J. Gustave Speth, "Against Plutonium Fuel," *New York Times* (September 27, 1976).

47. Energy Research and Development Agency, *U.S. Nuclear Power Export Activities,* pp. 4:10–4:18.
48. Joachim Hospe quoted in Craig Whitney, "Bonn's Atom Offered to Iran Stirs a Debate on Sharing," *New York Times* (April 18, 1976).
49. Stockholm International Peace Research Institute, *Armaments and Disarmament in a Nuclear Age* (Stockholm, 1976).
50. See Walske, "Nuclear Electric Power."
51. Lewis Dunn, "Nuclear 'Gray Marketeering,' " *International Security* (Winter 1976–1977).
52. Murrey Marder and Don Oberdorfer, "How West, Soviets Acted to De-fuse South African A-Test," *Washington Post* (August 28, 1977).
53. Reported in the *Washington Post* (May 3, 1977).
54. See David Rosenbaum, "Nuclear Terror," *International Security* (Winter 1976–1977).
55. See Paul Szasz, "International Atomic Energy Agency Safeguards," and Bernhard Bechhoefer, "Historical Evolution of International Safeguards," in Mason Willrich, ed., *International Safeguards and Nuclear Industry* (Baltimore: Johns Hopkins University Press, 1973).
56. See Energy Research and Development Agency, *U.S. Nuclear Power Export Activities, vol. 2,* section C–1.

SUGGESTED READINGS

1. C. Fred Bergsten, ed. *The Future of the International Economic Order: An Agenda for Research.* Lexington, Mass.: D. C. Heath, Lexington Books, 1973.
2. Seyom Brown, et al. *Regimes for the Ocean, Outer Space and Weather.* Washington, D. C.: The Brookings Institution, 1977.
3. Barry Buzan. *Seabed Politics.* New York: Praeger, 1976.
4. Energy Research and Development Agency. *U.S. Nuclear Power Export Activities.* Washington, D. C., 1976.
5. William Epstein. *The Last Chance: Nuclear Proliferation and Arms Control.* New York: The Free Press, 1976.
6. Robert Gilpin. *Technology, Economic Growth, and International Competitiveness.* Washington, D. C.: Joint Economic Committee, 1975.
7. Robert Goodin. *The Politics of Rational Man.* London: John Wiley & Sons, 1976.
8. Ted Greenwood, Harold Feiveson, and Theodore Taylor. *Nuclear Proliferation: Motivations, Capabilities, and Strategies for Control.* New York: McGraw-Hill, 1977.
9. Garrett Hardin. *The Limits of Altruism: An Ecologist's View of Survival.* Bloomington, Ind.: University of Indiana Press, 1977.
10. Garrett Hardin and John Baden, eds. *Managing the Commons.* San Francisco: W. H. Freeman, 1977.
11. Kiyoshi Kojima. *Japan and a New World Economic Order.* Tokyo: Charles E. Tuttle Co., 1977.
12. Nuclear Energy Policy Study Group. *Nuclear Power Issues and Choices* Cambridge, Mass.: Ballinger, 1977.

13. Mason Willrich, ed. *International Safeguards and Nuclear Industry.* Baltimore: Johns Hopkins University Press, 1973.
14. Mason Willrich and Theodore Taylor. *Nuclear Theft: Risks and Safeguards.* Cambridge, Mass.: Ballinger, 1974.
15. Edward Wonder. *Nuclear Fuel and American Foreign Policy: Multilateralization for Uranium Enrichment.* Denver: Westview Press, 1977.
16. The Union of Concerned Scientists. *The Nuclear Fuel Cycle.* Cambridge, Mass.: MIT Press, 1975.

Ecopolitics and Development

There are few aspects of the established dominant paradigm in international relations that have been as shaken by the new ecopolitical context as those associated with development and economic growth in the world's less developed countries. Over the last two decades, an image of a "developing" world successfully struggling to accumulate the capital essential for sustained industrialization and to better the lot of the poor has been predominant. The common belief in financial circles in industrial countries has been that the gap separating the rich and poor countries will narrow as the result of this development, that foreign aid will play an important role in helping Third World countries to industrialize rapidly, that multinational corporations will be benevolent forces in carrying modernization to less developed countries, that trade between the Third World and industrial countries will be a mutually beneficial process, and that the lot of all peoples in less developed countries will be improved through rapid growth in gross national product. But the oil price increases had a dramatic impact on the sparse foreign exchange reserves of most of the less developed countries and hastened the exposure of many anomalies already existing within this paradigm. The development record now has been found to be less than a success, and a major reassessment of objectives and methods is under way.[1]

The failures in reaching these old development goals are emphasized by the unfulfilled hopes of the UN's two development decades. In 1970, the General Assembly of the United Nations declared that during the second development decade, the developing countries as a whole should attain a real growth rate of 6 percent annually during the first half of the decade and an even higher rate during the second half. On a per capita basis, real GNP growth was to be 3.5 percent. This growth was to be facilitated by developed countries providing financial resource transfers of 1 percent of their gross national products to less developed countries. Official development assistance by developed countries to less developed countries was to equal .7 percent of gross national product.[2] None of these goals has been met. Instead, over the last decade, many of these less developed countries have had to make a tremendous economic effort simply to maintain the original low standards of living. In some countries, per capita standards have actually been declining.

The present international division of labor and system of trade have been called into question by Third World leaders as the rich countries continue to get richer while the plight of the poor remains much the same.[3] In the period 1970–1975, for example, forty of the world's poorest nations in Asia, Africa, and Latin America experienced a collective decline of 1 percent in gross national product per capita, while the industrial countries, with the exception of a significant adjustment pause in 1974–1975, continued to widen the gap between themselves and the poor (see table 7–1 and figure 7–1).[4]

Ironically, the OPEC price increase, which provided an important impetus to the development of ecopolitics, also precipitated a decline in the living standards in many less developed countries and a reassessment of commonly held beliefs about their industrialization prospects. The economic orthodoxy within the old paradigm held that most of the newly emerging nations were capable of following roughly the same energy-intensive path to industrialization orginally followed by the United States, the Soviet Union, and Western Europe. The optimists argued that through trade and modest amounts of aid, the less developed countries could slowly accumulate the capital necessary for a takeoff into a period of sustained economic growth. But the energy-resources-food dilemma has now triggered a dramatic reassessment of the economic growth philosophies and programs that were part of the old paradigm.

Underlying much of this rethinking of the old development paradigm is the fact that future opportunities for economic growth of a conventional sort in much of the Third World are no longer as great as they once were thought to be. A combination of rapid population growth,

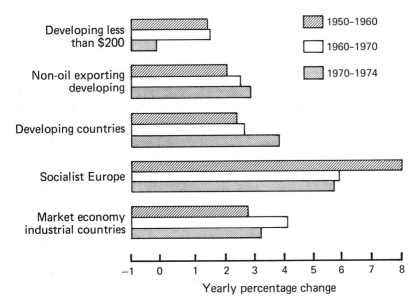

FIGURE 7–1. *Real per Capita GNP* [SOURCE: United Nations Conference on Trade and Development, *Handbook of International Trade and Development Statistics, 1976* (New York, 1976), tables 6.1b and 6.2.]

TABLE 7-1. *Economically Troubled Countries*

	Current Annual Population Growth (in percent)[1]	Average Annual Percentage of Growth Rate per Capita Food Production (1970–1975)[2]	Average Annual Percentage of Growth Rate per Capita GNP (1965–1973)[3]	Discomfort Index[4]	Energy Dependency[5]
Afghanistan	2.2	1.3	1.1	2.4	419
Bangladesh	2.7	0.0	-1.9	-1.9	32
Benin	2.7	-.7	.8	.1	0
Bhutan	2.3	—	-.2	—	0
Burma	2.4	0.0	.8	.8	94
Burundi	2.1	7.0	1.3	8.3	0
Central African Republic	2.1	-.9	.8	-.1	17
Chad	2.0	-6.1	-1.5	-3.3	0
Ethiopia	2.5	-4.8	1.5	-3.3	5
Gambia	2.1	.8	3.2	4.0	0
Guinea	2.4	-2.1	.1	-2.0	0
Haiti	2.0	.4	.7	1.1	7
India	2.1	-.6	1.3	.7	87
Kenya	3.3	-2.2	3.5	1.3	3
Laos	2.2	-1.1	2.0	.9	13
Lesotho	1.9	1.1	3.7	4.8	—
Malagasy Republic	2.9	-1.3	.3	-1.0	4
Malawi	2.4	.7	4.7	5.4	10

Mali	2.4	−6.8	.4	−6.4	0
Mauritania	2.0	−7.9	1.3	−6.6	0
Nepal	2.3	−.2	0	−.2	8
Niger	2.7	−4.3	−3.8	−8.1	0
Pakistan	2.9	−1.2	2.5	1.3	64
Rwanda	2.9	−1.6	1.4	−.2	40
Sierra Leone	2.4	−1.1	1.4	.3	0
Somalia	2.6	−.2	1.1	.9	0
Sri Lanka	2.0	−2.1	2.0	−.1	8
Sudan	3.0	2.5	4.3	6.8	1
Tanzania	2.5	−2.1	2.3	.2	4
Togo	2.7	−4.0	2.8	−1.2	0
Uganda	2.7	−2.8	.7	−2.1	16
Upper Volta	2.3	−3.8	−.5	−4.3	0
Western Samoa	2.8	—	1.3	—	0
Yemen Arab Republic	2.9	9.1	—	−3.5	0
Yemen People's Republic	2.9	.8	−4.3	.4	0
Zaire	2.5	−2.5	2.9	—	33

1. Taken from Population Reference Bureau, *1977 World Population Data Sheet* (Washington, D.C., 1977).

2. Adapted from Food and Agriculture Organization of the United Nations, *Production Yearbook, 1975* (Rome, 1976).

3. World Bank, *World Bank Atlas, 1976* (Washington, D.C., 1977).

4. This index is the sum of the figures in columns 1 and 2. The higher the negative number the worse the plight.

5. Adapted from United Nations, *Statistical Yearbook 1976* (New York, 1977). Energy dependence is figured by dividing yearly production by consumption and multiplying by 100. Zero denotes complete dependence on others while 100 indicates complete self-sufficiency.

depletion of natural resources, profligate consumption patterns in industrially developed countries, and domination of the world economic system by developed countries serves to constrain future possibilities. This fact was clearly demonstrated by the devastating impact of the quadrupling of petroleum prices on Third World development. By 1975, non–oil-exporting Third World economies had virtually ceased growing, and their debts were rapidly mounting. Not only were these countries hit by increased oil prices, they were the primary victims of the recession in developed countries, which cut into purchases of raw materials.[5]

There have been different opportunities for various kinds of economic growth in different historical periods and geographical locations. It now appears that the era of "cheap growth" relying on inexpensive sources of energy and technological innovations related to the fossil fuels has passed. Modern technology is wasteful in its use of natural resources because historically these natural resources have not been scarce or expensive in the countries in which the technology developed. But it is this wasteful technology that the industrial countries now are selling to the less developed areas of the world despite the fact that changing natural resource abundance and prices are making it inappropriate for sustainable economic growth there.

As Glenn Hueckel notes, "There seems to be a surprisingly wide range of alternative possible methods of getting a job done, each method being characterized by a different mix of capital, labor, and resource inputs; and the particular method chosen by society is determined by the prevailing structure of the relative prices of these inputs."[6] In the present trade structure, however, the less developed countries are having their choices made for them, in many cases by other countries that industrialized early under conditions where the mix of capital, labor, and natural resources was much different than it is at present or will be in the very near future. This failure to develop technology to meet the needs of less developed countries is particularly pronounced in agriculture. In less developed countries having a large surplus of labor it makes little sense to import mass production techniques and heavy equipment. But the green revolution often replaces workers with tractors, and the large landowners profit most from introduction of new seeds, fertilizers, and labor-saving devices while the peasantry is driven from the land.[7]

Thus, while over time the gap between the rich countries and the poor countries was expected to narrow, very little progress has been made. Although the precise extent of this gap between rich and poor varies with the array of countries included in each category, there is a consensus that it has widened, rather than narrowed, over the last decade.[8] While the developed market economies grew at an average per capita rate of 4.1 percent between 1960 and 1970 and 3.2 percent for the 1970–1974 period, the non–oil-exporting developing countries grew at a very modest 2.5 percent during the former period and 2.8 percent during the latter. And in 1975, their economic performance declined very rapidly in response to high oil prices.[9] The hard-core poverty cases, those countries with less than $200 gross national product per capita, increased their per capita product by only 1.4 percent during the 1960–1970 period and experienced a .4 percent decline in 1970–1974.

While the record of economic growth in all less developed countries in the 1960s could not be considered a complete disaster, this growth had little impact on the impoverished masses within the less developed countries. While the rich got richer, the poor remained poor, and the gap between the richest and the poorest classes in most developing countries widened. In Mexico, for example, real gross national product grew at between 6 and 7 percent in the period 1960–1975, but at the same time unemployment increased, and the income disparity between rich and poor actually widened. In the early 1950s, the total income of the top fifth of the Mexican population was ten times that of the lowest fifth. By 1969, it was sixteen times that of the lowest fifth.[10]

Thus, in spite of expectations to the contrary, the fruits of economic growth have not trickled down to the poorest segments of national populations. Instead, those who have profited first from growth have been able to use their political and economic leverage to prevent significant redistribution from taking place. The trickle-down theory depends upon a growing sense of social justice among ruling elites of less developed countries, altruism, or some unspecified economic mechanism to insure that additional increments of wealth will be directed to the poorest. But human nature doesn't seem to work in this way. To depend upon the rich to funnel resources to the poor is to ignore how most of the rich became that way. When the total resources available to any social group are increased, using them to create more equality is only one option. Particularly in very poor countries, the other option is for one class to use these resources to dominate the others.

In the past, development models concentrated on the *rate* at which a country could increase GNP. But now the focus is shifting to *how* this increase takes place. Not only is the total wealth available in less developed countries much less than in the industrialized countries, but most of the less developed countries show patterns of greater inequality than do the developed ones.[11] Furthermore, growth also has given rise to higher unemployment as labor-saving machinery has been introduced on farms and in factories. Thus, small farmers, often driven off the land by large landowners, have migrated to the cities in search of jobs that cannot be found. It is estimated that nearly one-third of the work force in Third World urban areas is now either unemployed or underemployed.[12]

In addition to these anomalies in the established development model, an ethical component has been added to the development debate. Meeting the most basic human needs of the poorest segments of national populations is rapidly becoming accepted as an ethical first principle. The International Labor Organization, for example, declared at its 1976 World Employment Conference that "development planning should include, as an explicit goal, the satisfaction of an absolute level of basic needs."[13] Greater equality is also coming to be accepted as an ideal. The reasons for this change are not completely clear, but they range from the moral to the very practical. The philosophical work of John Rawls, with its emphasis on distributive justice, is being taken seriously by some.[14] Still others have obviously been disturbed by the domestic political disorder that often is driven by grave inequality.[15] Whatever the driving motivation might be, an increased emphasis on basic human needs and greater income equality, both within and among nations, is a primary component of the new development paradigm.[16]

The problems of economic growth, development, and closing the gaps between rich nations and poor nations and between the rich and poor within nations will not be solved by pious statements, however. There are a number of problems within the old international economic order that have created the existing disparities. And it will take a fundamental shift in the way that development problems are perceived and goals are set before real progress can be made.

THE COLONIAL LEGACY

During the wave of colonial expansion that engulfed the territory of the presently less developed countries, little concern was evidenced for the future political or economic well-being of the populations in the occupied areas. Colonies were regarded as extensions of national territory where the resource needs of the colonial powers could be met. These areas were used to produce commodities desired, but lacking, in the technologically dominant countries. Many of the colonies became one-crop agrarian economies specializing in supplying coffee, tea, cocoa, sugar, or some other agricultural commodity. Very little industrial investment was made in the colonies, since most raw materials could be easily transported to and processed by factories in the industrial countries. The colonial labor force usually received only the minimal training that was required for menial labor in fields and mines. Because of this legacy, there were very few less developed countries that ever had a chance to industrialize rapidly within the old development model. A few of these countries were able to use cheap labor as a lure to multinational corporations and to escape the worst aspects of the poverty syndrome, at least in the short term, but a heavy price has been paid by an oppressed work force laboring long hours for extremely low wages.

The most important basic fact about the present international economy is that natural resources flow from the poor countries to the technologically developed rich ones where, by conventional economic definitions, they can be used more efficiently.[17] In the existing international division of labor, the industrial countries can more profitably transform raw materials exported by less developed countries into consumer goods that are much in demand around the world. As a result, almost all significant technological innovation now takes place in the industrially developed countries. Ninety-eight percent of all expenditure on research and development takes place there. And these innovations are protected by an international patent system that keeps less developed countries from using them.[18] Half of the research that takes place in the developed countries is in the fields of defense, space, atomic energy, and supersonic aircraft, research that has only marginal value to Third World countries.[19] Furthermore, by the time many of these technological developments are "transferred" to less developed settings, they have often become obsolete, making industries in less developed countries less than competitive with those in developed countries. In this manner, the industrial countries are able to keep one step ahead of their less developed counterparts through continued technological innovation.

The failure of colonial powers to locate "downstream" facilities in their possessions has spawned this most fundamental problem of development.[20] The highly complex and expensive industrial infrastructures, continual invention of new technologies, and economies of scale found in international marketing all give the industrial countries a great edge in the economically efficient use of natural resources. The less developed countries do not possess the expertise, facilities, or marketing capability that is essential to compete successfully in contemporary international trade in anything but labor-intensive products.

Natural resources have little intrinsic economic value; they become valuable only when they are used to create finished products. It is a combination of natural resources with technology that gives them added value. Technology thus creates demands for natural resources. In international trade, the flow of natural resources is in ever larger amounts to those high-technology countries where the most value can be added to them. Even though wages may be lower in many less developed countries, technology makes labor much more productive in the industrialized countries. Thus, it is unthinkable that a less developed country would develop an automobile competitive on the international market or an aircraft industry. So the metals and fuels that are used to make these high-technology products continue to flow to the developed countries as long as international transportation remains cheap relative to the final product costs. Technology gives the industrial countries a comparative advantage in almost every sector that they choose to develop and exploit, and the less developed countries have to make do with the markets that remain.

Tables 7–2 and 7–3 clearly illustrate the existing differences in the

TABLE 7-2. *Key Exports of Industrial Countries**

	1967 (Percent of World Exports)	1972 (Percent of World Exports)	1972 (Percent of all Industrial Exports)	Annual Percent of Change, 1967–1972
Motor Vehicles	96	95	10.1	21
Nonelectrical Machinery	93	91	5.8	16
Electrical Machinery	96	92	2.3	18
Ships and Boats	88	94	2.2	21
Power Machinery (nonelectrical)	80	97	2.2	15
Telecommunications Equipment	93	93	2.2	20
Iron and Steel Products	96	87	2.1	16
Nonfur Clothing	75	67	1.9	18
Organic Chemicals	97	96	1.9	14
Paper and Paperboard	99	96	1.8	12
Plastic Materials	99	98	1.8	19
Office Machines	94	96	1.8	20
Specialty Machines	86	84	1.8	14
Petroleum Products	45	45	1.7	12
Aircraft	98	93	1.6	14

*Ranked by value.

SOURCE: *United Nations Conference on Trade and Development*, Handbook of International Trade and Development Statistics *(New York: United Nations, 1976), table 4.3(b).*

TABLE 7-3. Key Exports of Less Developed Countries*

	1967 (Percent of World Exports)	1972 (Percent of World Exports)	1972 (Percent of all LDC Exports)	Annual Value Change, 1967–1972
Crude Petroleum	88	87	28.2	12
Petroleum Products	53	46	7.6	9
Coffee	96	93	4.7	7
Sugar	79	64	3.5	10
Nonfur Clothing	18	24	3.0	29
Copper	45	40	2.9	2
Cotton	63	58	2.8	9
Nonferrous Ores	52	43	2.3	10
Fruits and Nuts	42	40	2.0	8
Rubber (crude and synthetic)	70	61	1.7	2
Fresh Meat	18	22	1.7	23
Iron Ore	46	36	1.5	6
Wood	45	47	1.4	12
Animal Feed	39	35	1.3	9
Precious Stones	22	24	1.3	16
Cocoa	86	85	1.2	5

*Ranked by value.

SOURCE: *United Nations Conference on Trade and Development, Handbook of International Trade and Development Statistics (New York: United Nations, 1976), table 4.3 (c).*

export patterns of industrial and less developed countries. Industrial countries export automobiles, machinery, electrical appliances, and other costly high-technology products. These finished products are much more valuable than the simple sum of the component parts. Demand for them is great among the majority of human beings living in the less developed areas of the world, where the expertise, capital, and facilities to manufacture their own products are lacking.

Furthermore, in one of the more perverse twists of economics, Engel's law states that as incomes go up in any country the percentage of that income devoted to food diminishes. Thus, as countries develop economically, many agricultural commodities exported by less developed countries are in comparatively smaller demand. Markets for high-technology products expand rapidly along with industrial growth while food markets expand very slowly.

Most of the world's less developed countries export agricultural commodities. One-third of the world's sugar is exported by Cuba, Brazil, and the Philippines. Eight less developed countries earn more than one-third of their total export revenues from sales of sugar. Coffee is another commodity originally introduced to less developed economies in order to meet the perceived needs of the developed countries. Brazil and Colombia now account for nearly one-half of all the world's coffee exports, and a dozen less developed countries derive more than one-quarter of their total export revenue from coffee. One-quarter of world cocoa exports come from Ghana, and these account for two-thirds of Ghana's export revenue. Sixty percent of world tea exports come from India and Sri Lanka. Table 7-4 indicates that a total of thirty-seven less developed countries obtain more than two-thirds of their export revenue from the sale of food items and agricultural raw materials.

World demand for these commodities increases very slowly, since the markets are saturated. Furthermore, competition from the industrial countries, using mechanized equipment, fertilizers, and pesticides, has begun to cut into less developed country exports of even these basic agricultural commodities. For example, 55 percent of the world rice market was in the hands of less developed countries in 1967. By 1972, this share had dropped to only 43 percent, largely because of increased exports by the United States. A similar situation exists in the world sugar market, where less developed countries accounted for 78 percent of all sugar exports in 1967 but saw their share drop to only 64 percent by 1972.[21] Not only must less developed countries earn export revenues from these comparatively cheap commodities, industrial countries are now using technology to make inroads into relatively stagnant markets that were previously controlled by the less developed countries!

Furthermore, prices of these agricultural commodities shift considerably over time due to rapid fluctuations in supply caused by weather and similar factors. Revenues earned from such exports are,

TABLE 7-4. *Commodity Export Concentration*

Country	Number of Commodities Exported, 1972	Concentration Index, 1962*	Concentration Index, 1972*	Percent of Food Items Plus Agricultural Raw Materials**	Principle Commodities	Percent of All Exports Accounted for by Principal Export
Vietnam	4	.680	.982	98.16	Rubber	52.1
Zambia	66	.911	.952	1.31	Copper	94.1
Mauritius	65	.982	.916	95.06	Sugar	88.7
Iraq	95	.655	.915	4.42	Wool, petroleum	50.3
Cuba	7	.860	.795	82.23	Sugar	71.8
Cambodia	3	.488	.794	97.84		
Mauritania	57	.819	.786	13.40	Iron ore	77.3
Bolivia	6	.797	.779	1.53	Tin	50.1
Chile	116	.648	.754	6.84	Copper	71.6
Liberia	82	.624	.741	20.98		
Nigeria	82	.368	.736	12.07	Cocoa, petroleum	60.4
Surinam	43	.787	.729	5.84		
Algeria	114	.630	.667	20.49	Iron ore, petroleum	51.2
Chad	60	.766	.665	82.58	Cotton	62.4
Zaire	92	.539	.656	11.43	Copper	64.2
Ghana	70	.697	.650	87.70	Cocoa	61.1
Jamaica	117	.518	.629	22.59	Bauxite	25.4
Sierra Leone	31	.612	.627	22.23	Iron ore	12.0
Uganda	67	.544	.620	94.35	Coffee	58.8
Belize	9	.575	.602	91.54	Sugar	29.9
Gambia	7	.945	.597	99.56		
Sudan	46	.621	.596	98.71	Cotton	60.6
Sri Lanka	63	.638	.575	92.06	Tea	57.9
Somalia	57	.582	.574	92.76	Bananas	27.8
Dominican Republic	14	.579	.566	73.89	Sugar	48.9
Ecuador	7	.608	.563	38.08	Bananas	39.6
Uruguay	15	.470	.563		Beef	34.7

TABLE 7-4. Commodity Export Concentration (continued)

Country	Number of Commodities Exported, 1972	Concentration Index, 1962*	Concentration Index, 1972*	Percent of Food Items Plus Agricultural Raw Materials **	Principle Commodities	Percent of All Exports Accounted for by Principal Export
Colombia	147	.702	.550	68.02	Coffee	59.5
Guyana	20	.548	.549	44.88	Sugar	30.7
Panama	66	.550	.547	55.95	Bananas	53.9
Rwanda	12	.603	.544	76.38	Coffee	52.1
Western Samoa	17	.546	.506	95.03		
Malawi	66	.460	.488	95.56	Tea	20.0
Ethiopia	85	.543	.485	95.07	Coffee	53.8
Barbados	83	.908	.466	49.	Sugar	35.6
Central African Republic	60	.476	.453	61.24	Cotton	27.6
Honduras	86	.472	.451	89.01	Bananas	45.1
Egypt	117	.593	.447	64.88	Cotton	46.9
Congo	68	.478	.431	80.09	Sugar	8.9
Upper Volta	85	.615	.429	91.25	Cotton	21.7
Malaysia	156	.550	.422	62.	Rubber	28.2
Ivory Coast	121	.507	.415	87.60	Coffee	30.7
New Guinea	14	.431	.415			
Peru	10	.288	.412	33.69	Copper	21.7
Togo	110	.514	.399	44.92	Cocoa	36.0
Indonesia	71	.470	.394	43.40	Rubber	17.5
Burma	48	.620	.388	89.26	Rice	44.6
Niger	56	.635	.388	75.38	Cotton	2.7
Costa Rica	121	.608	.379	78.67	Bananas	29.3
El Salvador	130	.602	.378	68.48	Coffee	42.1
Tunisia	122	.310	.374	26.65	Iron	1.0
Syria	135	.471	.366	55.42	Cotton	38.3
Mali	72	.502	.363	89.50	Cotton	33.0

Country				Commodity	
Camaroon	134	.391	.362	83.52	Coffee	26.5
Angola	137	.442	.358	43.20	Coffee	30.8
Bangladesh	26	.218	.357	28.51	Jute	48.9
Jordan	78	.460	.348	82.58	Bananas	.8
Madagascar	137	.311	.326			
Guatemala	139	.643	.319	73.37	Coffee	33.0
Philippines	133	.345	.314	79.13	Sugar	18.0
Kenya	128	.356	.314	75.39	Coffee	26.5
Pakistan	132	.253	.309	35.63	Cotton	15.2
Afghanistan	25	.331	.298	71.18	Cotton	13.9
Nicaragua	116	.442	.296	83.65	Cotton	23.3
Morocco	138	.313	.278	55.31	Cotton	1.1
Tanzania	86	.363	.273	83.04	Coffee	16.0
Korea, Republic of	162	.245	.262	10.87	Iron ore	.3
Brazil	168	.534	.256	63.88	Coffee	28.0
Paraguay	56	.305	.240	63.17	Beef	12.9
Senegal	145	.498	.238	58.61	Cotton	1.0
Mozambique	124	.339	.234	73.87	Cotton	14.8
Thailand	142	.411	.230	69.58	Rice	18.1
India	172	.232	.153	38.42	Tea	9.3
Mexico	162	.216	.122	42.64	Cotton	8.3

*The closer the index approaches 1.0, the higher the concentration of exports.
**Most recent available data, 1967–1974.

SOURCES: *World Bank, Commodity and Price Trends, 1976 (Washington, D.C., 1976); United Nations, Yearbook of International Trade Statistics, 1974, vol. 1 (New York, 1975); General Agreement on Tariffs and Trade, International Trade 1973/74, (Geneva, 1974); David McNicol, Commodity Agreements and the New International Economic Order (Pasadena: California Institute of Technology, 1976).*

therefore, very undependable. For example, sugar on world markets rose dramatically from $99 per metric ton in 1971 to $654 per metric ton in 1974 when weather caused a poor harvest. By 1975, the price had dropped back to $450 per metric ton and has been steadily declining since.[22] And, when the bottom fell out of the world sugar market, the United States tripled its import duties to protect high-cost domestic producers, further worsening the plight of the exporters. The retail price of sugar in supermarkets did not fall back in proportion to the drop in raw sugar prices, as refiners, wholesalers, and retailers in industrial countries used falling prices to their advantage in increasing profits. A similar series of events recently struck the world coffee market. In 1971, coffee was selling for $984 per metric ton. Because of a hard freeze in Brazil in 1976, which severely damaged large numbers of trees, an earthquake in Guatemala, and civil war in Angola, the price of coffee skyrocketed to more than $2000 per metric ton in 1977 before dropping significantly.[23]

These weather-based price fluctuations create a dilemma for less developed countries. Prices for their exports rise rapidly during times of shortages. Yet these increased prices do not mean increased total revenue because they occur when production falls short of target. High prices sometimes lead to consumer resistance. And the unpredictability of weather and similar natural disasters makes long-term development planning difficult.

In spite of attempts to diversify, most less developed countries are still wedded to the one or two crops that remain from the colonial legacy. Table 7-4 summarizes the extent of export concentration. While the indices of concentration decreased for almost all less developed countries over the decade 1962–1972, the decline in many of the one-crop economies was very small. As late as 1972, there were twenty-seven less developed countries that received more than 50 percent of their export revenues from a single commodity, and there were forty-three less developed countries that received more than 50 percent of their export revenues from only three commodities. Furthermore, a total of thirty-seven less developed countries received more than two-thirds of export revenues exclusively from agricultural products.

A small number of less developed non-OPEC countries export one or two nonfuel minerals in an analogous one-crop situation. While the production of these "crops" is not hampered by changes in weather, minerals are very closely tied to the market for them, which is determined by economic conditions in industrial countries. For example, Zambia, Chile, and Zaire share 40 percent of the world export market in copper. Copper comprises 91, 67, and 58 percent of their export earnings, respectively. But whereas the less developed countries controlled 45 percent of the world copper trade in 1967, this figure dropped to less than 40 percent by 1972.[24] The rapid global economic expansion of 1972–1973 led to a substantial increase in copper prices followed by a precipitous decline associated with the world economic recession of

1974–1975. In 1971, copper sold for $1081 per metric ton. Prices peaked in early 1974 at more than $2000 per metric ton and subsequently dropped back to the earlier level in 1976. As a result of this extreme fluctuation in prices, Zaire overextended itself in international financial markets and defaulted on payment of $50 million in debts in 1976. In 1977, Zaire's external debt was estimated at 50 percent of gross national product and over three times the value of yearly exports.[25]

There are still other aspects of the colonial heritage that have dimmed development prospects for former colonies. Since these areas were viewed as extensions of the colonizers, their transportation infrastructures were designed to facilitate the flow of raw materials to the sea. Thus, in many contemporary less developed countries the railroads and highways are designed to move raw materials from inland areas to ports, where they can be shipped to industrial countries. It is now a difficult task to redirect these transportation networks to meet the countries' own domestic needs.

In addition, since diversification of trade and construction of facilities are very slow processes, the industrially developed countries still have significant neocolonialist influence over the economies of many of the less developed countries. Members of OPEC, for example, still refine very little of their own crude oil. Most of it is shipped to refineries in industrial countries and marketed by multinational oil corporations, giving these companies considerable leverage in their negotiations.

Finally, the boundaries drawn by the colonial powers did not include cohesive ethnic, tribal, or cultural units. Spheres of influence often were extended until they collided with the territorial ambitions of other colonial powers. When the industrial countries divested themselves of these colonies in the 1960s and 1970s, little consideration was given to the fact that state boundaries did not always coincide with national aspirations. Diverse tribes or cultures often were trapped within the same newly independent state. Thus, Nigeria received independence from Great Britain in 1960 and fell almost immediately into civil war. The Ibo tribe attempted to take over the government in a coup in 1966 only to face the wrath of the Hausa, Fulani, and Yoruba tribes, which quickly took revenge. Tens of thousands of Ibos were massacred, and their attempt to form Biafra as a breakaway state failed. These types of quarrels have been common in many newly independent states and have created an atmosphere in which economic development and political stability have been impossible.[26]

In summary, the colonial experience stacked the deck against industrialization efforts in contemporary less developed countries. Most of these less developed economies were deliberately kept agrarian by the colonial powers. The mix of commodities grown or mined was related to the needs of the home country and not to any economic needs of the colonized areas. Technologically sophisticated facilities were introduced into these countries only when there were no other options. The economic ties with the former colonial powers persist, and, in many cases, the negative aspects of outright imperialism have been replaced by a neoimperialism characterized by control of downstream facilities and markets for the basic commodities exported by these less developed countries.[27] And this whole set of colonial and neocolonial issues is now being raised as an integral part of the North-South ecopolitical dialog.

PROBLEMS OF CAPITAL ACCUMULATION

Within the old development paradigm, the key to economic growth was the accumulation of capital and the use of it to create the base for heavy industry. But the methods by which less developed countries were to accumulate capital were never clearly explained, and this omission has led to many of the anomalies that beset the old paradigm. Mahbub Ul Haq claims that development planning has gone through several phases. Using Pakistan as his example, he points out that planners first encouraged less developed countries to invest in industries that could produce substitutions for imports, thereby preserving scarce foreign exchange for essential items. Then, as "fashions" changed, the planners switched their emphasis from import substitution to export expansion, then to expansion of the agricultural sector, then to population control. Finally, in more recent years, planners have "discovered" that the poor in less developed countries really haven't gained much at all and are now suggesting that wealth redistribution take priority over growth.[28] Despite all of the development approaches tried, the old paradigm did not take the welfare of the lower classes into consideration, nor did it provide an appropriate role for the huge, unemployed labor force in underdeveloped countries. Thus, Ul Haq points out that in Pakistan the level of literacy declined from 18 percent in 1950 to 15 percent in 1970 while rapid economic growth was supposedly taking place.[29]

Keith Griffin has found a similar situation in world agriculture. In many nations where there has been substantial technological innovation in agriculture there has been little simultaneous increase in per capita food production.[30] John Mellor has found that India's second five-year plan, which moved it away from a program of labor mobilization and small-scale production and instead stressed capital goods and the growth of heavy industry, led to very low growth rates and significant increases in idle workers. Most growth that did later take place was closely tied to foreign aid.[31]

Shifts in development "fashions" reflect the frustrations of development planners and leaders of less developed countries as their faith in old development models has been shaken. Development has been taken by them to be a cooperative endeavor. Trade with industrial countries was assumed to be the key to mutual prosperity. Growth in the industrial world would supposedly trickle down to the less developed countries as industrial prosperity would create new markets for Third World exports. Prosperous countries would be more willing to increase their foreign aid, and foreign investment would increase along with growth in the industrial world. Unfortunately, this mutual self-interest theory of development has proved to have little validity. Aid commitments have diminished even during recent times of economic prosperity.

Trade, of course, should be a major source of foreign exchange to be used to facilitate industrial growth in less developed countries. Terms of trade are a measure of the relative value or change in relative value of the commodities exported and imported by any country or group of countries. They are found by comparing a weighted index of the price of all exports against a similar weighted index of all imports. The terms of trade for less developed countries are an important measure of the rate at which foreign exchange can be accumulated. The more favorable the terms of trade, the more likely a developing country will be able to obtain foreign exchange and thereby profit from its involvement with the world trade system. If the terms of trade deteriorate, this involvement becomes much less satisfactory.

Figure 7–2 summarizes terms of trade for four groups of countries over the last two decades. Over the first fifteen years of this period

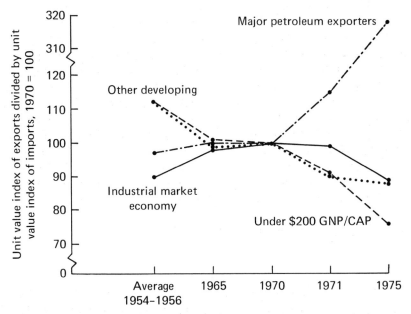

FIGURE 7–2. Terms of Trade [SOURCE: United Nations Conference on Trade and Development, *Handbook of International Trade and Development Statistics, 1976* (New York, 1976), table 2.5.]

(1955–1970), the industrial countries witnessed a steady improvement in their terms of trade. In the early 1970s, however, there was a deterioration in these terms of trade due largely to the large increase in the price of imported oil. As a result, the terms of trade for industrial countries were roughly the same in 1975 as they were in 1955. The terms of trade for the non–oil-exporting developing countries, by contrast, have deteriorated steadily over the entire twenty-year period. This deterioration subtracted about 21 percent from the value of the typical export item in relation to the price of imports. But the poorest less developed countries witnessed an even more extreme deterioration in their terms of trade, dropping nearly 31 percent over the two decades. There have been only two short periods of improvement in terms of trade for these countries since World War II, and both were associated with periods of military confrontation. The first was during the Korean War in the early 1950s and the second during the latter years of the Vietnam War in the early 1970s. In both cases, the favorable movement in the terms of trade quickly reversed once the panic mentality associated with international turmoil subsided.

There are a number of explanations for this turn of events. The terms of trade problem for less developed countries is related to the technology gap. The less developed countries export basic commodities. The markets for these commodities are limited. Furthermore, should the price of a commodity rapidly increase, the technologically developed countries can usually synthesize a substitute. But most important, basic commodities are relatively undifferentiated, and there are many less developed countries seeking to expand exports of the same commodity. Thus, periodic commodity gluts drive prices down.[32]

But on the industrial side of the technology gap there is an increasing demand for the manufactured items produced in industrial countries. These goods are in heavy demand because they are essential to progress in the large number of countries that seek to follow the traditional energy-intensive path to industrialization. Furthermore, highly organized labor unions in industrially advanced countries insure that workers there, rather than consumers in less developed countries, receive the economic benefits of any increased productivity. Thus, prices of exported industrial products remain high even when technology permits larger quantities to be produced with the same amount of labor because the cost of labor now increases more rapidly than productivity in the technologically advanced countries. But in the less developed countries there is a vast pool of unemployed labor, and trade union activity cannot force wages up, even if productivity increases.[33]

Arghiri Emmanuel has developed this thesis further; he claims that prices of exports in any country are determined mainly by wage levels. Wages are not directly linked to productivity but depend on institutional factors in various countries. Labor is restricted by natural boundaries, but capital moves freely across them. Thus, rates of profit tend to be similar in all countries. The differences in prices of goods, however, are determined by differences in wages. This leads to "unequal exchange," high-priced goods from industrial countries being traded for low-priced goods from less industrial countries. The only ways for a less developed country to escape from this dilemma, according to Emmanuel, are to increase trade with other developing countries or to increase their self-reliance.[34]

Thus, for many of the less developed countries, involvement in trade with industrial countries has siphoned off rather than added to investment capital. These unfavorable terms of trade have even partially negated the impact of foreign aid. Increased awareness of the role of trade in creating a "development treadmill" has led some Third and Fourth World leaders to call for dissociation from the present international economic order and for an increase in mutual self-reliance.[35]

Development assistance is a second possible source of investment capital. Assistance can come from two sources: official developmental assistance and private capital flows. Official assistance is preferred by less developed countries because it usually consists of a large concessionary element, grants or loans with low rates of interest. Private capital comes either in the form of direct foreign investment by private corporations or by loans from financial institutions at market rates.

Table 7–5 contains data on the net official governmental assistance of industrial nations as a percentage of their gross national products. For all Development Assistance Committee (DAC) members, net offered assistance increased from $5.7 billion per year, in the period 1964–1966, to $12.8 billion in 1975. While this doubling looks impressive, it represents an increase of only about 8 percent each year, which was much less than the increased prices of goods and services to be purchased with this aid. During the ten-year period 1964–1974, the *real* value of foreign aid given by DAC countries declined by 9 percent.[36] Total net official aid given by all DAC members dropped from .42 percent of gross national product in 1964–1966 to .34 percent of collective gross national product in 1975.

Sweden and the Netherlands have been the only industrial countries to meet the original United Nations wealth transfer target of .7 percent. The Scandinavian countries, Sweden, Norway, and Denmark, are all at the top of the donor list, and all of them have increased substantially the portion of GNP given to assistance. The larger industrial countries, in contrast, have made a very dismal showing. Official assistance from the United States has dropped substantially in constant dollars over the last decade. And the proportion of GNP going to aid has been cut in half. In 1975, the United States gave aid equivalent to only .25 percent of gross national product. Japan, Germany, and Great Britain have only slightly better records.

It might seem that the more highly developed countries should give greater amounts of foreign assistance, but this is not the case. Swit-

TABLE 7-5. DAC Members' Net Official Assistance to Less Developed Countries*

	Average 1964–1966		1970		1972		1975	
	Dollars	Percent of GNP	Dollars	Percent of GNP	Dollars	Percent of GNP	Dollars	Percent of GNP
Sweden	43	.21	116	.38	197	.48	563	.81
Netherlands	68	.36	190	.60	299	.66	584	.73
Norway	12	.17	37	.32	63	.43	184	.66
France	743	.74	927	.63	1,257	.64	1,979	.58
Denmark	15	.14	59	.37	95	.45	205	.58
Australia	115	.51	202	.59	267	.59	505	.61
Canada	121	.23	346	.42	491	.47	879	.58
Belgium	83	.49	119	.46	192	.55	375	.59
Germany	404	.35	518	.28	723	.28	1,526	.36
Great Britain	411	.41	390	.32	539	.35	778	.34
New Zealand	10	.19	14	.23	21	.25	66	.52
Japan	202	.22	408	.21	538	.18	1,018	.21
United States	3,366	.48	2,869	.29	3,106	.27	3,731	.25
Finland	3	.03	7	.07	20	.15	48	.18
Austria	9	.09	7	.05	16	.08	64	.17
Switzerland	11	.08	29	.14	64	.21	102	.18
Italy	43	.07	127	.14	76	.06	165	.09
Total	5,656	.42	6,364	.31	7,963	.31	12,770	.34

*Outflows of assistance less amortization and interest recovered; data in millions of dollars.

SOURCES: Organization for Economic Cooperation and Development, Development Cooperation 1975. (Paris, 1975), p. 198, and Organization for Economic Cooperation and Development, Development Cooperation 1976. (Paris, 1976), p. 210.

zerland, the United States, Sweden, Canada, and Germany were the five most highly industrialized countries in 1975 according to gross national product per capita rankings. In that year, Switzerland, the United States, and West Germany all ranked in the bottom half of DAC countries in percentage of GNP given as aid, and Canada ranked eighth.[37]

There is also little economic logic to the process by which countries are selected to be aid recipients. Pierre Uri has studied the relationships between amount of aid received by less developed countries and gross national product per capita. He has found that the pattern of aid-giving is quite chaotic. The poorest countries, which have the greatest objective need, often receive little aid. The richer less developed countries receive more official assistance, on the average, than their poorer counterparts. The relationship between GNP per capita and direct private investment in less developed countries is also almost random.[38] Unfortunately, the criterion for aid that seems to predominate in international transactions at present is political and seems to be based on donor self-interest. Industrial countries and OPEC nations, with very few exceptions, rarely give aid for altruistic reasons. Concrete benefits are expected in return.

United States assistance patterns offer a good example. Most US assistance has been given as military aid. Other assistance has had strings attached that forced recipients to buy American goods, often at inflated prices. In 1977, three out of every four dollars of US bilateral assistance was used to purchase goods and services from the US.[39] The initial US foreign aid appropriation for fiscal 1977 was $5.1 billion. Of this, over half, $2.7 billion, was for military grants and loans and only $1.4 billion went to bilateral economic assistance. The remainder of the appropriation went to the support of several multilateral efforts. Of the total given, Israel received nearly 20 percent of all aid, most of it for military purposes. In fiscal years 1970–1974, Vietnam received nearly the same proportion of US assistance that now goes to Israel.[40] The United States also frequently gives aid in return for military bases. The Philippines was offered $1 billion over five years in 1976 in return for continued use of military bases.

The behavior of industrial nations as foreign aid donors supports the ecopolitical and neocolonial arguments made by leaders of less developed countries. Most industrial countries reduced aid commitments as a percentage of gross national product in the early 1970s, before the North-South confrontation became heated. Closing the gap between rich and poor countries does not seem to have high priority for them. When aid is given it is usually military aid or economic aid given to influence the internal affairs of recipient countries. Other aid is offered mainly to meet the needs of donor countries. In 1976, for example, Secretary of State Henry Kissinger offered to set up a loan fund to help Third World countries exploit their natural resources in order to expand mineral exports to highly industrialized countries. The less developed countries, of course, refused the offer.

THE NEW SCARCITY AND DEVELOPMENT

The oil price increases of 1973–1975 dealt additional devastating blows to development plans. One of the results of this dislocation was the removal of nearly three dozen countries from the Third World (the developing world) category and creation of a Fourth, or "economically troubled," category by the World Bank. These are countries that now have few prospects for coping with increased raw materials prices because they have little of value with which to participate in international trade.

The non–oil-exporting less developed countries suffered several interrelated economic setbacks at different points in time as a result of the petroleum price increases. The most obvious setback directly depleted foreign exchange reserves as prices for imported petroleum rapidly rose. At the lowest end of the income scale, less developed countries are not heavily dependent upon imported petroleum because little industry exists. Their economic performance is more closely linked to agriculture and is determined by weather. But the poorest countries also have the smallest exchange reserves, and the impact of the price increases on these modest petroleum imports created significant problems.

Higher levels of industrialization are associated with significant increases in per capita energy consumption. Imported petroleum is the major source of energy for many of the rapidly growing developing countries. They lack storage and transportation facilities for natural gas, and very few have significant reserves of coal. Of a sample of twenty-three developing African countries, for example, thirteen derived *all* of their measured energy consumption from imported petroleum.[41] Many development experts now concede that quadrupled and quintupled petroleum prices may have created a "never-to-be-developed" world, countries that now have no prospects for industrial development within the conventional way of thinking about it. It is estimated that seventy-three less developed countries were forced to borrow $60 billion in 1974–1975, largely to finance their increased bill for petroleum imports.[42] In 1976, the estimated debt of these countries was between $180 and $250 billion.[43]

This direct impact of oil price increases is only a part of the problem that has been faced by the less developed countries. The petroleum-related recession in the industrial countries that peaked in 1975 also had a negative impact on the economic performance of the less developed countries. It dried up markets for basic commodities and drove down prices for these exports, which are essential to the economic health of the less developed world. Thus, the giant increase in oil bills in 1974 was followed in many less developed countries by a substantial drop in export revenue in 1975.

By 1976, another perverse result of the oil price increase rebounded to the disadvantage of these countries. Rampant inflation in the industrial countries, triggered by the petroleum price increases, drove up prices of industrial exports. Many industrial countries were able to pass through most of the impact of the OPEC price increase and balance their payments by increasing export prices. Faced with depressed markets for their own basic commodities, the less developed countries took the brunt of these inflationary dislocations in world trade.[44]

The net result of all of these problems has been a substantial drop in foreign exchange reserves, fears of bankruptcy, and drastic setbacks for development projects. Table 7-6 traces the change in reserve positions for the five-year period 1970–1975 for twenty countries with the smallest reserves. Nearly half of these countries had no reserves at all and the rest had less than one month's worth of imports equivalent in reserves in 1975. Many of the less developed countries have borrowed heavily to meet their

TABLE 7-6.   *Countries with Smallest Reserves of Foreign Exchange*

	Months of Imports			Millions of Dollars (1975)
	1970	1973	1975	
Chile	4.9	0.7	−1.6	−278
Sri Lanka	−1.2	0.0	−1.4	− 88
Sudan	−0.3	0.6	−1.4	− 96
Mali	−1.8	−0.5	−0.6	− 8
Central African Republic	0.4	0.5	−0.5	− 2
Zaire	4.1	3.1	−0.4	− 27
Pakistan	2.0	2.9	−0.3	− 55
Bangladesh	—	0.8	−0.2	− 22
Tanzania	2.2	2.7	−0.1	− 8
Chad	0.0	0.0	0.0	0
Senegal	1.3	0.4	0.2	9
Bahamas	0.6	0.4	0.3	58
Costa Rica	0.6	1.0	0.3	16
Camaroon	4.0	1.6	0.4	19
Netherlands Antilles	0.6	0.4	0.4	93
Ivory Coast	3.6	1.3	0.5	49
Liberia	−0.3	0.0	0.6	16
Madagascar	3.3	2.3	0.7	19
Argentina	4.5	4.6	0.8	281
Zambia	11.9	2.3	0.8	56

SOURCE: *United Nations Committee on Trade and Development,* Handbook of International Trade and Development Statistics 1976 *(New York: United Nations, 1976), table 5.9.*

obligations. Those with relatively good credit ratings, such as Brazil, Mexico, Taiwan, and South Korea, have been able to weather the storm fairly well. Others have been much less fortunate. Zaire, Zambia, Peru, and Argentina all came perilously close to defaulting on their obligations in 1976 and 1977. During 1976, the less developed countries had a trade deficit of nearly $32 billion.[45] Interest and amortization costs on their tremendous debt alone are now equal to more than 10 percent of gross foreign exchange earnings in these countries.[46]

The impact of any future price increases on the less developed countries, based on real or contrived scarcities, could yield similar results. Future increases in petroleum prices certainly will add to large existing deficits. Should prices for nonfuel minerals increase sharply, the less developed countries would be more severely affected than many of the industrial countries. Few of the less developed countries earn significant export revenue from nonfuel minerals. Zambia, Zaire, and Chile earn more than 50 percent of their export revenues from copper; Mauritania more than 50 percent from iron ore; and Jamaica more than 50 percent from bauxite. But, of the list of commodities that have been suggested as candidates for international price stabilization programs, there are more commodities for which price increases would be of greater benefit to selected industrial countries than there are that would benefit the less developed countries taken as a whole.[47]

In the middle of 1970s, the industrial countries were neither in a financial position nor predisposed to step up foreign assistance programs to help cover these additional deficits. The non–petroleum-exporting less developed countries turned to OPEC as a source of loans and grants, but OPEC was very guarded in its response (see table 7–7). A suggestion for a two-tiered price system, including cheaper petroleum for

TABLE 7–7. *Major Recipients of OPEC Aid, 1973–1975**

	1973	1974	1975	Total
Egypt	580.09	934.76	1145.83	2660.68
Syria	182.47	578.66	200.13	961.26
Pakistan	33.78	200.84	237.10	471.72
Jordan	94.38	190.22	75.08	359.68
India		247.64	16.90	264.54
Oman	9.62	125.46	51.73	186.81
Sudan	4.32	138.64	30.01	172.97
Algeria	57.71	82.38	2.63	142.72
Lebanon	2.45	120.97		123.42
Bangladesh		60.04	48.76	108.80
Total Aid to Developing Countries	1,176.79	3,437.48	2,344.53	6,958.80

*Millions of dollars.

SOURCE: *United Nations Conference on Trade and Development,* Handbook of International Trade and Development Statistics 1976 *(New York: United Nations, 1976), table 5.8.*

less developed countries, was rejected. It has been estimated that OPEC received nearly $12 billion annually in added oil revenues from Third World countries in 1974 and 1975. In each of those years, OPEC returned only about $4.6 billion in aid to this group of countries, a net loss to them of $7.4 billion.[48]

When OPEC countries have given aid, they have not given it to the most needy countries. In this respect, OPEC countries have acted like their industrial counterparts. Two-thirds of 1975 aid went to Syria and Egypt, both net exporters of oil, as "good faith" money in the political struggle against Israel. Less than 10 percent of direct aid went to non-Moslem countries.[49]

Saudi Arabia claimed in 1976 that its foreign aid had reached its peak and would be declining. Although Saudi Arabia had a $20 billion current accounts surplus in 1975, it reportedly gave only $4 billion in foreign aid, most of it to other Arab countries in the form of loans. Thus, the only sacrifice by Saudi Arabia was a small percentage interest that represented the difference between the interest the money would have earned at commercial rates and the lesser interest earned from most of the loans. In the words of Saudi Arabia's Minister of Planning, Hisham Nazer, "to call Saudi Arabia a rich country is a mistake, a misconception. Saudi Arabia is depleting its resources and eating up its only capital. . . . Saudi Arabia comes first."[50]

OPEC did collectively agree to set up a $1 billion development fund in 1976, but only agreed to do so for one year. Part of the money, $400 million, was to go to the International Agricultural Development Fund provided that the industrial countries contribute $600 million. The other portion of the OPEC money was to be given as direct loans and not grants.

In summary, the petroleum price increase triggered by the OPEC cartel did lead to a large shift in purchasing power in the international economy. But only the oil exporters within OPEC reaped extensive economic benefits. Initially, it was the industrial countries that felt the brunt of the price increases in 1974, but most of these economies were able to rebuild and begin to right their trade deficits by raising prices on industrial goods in 1975 and 1976. The less developed countries, however, were hit by three separate phases of the petroleum crisis. The price increase itself depleted most exchange reserves, the ensuing drop in demand for basic commodities kept them from replenishing these reserves, and the increase in price of high-technology imports further diminished economic development plans. The net result was the creation of a Fourth World, countries with no real prospects for substantial economic development.

Technology has changed the rules of the industrialization game and created a different development context. The new medical technologies applied to disease problems in less developed countries have resulted in a population explosion. These exploding populations now must be fed and housed. In many cases, this means doubling facilities every fifteen to twenty years just to stay even. Growth in per capita living standards is even more difficult. Yet, the ecopolitical events of the last decade have shattered the paradigm that has thus far guided development planning. Increases in petroleum prices, recession accompanied by inflation in the industrial countries, chaos in basic commodity markets, declining foreign aid from some industrial countries, and lack of perceived economic progress in the less developed countries have all combined to cast doubt on many aspects of the old development thinking. A search for a new model for growth is closely related to demands for a new international economic order.

The presently industrialized countries developed under a set of circumstances much different than those facing contemporary less developed countries. Natural resources of all types were in abundant supply in relation to human demands. Most important, the fossil fuel subsidy was very large, and the free energy from the subsidy triggered a series of fossil fuel–related technological innovations that had a multiplier effect on economic growth. If natural resources were not readily available at home, the old path to development led to their seizure from colonial areas.

But most contemporary less developed countries do not have these advantages. Few of them have substantial natural resources with which to work. And the cheap energy from the fossil fuel subsidy is disappearing. There are now no possibilities for less developed countries to build a network of colonies to aid them as did their predecessors. Military conquest is no longer permitted as a method of increasing territory, and there are no sparsely settled areas that can be seized.

Another reason that less developed countries cannot follow the established energy-intensive colonial model of development is that the time available to them to modernize is much more compressed than it was for developing countries three hundred years ago. Western European countries spent more than two centuries moving from the equivalent of $100 gross national product per capita to $1000 per capita. To suggest a similar timetable for contemporary less developed countries is to invite the derision of their political leaders, who must deal with an externally induced revolution of rising expectations. The countries that developed early had no affluent examples to follow, and political leaders did not have to deal with relative deprivation on an international scale. Contemporary industrialization thus takes place in a "catch-up" environment created by what are perceived to be very high standards of living in the presently industrialized countries.

Finally, the ethical principles governing contemporary industrialization have changed dramatically. Old capital accumulation schemes are now in disfavor. Child labor, sixty-hour work weeks, and subsistence-level wages have been replaced by minimum wage laws, social security, the eight-hour day, early retirement, and a number of other economic benefits. It is now considered to be morally wrong to use slaves or captive workers living in company barracks, or to employ ten-year-old children. The old standards were an important aspect of getting the industrialization job done, both in Western Europe and later in the Soviet Union. But in an era of increasing emphasis on human rights, no one would suggest a return to what are perceived to be barbaric standards in the interest of contemporary modernization.

One answer to these dilemmas is to create new alternatives and a new development paradigm by selecting various positive aspects of the old.[51] Historically, energy-intensive industrialization has been the driving force behind the modernization syndrome. Heavy industry has been taken to be the primary component of a social mobilization process that transforms agrarian societies into industrial ones.[52] This fossil fuel–based modernization cluster consists of closely related industrial, economic, psychological, social, political, and demographic components. Modernization also contains an important psychological component. Modern individuals have different personalities than do those living in traditional societies. They can be identified by feelings of efficacy toward physical and social environments, respect for the opinions of others, high levels of trust in other people, a feeling that human beings can triumph over nature, openness to new experiences, belief in the importance of planning, a time orientation to the present and future rather than the past, and educational and occupational aspirations.[53]

Historically, these components of modernization have occurred simultaneously with industrialization. Modern individuals could emerge only in a standard industrial setting, or so the common wisdom said. But there is no reason that the various components of modernization cannot be separated from energy-intensive industrial growth as part of a deliberate social design process.[54] Modernization can take place without heavy industry. Modern individuals can emerge outside of a factory setting. Furthermore, there is no direct evidence that conventional industrialization increases total human happiness.[55] Development experts have highlighted the favorable aspects of modernization and ignored the shattered family life, urban squalor, mass unemployment, alcoholism, wealth disparities, mental disturbances, and crime that have also been triggered by conventional development. The record of growth in contemporary developed countries has not been an enviable one in terms of creating human happiness.

It is possible now to look forward to the emergence of a postindustrial human being in a postindustrial society, free from the anxieties induced by industrialization.[56] There are alternative ways to create the happiness that supposedly results from energy-intensive modernization. Switzerland offers an example. By most objective indicators, the Switzerland of the 1960s was not an industrial country. But it was certainly a country inhabited by modern individuals who appeared to be reasonably content.

A new development paradigm requires splitting up the components of the old modernization syndrome in order to assess their impact on the quality of life of the human beings involved. There are certain aspects of modernization that are universally considered to be desirable. Among these are those directed at meeting basic human needs, including medical care, adequate diet, basic shelter, clothes, and so on. Beyond the basics there also is considerable agreement that education, literacy, development of mass communication, and political democracy are worth striving for. But none of these items need be energy-intensive. It is only when industrialization, urbanization, and mass transportation become goals that natural-resource-intensive processes become part of the modernization syndrome.

Pieces of this nascent paradigm are already falling into place as a result of the anomalies that have been identified in the old one. Griffin, for example, has argued for a development strategy that eschews urbanization and capital-intensive industrialization while concentrating on agriculture and rural development.[57] Mellor has suggested a labor-intensive strategy that would take advantage of the extensive labor supply in less developed countries.[58] Meier has speculated on ways to modernize while avoiding urban crowding and deterioration in the quality of life.[59] Many others have been investigating the role of "safe" or "appropriate" technologies in facilitating non–energy-intensive, decentralized, non–capital-intensive, easy-to-understand approaches to economic growth.[60]

A new philosophy of development is also emerging in support of this new paradigm. Goulet has argued for a new ethics of development that, at a minimum, would assure the satisfaction of basic physiological, psychological, and aesthetic needs of all members of the human race, eliminate the flagrant economic and social inequalities within and among societies, and optimize the potential freedom of each person and each cultural group to resist manipulation by others.[61] Ul Haq has similarly argued for a new development strategy based on the satisfaction of basic human needs rather than market demand, and development styles built around people rather than people around development.[62] While a new development paradigm will not be constructed overnight, continued exposure of the anomalies in the old one and creative attempts to envision and construct a new one can lead to sustainable modernization in contemporary less developed countries. This design process could yield more human satisfaction with less capital and resource consumption than the energy-intensive type of modernization that has been experienced by the presently industrialized countries.

ENDNOTES

1. See Aidan Foster-Carter, "From Rostow to Gunder Frank: Conflicting Paradigms in the Analysis of Underdevelopment," *World Development* (March 1976).
2. United Nations, *International Development Strategy* (New York, 1970).
3. See Samin Amin, *Unequal Development* (New York: Monthly Review Press, 1974).
4. World Bank figures cited in the *Washington Post* (January 16, 1977).
5. See Edward Woodhouse, "Re-visioning the Future of the Third World," *World Politics* (October 1972).
6. Glenn Hueckel, "A Historical Approach to Future Economic Growth," *Science* (March 14, 1975).
7. See Keith Griffin, *The Political Economy of Agrarian Change* (Cambridge, Mass.: Harvard University Press, 1974), chap. 3.
8. Ul Haq claims the developed world has a per capita income of $2400, compared to an average of $180 in the less developed countries. He expects this $2220 gap to widen by another $1100 between 1976 and 1980. See Mahbub Ul Haq, *The Poverty Curtain* (New York: Columbia University Press, 1976), p. 40.
9. Davis Bobrow, Robert Kudrle, and Dennis Pirages, "Contrived Scarcity: The Short-Term Impact of Expensive Oil," *International Studies Quarterly* (December 1977).
10. James Grant, "Development: The End of Trickle Down?" *Foreign Policy* (Fall 1973).
11. Montek Ahluwalia, "Income Inequality: Some Dimensions of the Problem," in Hollis Chenery, et al., *Redistribution with Growth* (London: Oxford University Press, 1974).
12. International Labor Organization, *Employment, Growth and Basic Needs* (New York: Praeger, 1977), pp. 18–19.
13. Ibid., p. 31.
14. John Rawls, *A Theory of Justice* (Cambridge, Mass.: The Belknap Press, 1971).
15. See Dee Pak Lal, "Distribution and Development: A Review Article," *World Development* (September 1976).
16. See, among others, John Mellor, *The New Economics of Growth* (Ithaca, N.Y.: Cornell University Press, 1976); Irma Adelman and Cynthia Morris, *Economic Growth and Social Equity in Developing Countries* (Stanford: Stanford University Press, 1973); and Chenery, et al., *Redistribution with Growth.*
17. See Earl Cook, *Man, Energy, Society* (San Francisco: W. H. Freeman, 1976), pp. 412–417.
18. See Constantine Vaitsos, "The Revision of the International Patent System:

Legal Considerations for a Third World Position," *World Development* (no. 2, 1976).

19. Richard Jolly, "International Dimensions," in Chenery, et al., *Redistribution with Growth*.

20. See Marian Radetzki, "Where Should Developing Countries' Minerals Be Processed? The Country View Versus the Multinational Company View," *World Development* (April 1977).

21. See United Nations Conference on Trade and Development, *Handbook of International Trade and Development Statistics, 1976* (New York, 1976), table 4.4.

22. Ibid., table 2.8.

23. Summary figures for fluctuations for all agricultural commodities can be found in ibid., tables 2.7 and 2.8.

24. Ibid., table 4.4.

25. Reported in *Business Week* (January 31, 1977).

26. See Robert Clark, Jr., *Development and Instability* (New York: The Dryden Press, 1974), chap. 8.

27. See Samir Amin, *Neo-Colonialism in West Africa* (New York: Monthly Review Press, 1973), for additional perspectives and case studies of African countries.

28. Ul Haq, *The Poverty Curtain*, p. 20.

29. Ibid., p. 23.

30. Griffin, *The Political Economy of Agrarian Change*, pp. 61–62.

31. Mellor, *The New Economics of Growth*, pp. 1–10.

32. See F. Stewart, "Trade and Technology," in Paul Streeten, ed., *Trade Strategies for Development* (London: Macmillan, 1973). See also John Spraos, "Why Inflation Is Not Relative Price-Neutral for Primary Products," *World Development* (August 1977).

33. See Raul Prebisch, "The Role of Commercial Policies in Underdeveloped Countries," *American Economic Review, Papers and Proceedings* (May 1959).

34. Arghiri Emmanuel, *Unequal Exchange* (London: New Left Books, 1972). See also Kathryn Morton and Peter Tulloch, *Trade and Developing Countries* (New York: John Wiley & Sons, 1977), chap. 1.

35. See Guy Erb and Valeriana Kallab, eds., *Beyond Dependency* (Washington: Overseas Development Council, 1975), section I.

36. Organization for Economic Cooperation and Development, *Development Cooperation* (Paris, 1976), pp. 16, 210.

37. Ibid.

38. See Pierre Uri, *Development without Dependence* (New York: Praeger, 1976), pp. 33–51.

39. For examples, see Felix Greene, *The Enemy* (New York: Random House, 1970), chap. 3. The 1977 figures are taken from the *Washington Post* (March 5, 1978).

40. James W. Howe, *The U.S. and World Development* (Washington, D.C.: Overseas Development Council, 1976), p. 260.

41. Figures are derived from United Nations, *World Energy Supplies* (New York, 1976).

42. Figures are from Harland van B. Cleveland and W. H. Bruce Britain, "Are the LDC's in over Their Heads?" *Foreign Affairs* (July 1977).

43. The low estimate is from Morgan Guaranty Trust Company, *World Financial Markets* (January 1977), p. 1. The high estimate is from Donaldson, Lufkin and Jenrette Securities Corporation, *The Banking Industry Lending to Less Developed Countries* (December 1976), p. 6.
44. See Wouter Tims, "The Developing Countries," in Edward Fried and Charles Schultze, eds., *Higher Oil Prices and the World Economy* (Washington, D.C.: The Brookings Institution, 1975).
45. Figures are from David Beim, "Rescuing the LDCs," *Foreign Affairs* (July 1977).
46. Reported in *Business Week* (March 1, 1976).
47. See David McNicol, *Commodity Agreements and the New International Economic Order* (Pasadena: California Institute of Technology, 1976), chaps. 6 and 7.
48. Maurice Williams, "The Aid Programs of the OPEC Countries," *Foreign Affairs* (January 1976).
49. Figures derived from Organization for Economic Cooperation and Development, *Development Cooperation*, pp. 116–117.
50. Statement reported in the *Washington Post* (August 14, 1976).
51. See Paul Streeten, "Alternatives in Development," *World Development* (February 1974). See also the other articles in this same volume.
52. Karl Deutsch, "Social Mobilization and Political Development," *The American Political Science Review* (September 1961).
53. See Alex Inkeles, "The Modernization of Man," in Myron Weiner, ed., *Modernization: The Dynamics of Growth* (New York: Basic Books, 1966); Robert Clark, Jr., *Development and Instability* (Hinsdale, Ill.: Dryden Press, 1974), chapter 2; and Alex Inkeles and David Smith, *Becoming Modern* (Cambridge, Mass.: Harvard University Press, 1974).
54. Dennis Pirages, "A Social Design for Sustainable Growth," in Dennis Pirages, ed., *The Sustainable Society* (New York: Praeger, 1977).
55. See Tibor Scitovski, *The Joyless Economy* (New York: Oxford University Press, 1976).
56. See Daniel Bell, *The Coming of Post-Industrial Society* (New York: Basic Books, 1973).
57. Griffin, *The Political Economy of Agrarian Change.*
58. Mellor, *The New Economics of Growth.*
59. Richard Meier, "A Stable Urban Ecosystem," *Science* (June 4, 1976), and Richard Meier, *Planning for an Urban World* (Cambridge, Mass.: MIT Press, 1975).
60. See Nicolas Jequier, ed., *Appropriate Technology: Problems and Promises* (Paris: Organization for Economic Cooperation and Development, 1976), and Richard Eckaus, *Appropriate Technologies for Developing Countries* (Washington, D.C.: National Academy of Sciences, 1977).
61. Denis Goulet, *The Cruel Choice* (New York: Atheneum, 1971).
62. Ul Haq, *The Poverty Curtain.*

SUGGESTED READINGS

1. Irma Adelman and Cynthia Morris. *Economic Growth and Social Equity in Developing Countries.* Standford: Stanford University Press, 1973.
2. Samir Amin. *Unequal Development.* New York: Monthly Review Press, 1974.
3. George Beckford. *Persistent Poverty: Underdevelopment in Plantation Economies of the Third World.* New York: Oxford University Press, 1972.
4. Norman Brown, ed. *Renewable Energy Resources and Rural Applications in the Developing World.* Denver: Westview Press, 1978.
5. Hollis Chenery and Moises Syrquin. *Patterns of Development 1950–1970.* New York: Oxford University Press, 1975.
6. Hollis Chenery, et al. *Redistribution with Growth.* London: Oxford University Press, 1974.
7. Charles Elliott. *Patterns of Poverty in the Third World.* New York: Praeger, 1975.
8. Arghiri Emmanuel. *Unequal Exchange.* London: New Left Books, 1972.
9. Charles Frank and Richard Webb, eds. *Income Distribution and Growth in the Less-Developed Countries.* Washington, D.C.: The Brookings Institution, 1977.
10. Denis Goulet. *The Cruel Choice: A New Concept in the Theory of Development.* New York: Atheneum, 1971.
11. Denis Goulet. *The Uncertain Promise: Value Conflicts in Technology Transfer.* New York: IDOC, 1977.
12. Keith Griffin. *Land Concentration and Rural Poverty.* New York: Homes & Meier, 1976.
13. Keith Griffin. *The Political Economy of Agrarian Change.* Cambridge, Mass.: Harvard University Press, 1974.
14. Mahbub Ui Haq. *The Poverty Curtain.* New York: Columbia University Press, 1976.
15. Irving Horowitz, ed. *Equity, Income, and Policy: Comparative Studies in Three Worlds of Development.* New York: Praeger, 1977.
16. International Labor Office. *Employment, Growth, and Basic Needs: A One-World Problem.* New York: Praeger, 1977.
17. John Mellor. *The New Economics of Growth.* Ithaca: N.Y.: Cornell University Press, 1976.
18. Theodore Moran. *Multinational Corporations and the Politics of Dependence: Copper in Chile.* Princeton: Princeton University Press, 1974.
19. Kathryn Morton and Peter Tulloch. *Trade and Developing Countries.* New York: John Wiley & Sons, 1977.
20. Edgar Owens and Robert Shaw. *Development Reconsidered: Bridging the Gap Between Government and People.* Lexington, Mass.: D. C. Heath, 1972.
21. Cheryl Payer. *The Debt Trap: The International Monetary Fund and the Third World.* New York: Monthly Review Press, 1974.
22. Ronald Ridker, ed. *Changing Resource Problems of the Fourth World.* Washington, D.C.: Resources for the Future, 1976.
23. Robert Rothstein. *The Weak in the World of the Strong.* New York: Columbia University Press, 1977.
24. Gordon Smith. *The External Debt Prospects of the Non–Oil-Exporting Developing Countries.* Washington, D.C.: Overseas Development Council, 1977.

25. Farvar Taghi and John Milton, eds. *Careless Technology: Ecology and International Development.* Garden City, N.Y.: The Natural History Press, 1972.
26. Louis Turner. *Multinational Corporations and the Third World.* New York: Hill & Wang, 1973.
27. Pierre Uri. *Development without Dependence.* New York: Praeger, 1976.

8

Toward a Global Perspective:
Some First Steps

Having analyzed the major ecopolitical issues and pressures that are leading to a new context for international relations, it remains to suggest what can be done to adjust to or even facilitate the paradigm shift that has now begun. Analysis of these problems in the absence of suggestions for taking action can lead to despair. Periods when value systems are overthrown and expectations are shattered are uncomfortable times. People sense that old beliefs and values are inappropriate guides for future behavior, but they find it difficult to attach themselves to new ones. And those vested interests who profit most within the existing paradigm can be expected actively to oppose efforts to change the established rules of the game.

There is no way that the rapid and complete transformation of world view that must take place over the next few decades can be simultaneously painless and meaningful. Very rapid change, catalyzed by the specter of scarcity, is necessary, but there will be few obvious and immediate rewards for proponents of the new paradigm.

The impetus for the impending great transition, unlike the industrial transformation that seduced through abundance, is coming from the gradual loss of the fossil fuel subsidy, the related inability to channel technological innovation in less fossil fuel–intensive directions, and the increasing disruption potential of the poor within and among nations. The vast majority of humanity finds itself running harder just to stay in place on an economic treadmill that signals the bankruptcy of the old way of looking at things. Energy prices continue to rise, and more capital is poured into technologically sophisticated and centralized alternative energy sources. In the near future, nonfuel minerals will increase in price as more energy is needed to mine and process less rich grades of ore. Even the price of food will rise if more expensive fertilizers are to be used to increase agricultural productivity. The basic causes of this syndrome of increased costs and related decline in perceived quality of life are well disguised and not fully understood by the individuals most affected. Scapegoats are blamed: the Arabs, the oil companies, greedy politicians, even the Communists. But until the central problems are identified and dealt with through the development of appropriate technologies and new social institutions, the world economy will remain in a condition of aimless drift and apparent loss of purpose.

Perceived problems such as these are normal for periods of rapid change in world view. L. S. Stavrianos likens the present era to that which preceded the fall of Rome. He sees four basic similarities between these two periods, including economic imperialism, ecological degradation, bureaucratic ossification, and flight from reason.[1] Both the Roman Empire and the Western European industrial empire were sustained by the subjugation of peripheral territories and degradation of physical environments. The parallels are striking. The industrial countries have lost their colonial sources of raw materials, and the new international economic order threatens to further exacerbate this loss. And the law of diminishing returns would seem to apply to future technological innovations built around more expensive and centralized energy sources.

While periods of paradigm shift are uncomfortable for many, the impending changes might well benefit the majority of human beings. Stavrianos sees great promise in the "coming dark age" because he sees it as an opportunity to reevaluate the basic tenets of the corrupt civilization that has grown out of the fossil fuel–based abundance. He argues that it is a problem of the "retarding lead" that hobbles the presently industrialized countries in developing creative responses to contemporary global problems. The less developed countries, in contrast, have not yet become locked into the growth syndrome based on fossil fuels and will, therefore, be able to adapt to new realities much easier than the "retarded" industrial countries, which are now plagued by the fact that their technological lead is not suited to the new world that is being created.[2] Thus, in the long run, the "backwardness" of many less developed countries may be to their advantage in adjusting to a postindustrial world.

HE DYNAMICS OF TRANSITION

Changes in human social systems are governed by two types of evolutionary processes, biological and social. If the parallels between these types of evolution are understood, directed social evolution can facilitate the transition to a new dominant social paradigm. Biological evolution takes place within a pool of genetic information that is passed from generation to generation through differential reproduction. Natural selection results from interactions between human genes and conditions in the physical and social environments. Those phenotypes that are in harmony with environmental conditions reproduce more successfully than those that are not. Natural selection is a slow process, and evolution within human gene pools takes place only over very long periods of time.

A parallel evolutionary process takes place within human cultures.[3] This sociocultural evolution occurs within the social paradigm that is passed from one generation to the next. The information and value content of the social paradigm is altered, but not wholly determined, by changing conditions in the physical and social environments. Sociocultural evolution also responds to society's "terminal values which have their own shaping capacity."[4] These preferred end-states can transcend physical realities and develop momentum of their own.

The major difference between biological and sociocultural evolution is that the latter is amenable to human understanding and control. Although a social paradigm may be very complex, it can be studied, evaluated, and modified by human efforts, since the socialization processes by which it is passed from generation to generation are understood.[5] The extent to which the contents of any social paradigm reflect valid evaluation of the existing physical and social worlds is related to the survival of the relevant civilizations.

Social paradigms are passed from generation to generation through mimicry, socialization, and learning experiences. Their contents normally change very slowly in response to the experiences of each generation—a complete transformation of any key political, social, or economic component of a social paradigm is likely to take longer than three generations.[6] During most of human history, physical and social environments have also changed very slowly and, over time, a basic congruence has usually been maintained between collective social beliefs and the physical and social worlds.

But history is also littered with the remains of civilizations and societies in which social belief systems did not give valid guidance for dealing with empirical reality. Divergence can occur if physical environments change more rapidly than social paradigms, if human activities alter these environments more rapidly than paradigms can adjust, or if the terminal values within a social paradigm shape human behavior in a way that is antithetical to survival. In other words, for a successful adjustment to be made to a changing world, a social paradigm must give valid survival information in conformity with real-world laws and conditions. If it does not, individuals who have internalized it may become alienated and experience cognitive dissonance when they follow laws, moral imperatives, and common wisdoms that lead to failure rather than to success.[7]

The aging dominant social paradigm is one within which both individuals and nations accept as a primary principle the inevitability and goodness of resource-intensive growth. The moral system within which this growth and abundance are to be secured is shaped by the pursuit of self-interest. In a world of rapid growth, the pursuit of self-interest and the absence of a supporting social principle may have been useful, but not necessarily morally desirable, as an organizing principle. But as real growth opportunities diminish, pursuit of self-interest can spark irreconcilable conflicts as easily as it contributes to any common good. It is now no longer obvious that each individual person or nation acting in perceived short-term self-interest can contribute to any collective welfare.[8] Self-interest of nations, or a "national interest" philosophy, has also been the organizing principle in international affairs. Within the industrial expansionist paradigm, the good of the international community of nations has been assumed to be maximized by self-seeking on the part of its members, at least self-seeking within a mutually acceptable set of rules. The balance of power tactics of the eighteenth and nineteenth centuries were predicated on individual actors acting only on their own behalf.

At the present time, the human race is at a fundamental turning point in its evolutionary history.[9] Technology has shaped a value system in which nations are to survive with a minimum of human intervention in what are perceived to be natural social processes. In part, this system is due to the perceived general increase in levels of affluence. Under rapid growth conditions, there was little reason to tinker with self-interest–centered institutions that seemed to be working so well. But during the last two decades of the twentieth century, the environmental constraints within which social evolution takes place have changed so rapidly that these old self-interest morals, values, beliefs, habits, and institutions, shaped in another era, increasingly lead to conflict. Humanity can continue to follow this laissez-faire noninterventionist evolutionary path for a considerable period of time without total self-destruction taking place. The rich and technologically advanced can continue to maintain their hold over the poor and technologically backward for sometime to come. But the eventual result will be the same as that which occurred in the Roman Empire. The expansion of the industrial period will inevitably be followed by a postindustrial contraction as the anomalies giving birth to a new international political and economic order become more intense. The presently industrialized world can postpone this birth of a new international paradigm, but the longer it is postponed, the more traumatic the labor pains will be.

This does not mean that the world will collapse in the very near future if the human race continues to follow its present course. World population, for example, will eventually stabilize, but through mass starvation rather than sensible family planning. The gap between rich and poor nations will narrow over time, but through conflict and pulling the rich down to the level of the poor rather than raising the levels of living for the poor. The world's energy problem can probably be solved by a crash program to build nuclear reactors, but this solution could well lead to authoritarian regimes made necessary by security problems.[10] In short, the present world can survive a few more decades if the industrial countries embrace lifeboat ethics and triage, selectively ridding the world of the most problematic populations, as principles of international conduct. But cutting off the world's less fortunate nations from the international community and denying them the provisions in industrial lifeboats—that is, economic assistance—could well create strife and terror for all as ever greater levels of repression would become necessary to keep hungry mobs from storming the lifeboats.[11]

An alternative path that is available to the human race is to intervene deliberately in social evolutionary processes and design a sustainable and equitable preferred future for the whole planet. This generation is the first to understand both the causes of human misery and its planetary dimensions. It is also the first to consider carefully directing science and technology to reach collective goals rather than simply adjusting society to technological imperatives.[12] The potential now exists for designing a preferred future for the planet as a whole and implementing a transition strategy, including a program to change deliberately the values governing international relations, for creating that future. As a shift in paradigms takes place, such a preferred future can be created by understanding those processes that are naturally taking place and using them to reach collective goals.[13]

A NEW VALUE PERSPECTIVE

In relations among nations, it can no longer be assumed that following a "natural" evolutionary path will lead to outcomes consonant with professed terminal values. A new way of looking at the international system, a new method for conducting relations among nations, is clearly needed if the impending human misery is to be minimized. But the new paradigm is now only in the early stages of development, and the pieces have not yet fallen into place.

One of these pieces is provided by Richard Sterling, who suggests a "macropolitical" perspective for future international relations. This perspective views the international system as a complex whole rather than a set of isolated individual actors. Macropolitical analysis begins "with the questions central to its global concerns: what is the international interest? . . . What policies and institutions appear to benefit all men, and what appear to benefit some but not others?"[14] This macropolitical perspective on international affairs is in direct conflict with the old national interest justifications for political actions that are a cornerstone of the present system.

The macropolitical perspective represents a significant departure from the one that has evolved during the centuries of industrial growth and abundance. It stresses the interdependence of all human beings. It leads to concern for the welfare of the whole rather than that of a few of the parts. Within this context, technological domination of the planet by a few industrial countries is not seen to be in the interest of all mankind. Most important, this perspective takes a holistic view of global problems and possible solutions. It helps individuals get beyond pure self-interest in making complex foreign policy decisions.

A macropolitical perspective in international affairs begins by stressing values as forces that should shape the evolution of international events rather than as simple products of this evolution. Among the values and objectives to be stressed within a macropolitical paradigm are equity, compassion, empathy, and meeting the basic human needs of all human beings before catering to the wants of a small minority. The principal goal is to maximize the welfare of all human beings in both present and future generations. The macropolitical perspective is a utopian one that will not be immediately accepted. But as the impending paradigm shift gathers momentum, the value context governing international relations will also begin changing in response to changes in the social and physical environments.

The shift toward a macropolitical, or global, perspective that is now under way has implications for all nations, both internally and in international relations. For the industrial countries that import large quantities of fuels, minerals, and food, the new value context will focus attention on their overconsumption. The key problem for them will be one of coping with future price increases and shortages and bringing consumption patterns into line with new physical realities. For the less developed countries, the most important task is to avoid the pitfalls inherent in the old view of modernization and growth. They must plan for sustainable growth in a world in which petroleum and natural gas are no longer cheaply available and adjust their development programs accordingly. Internationally, a new planetary agreement must be forged that will lead to increased opportunities for the less developed nations to meet the basic needs of all their citizens.[15] Such an agreement must also make provisions for changing the values shaping the present international political and economic order and move it away from principles of self-interest and competition to ethical principles, including human needs, cooperation, and concern for future global welfare.

Facilitating and smoothing the future rapid social, economic, and political changes requires both a vision of preferred futures and a transition strategy for reaching them. A vigorous debate is already under way on the nature of preferred futures.[16] While the visions are varied, a common value core is developing that includes maximizing human welfare, social justice, and environmental integrity while minimizing conflict among peoples and nations.[17] But utopian visions in the absence of a concrete transition strategy through which a new international order can be created are not particularly useful. Such a strategy must adequately take account of the dynamics that underlie the present system and suggest the short-term and long-term policies that can change these dynamics.[18] Individual values and beliefs must also change as part of this strategy. In most cases, this simply means creating a supportive environment within which people can live up to the values that they already profess. It also implies taking a long-range view of human survival prospects within the present international order, a view that should make even the most hardened self-interest cases see that their long-term self-interest is best served by a rapid change in established behavior patterns. It is said that *Homo sapiens* differs from other species by virtue of his rationality, his ability to conceptualize and plan, and his tendency to introduce ethical and moral considerations into social and political life. It remains to be seen whether these assets can be harnessed in the creation of a new global perspective within which it will be possible to solve the ecopolitical problems of the twenty-first century.

THE INDUSTRIAL AGENDA

A new international political and economic order must attend to the problems of narrowing the gap between rich nations and poor, increasing perceived "fairness" in relations between industrial and nonindustrial countries, and halting the dangerous drift toward nuclear anarchy and terrorism on the part of those who perceive themselves to have no stake in the system.[19] All of this must take place within the constraints of a long-term sustainable growth paradigm rather than within the continued undifferentiated growth and resource-intensive industrial paradigm. As Eduard Pestel and Mihajlo Mesarovic have put it, "It is this [past] pattern of unbalanced and undifferentiated growth which is at the heart of the most urgent problems facing humanity—and the path which leads to a solution is that of organic growth."[20] But organic growth requires subscribing to a macropolitical master plan that has implications for all nations.

It is impossible to map out all of the details of a master plan for a global paradigm shift in this brief chapter. That is a task for another complete book. But there are dozens of short-range, medium-range, and long-range proposals for reshaping the international order that have been suggested elsewhere and that are worth addressing. An attempt is made here only to identify an agenda of *most pressing* critical problems that an ecopolitical analysis suggests and to outline some possibilities for dealing with them from a macropolitical perspective. Such an agenda consists of at least three separate sets of tasks to be accomplished on three different levels. First, the industrial countries must begin to put constraints or ceilings on the consumption of certain nonrenewable raw materials and to direct the growth of technology to meet basic human needs outside of increasing dependence on fossil fuels. Second, the nonindustrial countries must abandon their attempt to mimic the development path previously followed by presently developed countries.[21] An attempt to follow their lead will ultimately cause failure and disillusionment in most cases. For the less developed countries, it is a matter of finding creative alternatives to the industrialization model that has been thrust upon them by the colonial experience.[22] Finally, new international arrangements and institutions can be suggested to solve those problems that cannot be handled by individual countries or by existing international machinery.[23]

Many of the world's industrially developed countries now live too far beyond the limits of their current carrying capacity. There are too many people living at high levels of natural resource consumption in these countries. The solution to this dilemma within the old international economic order has been the export of high-technology products to less developed countries in return for raw materials. But the colonies that once provided these raw materials are gone and, as the new international economic order gathers strength, the terms of trade that favored high-technology products may soon be turned around. Thus, industrial countries may soon be experiencing a decline in perceived quality of life because of rising resource prices.

The dependence of many industrial countries on others for nonrenewable resources continues to grow, and this uneven growth in natural resource consumption has serious implications for the future of planetary stability. Energy- and resource-intensive growth must be turned around. This does not mean that everyone in industrial countries must return immediately to living by current solar income alone. A return to the land and an agrarian style of life in these countries would surely result in mass starvation. But it does mean that social and technological innovation should be directed at new efficiencies in using natural resources. Future development in industrial countries must also focus on an increase in the *quality* of life rather than just *quantity*. Progress within a new social paradigm might be defined as the amount of output or satisfaction per unit of energy or other natural resource expended instead of per man-hour worked.

The agenda for industrial countries includes planning and designing future growth to require less energy and fewer resources. Cutbacks in energy consumption can be justified on both ethical and realistic grounds. From a *realpolitik* perspective, such cutbacks are necessary in these countries to stem increasing balance of payments problems. Without more judicious use of key natural resources, rising prices for them could lead to a diminution of overall quality of life even while measured gross national products apparently would continue to grow. But most important, from an ethical perspective, conservation actions taken by industrial countries could be interpreted by less developed countries as a sign that the industrial world is heeding demands for more equity in using the world's production of nonrenewable resources.

The recent record on energy consumption in industrial countries is not a good one. Energy conservation figures for 1975 show that the industrial countries collectively were 14 percent below the level of energy consumption projected by relying on 1968–1973 growth rates.[24] But by 1976, most industrial countries had adjusted economic processes to higher energy prices and were continuing along their normal growth paths in energy consumption. The United States increased energy consumption by 4.8 percent. Furthermore, much of the energy saved in 1974–1975 came from depressed economic activity. When total use of energy is compared with gross domestic product, a much different picture emerges. The energy intensiveness of gross domestic product declined only slightly in the industrial countries in the 1973–1975 period. In Canada, Spain, the United States, and Switzerland energy intensiveness of productivity either remained the same or actually increased during this period.[25]

The United States is particularly noteworthy as a heavy consumer of world natural resource production. At present, the population of the United States consumes nearly twice as much energy on a per capita basis as do those of other countries situated at similar levels of development. In Sweden, for example, a quality of life equal to or exceeding that in the United States requires a per capita energy consumption only 49 percent of that in the United States. The main difference between the two countries is found in transportation, where 24,025 kilowatt hours of energy equivalent are consumed per capita in the United States and only 7350 kilowatt hours are consumed per capita in Sweden.[26] New transportation alternatives, better automobile mileage, better construction and insulation of homes, limits on decorative and commercial lighting, and new energy efficiencies in industry could substantially reduce US energy consumption.[27] The economy can grow at acceptable rates without an increase in total energy consumption.[28] Other industrial countries have similar opportunities. A study of Denmark's energy future, for example, indicates that all needs could be met from renewable energy resources by the year 2000.[29]

Even if growth in energy consumption cannot be halted, there are other methods by which industrial countries can build more energy autarky and less developed countries can avoid the pitfalls of energy dependence. Amory Lovins has suggested scenarios in which projected growth in world energy consumption could be handled by nonnuclear technologies primarily based upon recurring current solar income. This would obviate the need for increased reliance on oil and natural gas imports as well as for proliferation of nuclear reactors with their attendant risks. Lovins claims that even the Japanese, now considered to be desperately short of land and energy, could take advantage of solar energy, offshore winds, geothermal, tidal, and seathermal power and meet their energy needs from renewable sources.[30] On a global scale, Lovins argues for launching an international effort to avoid the pitfalls of nuclear power through a concerted effort to develop "soft energy technologies" that could meet future energy needs for most nations.[31]

While fuels are the most important nonrenewable resource to be conserved, some nonfuel minerals also present depletion and rising cost problems in the medium and long term. Economist Herman Daly has suggested both the desirability and the necessity of establishing "steady-state" economies, first in the overdeveloped and eventually in the presently less developed countries. A steady-state economy is an economy "with constant stocks of people and artifacts, maintained at some desired, sufficient levels by low rates of maintenance throughput."[32] He argues that only over the last two hundred years has the human race moved away from something resembling a steady-state economy. The present concept of growth in life quality is measured by flows of resources (GNP) rather than by stocks (wealth). Thus, progress has been equated with resource consumption rather than with existing economic wealth.

While not everyone would agree with Daly's utopian economic ideas, his suggestions that overdeveloped industrial economies seek to minimize throughput of raw materials while sustaining relatively constant stocks of people and artifacts is a good one. It is not clear that all natural resources are in equally scarce supply, nor is it clear that constant stocks of people and artifacts can yet be an accepted social goal. But within a postindustrial paradigm, new technological breakthroughs will certainly permit people to do more with less and thus sustain growth in stocks while holding constant or even decreasing the use of nonrenewable resources.

Conservation of nonrenewable and scarce natural resources combined with increased use of renewable ones is a viable alternative growth path that most industrial countries could now begin to follow. But it does imply a reversal of the historical momentum toward increased natural resource–intensive development. This change, in turn, requires education, planning, political will, a transition strategy, and a value perspective that stresses the logic and ethics of sustainable growth principles.[33] Industrial growth concepts have been created and internalized in an era of natural resource abundance. Now that this abundance is much less assured, it is only prudent to use our understanding of social evolution to begin to deflect industrial civilization from its present dangerous developmental path.

There are other steps that can be taken to diminish the gaps between the rich and poor nations. Aid programs must be expanded so that a much more significant fraction of gross national product in industrial countries is transferred to those countries in greatest need.[34] Further, aid should not be given for military purposes or tied to purchases from donor countries. It should be devoted to development projects giving priority to meeting basic human needs. First on the list of these needs is an adequate diet and decent shelter. Whereas past aid programs have benefited a very small class in the less developed countries in the belief that wealth would trickle down to the poor, new aid programs should stress the economic and political participation of the poor in determining development priorities.

Steps should also be taken to curb the transfer of "inappropriate" technologies to the less developed countries. The definition of "inappropriate" is informed by the ecopolitical perspective developed previously. Energy-intensive industrialization should be discouraged in countries where there is unlikely to be a domestic source of or easy access to fossil fuels over the middle range. E. F. Schumacher has used the terms "appropriate" or "intermediate" to describe the small-scale labor-intensive technologies that should be essential aspects of development efforts in many countries.[35] It is desirable for industrial countries to use their research and development institutions to create and to export technologies that are more suited to a frugal future, both from the perspective of their customers and in their own self-interest in capturing future markets.

Finally, domestic political pressures in industrial countries must not be permitted to subvert altruistic moves in foreign assistance. The next few decades will be characterized by many economic dislocations within the industrial countries, and these will generate heavy protectionist pressures from politically powerful interest groups. These pressures must be resisted, and preferential treatment must be given to imports from less developed countries if they are ever to be able to acquire necessary development capital. This admittedly will require significant educational efforts aimed at exposing inequities in the present structure of trade as well as demonstrating the growing interdependence of both rich and poor countries.

THE THIRD WORLD: INITIATIVES AND PRESCRIPTIONS

While much can be done by the industrial countries to help give birth to a new international order, the less developed countries have responsibilities of their own. The most important principle for Third World development should be increased self-reliance. Self-reliant development means rejecting simple imitations of the processes that have taken place in industrial countries. The dynamics of development for Third World countries in a world of rising energy and other resource prices must, of necessity, be different from those characteristic of the countries that developed early. Each developing nation should finance much future growth with its own domestic natural resources. For many countries, this will mean following development paths that are much different than those now being pursued. But a *quality* life can be built in these countries without falling into the *quantity* and material consumption trap of contemporary industrialization.

Self-reliance also implies greater concern with social justice and institutional change. In poor countries, development efforts should be devoted to meeting the basic human needs of all persons before the wants of the dominant few. Capital accumulation and trickle-down theories of development should be set aside, along with imitative development approaches.[36] In many less developed countries, distribution of available wealth is much more inegalitarian than it is in the industrial world. These grave disparities must be eliminated before demands for increased transfers of wealth from the industrial world can be morally justified. In other words, human development stressing economic and political participation by the many, rather than only the few, should be a primary goal of development. And there can be little doubt that such changes will require painful and sometimes bloody social adjustments.

Increased cooperation among Third World countries is another dimension of self-reliance. The recent proliferation of regional and international organizations offers them a new environment within which to launch cooperative ventures.[37] One of the areas that is ripe for cooperation is economic integration. The Latin American Andean Pact, although far from perfect, is an example of a prototype common market agreement with great potential.[38] These types of agreements in other regions and perhaps the establishment of global Third World trade agreements would go far toward reducing economic dependence on industrial countries.

Third World cooperation in scientific research and development could also facilitate self-reliant development. There are many scientific research and development efforts that could attack problems common to all less developed countries, but these undertakings require a minimum critical mass of scholars, large financial risks in relation to the scope of Third World economies, or profit from economies of scale.[39] Joint Third World scientific research projects tailored to Third World needs can overcome these problems and are an important way of avoiding the technological domination by industrially advanced countries that is characteristic of the old international economic order.

Self-reliant development also suggests, as noted earlier, an emphasis on "appropriate" or "intermediate" technologies. While there are no precise definitions of what appropriate technologies are, they do represent an alternative to the energy- and capital-intensive technologies developed in industrialized countries, where labor has been scarce and expensive and capital and energy have been relatively abundant. Labor-saving machines and large factories may well be inappropriate in most Third and Fourth World countries. By the same token, free markets, piecework incentive systems, and assembly lines may not lead to an increase in the overall quality of life in these countries. What has worked in one setting (Western Europe) may very well be inappropriate within a completely different set of cultural constraints.

Most descriptions of appropriate technologies describe them as labor-intensive, decentralized, easy to repair and understand, non–energy- and capital-intensive, and simple to construct. Intermediate technologies are suited for the less developed countries because labor is abundant and capital and sophisticated expertise are in short supply. When modern advanced industrial technologies are transplanted into less developed environments they are likely to operate under conditions for which they were not designed—an expensive mistake. Adopting sophisticated technologies usually means concentrating on a few large plants while the rest of the economy falters. While the few modern plants in such an economy may reap big profits, this does not necessarily mean that profits for the country as a whole will necessarily be greater.

A useful distinction can be made between technological hardware and software or apparatus and technique.[40] Hardware and apparatus refer to the physical objects that are employed in production, such as tractors, roads, machines, and so on. Software and technique refer to the less tangible aspects of production, such as knowledge, education, experience, marketing systems, communications, incentives, and organization. In contemporary less developed countries, growth policy must stress both appropriate hardware and appropriate technique.

It may also be inappropriate for many less developed countries to attempt heavy industrialization on a large scale. The abundant resources in many Third and Fourth World countries are land and labor. Under these conditions, it may make more sense to devise strategies to keep people on the land and develop a vigorous agricultural sector accompanied by cottage industries.[41] While this development strategy lacks the "glamour" of heavy industrialization and automation, it has a more immediate payoff: it focuses on meeting the most basic of human needs and is a sustainable type of development that cannot be undermined by external forces. Certain aspects of the Chinese model of development, with its emphasis on reduced vertical division of labor, local self-reliance, and full employment of the entire work force are certainly worthy of further study, if not emulation, in many less developed countries.[42]

Finally, perhaps the most essential component of self-reliant development is use of renewable energy resources. The less developed countries can ill afford to become dependent upon OPEC petroleum during the coming decades of rising prices and international competition for fuels. Since most of these countries have no significant fossil fuel reserves at all, the answer may lie in their exploitation of energy sources already in their possession.[43] For example, many less developed countries are located in semitropical areas, ideal locations for using solar energy for heating, cooking, and eventually production of electricity. In areas where solar energy cannot be tapped effectively, biogasification is an economically feasible alternative.[44] Hydroelectric power and electricity from windmills are other alternatives that could help the less developed countries avoid the pitfalls of fossil fuel–intensive development.

Finally, there are changes that can take place only through new international arrangements. In some sectors, nations have become so interdependent or issues have become so complex as to require completely new sets of rules and arrangements. To use Nye and Keohane's terminology, a change in international regimes must take place.[45] Two of these areas in which change must take place soon are nuclear proliferation and global food policy. As a more general paradigm shift in international relations takes place, there will undoubtedly be many other areas in which other changes will occur. In the case of nuclear proliferation, the old rules governing transfer of technologies that could lead to fabrication of nuclear weapons broke down in the mid-1970s. No new set of agreements has yet arisen to take their place. This is a case of technological development outstripping the capacity of the existing regime to cope. A global food regime is also now needed where none has existed in the past because of added population pressures and changes in the physical environment, such as less available land and likely climatological shifts over the next few decades.

The need for a new set of rules and arrangements in the nuclear field arises from the rapid pace of development in nuclear technology, the impossibility of segregating peaceful and military applications, the powerful economic incentives for exporting dangerous technologies, and the relative weakness of existing control mechanisms. In its present state, the International Atomic Energy Agency is neither powerful enough nor adequately staffed to check nuclear proliferation violations. Nor is the Non-Proliferation Treaty an adequate document to insure against the spread of nuclear weapons.[46] Many key nations have not yet ratified the document and are unlikely to do so. And the sanctions for violating the spirit of the agreement are not clear.

One solution to this dilemma might be to explore international cooperation in separating the weapons-creating technologies from nuclear sales in general by developing regional enrichment and reprocessing centers. Many of the less developed countries will never build enough nuclear reactors to justify economically domestic reprocessing facilities.[47] The decision to build reprocessing facilities could arise from fear of being cut off from reprocessing facilities in industrial countries or from a desire to develop weapons capability. In the latter case, nuclear technology should definitely not be transferred under any circumstances. In the former case, geographically dispersed reprocessing facilities under international supervision might alleviate the fears driving such countries to develop costly domestic facilities.

There are several prerequisites for the establishment of any international regime to handle enrichment and reprocessing. First, such facilities must service an adequate number of reactors to make their operation viable. Second, the International Atomic Energy Agency, or an equivalent organization, must be upgraded and adequately staffed to oversee the operations. Third, there must be adequate geographical distribution of the facilities so as to guarantee an uninterrupted supply of reprocessed fuel to states subscribing to the agreement. Fourth, the location of these facilities must be politically acceptable to those countries that might otherwise develop their own. And finally, a decision must be made on the disposition of plutonium accumulated from reprocessing.[48]

There are formidable obstacles to the acceptance of such an agreement. The surrender of such authority to an international organization requires a dramatic change in perspective on the part of both exporting and importing countries. Perhaps fear of nuclear proliferation can foster such a change. Exporters must agree to forego an immediate economic gain in the interest of long-term stability. Importers must trust the international organization to protect their interests. And all countries must adequately support the institution in charge of overseeing the arrangements.

The world food market is a second area in which basic changes are needed. The need for a new regime stems from the growth of a global food market, rapid increases in population, and predictions that the next few decades may be characterized by climate instabilities. Possibilities for significant crop failures will increase as more marginal land is brought into production. More important, however, are suggestions by climatologists that indicate that the period 1930–1970 might well have been one of the best in recent history for agricultural production from a climatological point of view. As late as 1850, the Northern Hemisphere was recovering from a "Little Ice Age" that began nearly three hundred years earlier. Since 1850, however, an apparent warming trend has produced weather that is optimal for world food production. The sudden return of cold winters in the 1970s could be part of a temperature shift back toward the more "normal" cooler periods that have been common throughout recent history.[49] If this is the case, or even if only wider fluctuations in temperatures from year to year result from these shifts, world food production is likely to be significantly impaired.

Many suggestions have been made for an international granary to overcome the problem of periodic crop shortages. Some people have come up with schemes to prevent famine in poor countries during periods of international production shortfalls. These plans include aid arrangements that provide for meeting crop shortfalls in less developed countries before food is sold on the international market.[50] Philip Trezise has suggested that there are six points that must be considered when setting up such an international grain reserve. The first is to determine the optimal size and composition of the reserve. The second is to determine membership. Third, the cost of carrying the reserves, if any, must be apportioned. Fourth, someone must be appointed to carry out managerial responsibilities. Fifth, some provision must be made for a famine reserve for less developed countries. Finally, national farm policies must be coordinated with the international reserve.[51]

The main obstacle to the establishment of a world food regime is inertia. During the shortfall years when world food stocks were down, there was a flurry of international concern over this issue. But bad years have always been followed by years of abundance, and as stocks are rebuilt the problem no longer seems pressing. At some point in the very near future, however, a longer string of bad years could catch the world totally unprepared, and a tremendous human toll could be exacted because of this neglect.

These suggestions for new international regimes represent only a sample, albeit an important one, of international initiatives that could be taken to deflect the planet from the very dangerous course that is now being followed. They are not particularly utopian and depend mainly on an expanded perception of self-interest. They do not require a high degree of idealism among the actors involved. Thus, creating a new post-industrial paradigm is not only a matter of wishing that people would become more decent. It is an incremental process dependent not only on concern for the welfare for all human beings but also on creating a new appreciation of how pursuing short-term self-interest can lead to longer-term self-defeat.

The aim of this book has been to clarify a number of international problems by viewing them from an ecopolitical perspective. Understanding this complex network of interrelated problems and suggesting a range of ethical and humane solutions to them represent two steps in moving toward a new global consciousness. What is now lacking is the political determination to implement some of these solutions, particularly when the short-term advantages of some of them may not be shared equally by all parties involved. Perhaps this third step can be taken only when the folly of trying to patch up the outmoded industrial paradigm becomes obvious through the problems and anomalies that it continues to create. By that time, perhaps, support will have grown for a new and more ethical international order, and this vision of a new order will help ease the pains of the coming transition.

ENDNOTES

1. L. S. Stavrianos, *The Promise of the Coming Dark Age* (San Francisco: W. H. Freeman, 1976), chap. 1. See also Roberto Vacca, *The Coming Dark Age* (Garden City, N. Y.: Anchor Books, 1974).
2. Stavrianos, *The Promise*, pp. 181–196.
3. See C. H. Waddington, *The Ethical Animal* (London: George Allen & Unwin, 1960), chaps. 10 and 11.
4. The nature of terminal values is discussed in Milton Rokeach, *The Nature of*

Human Values (New York: The Free Press, 1973), pp. 11–17.

5. See Dennis Pirages, ed., *The Sustainable Society* (New York: Praeger, 1977), introduction.

6. Attempts were made in socialist (Communist) countries to alter key economic components of the dominant social paradigms when Communist parties took power. The evidence that is available shows that it is only in the third generation that new values begin to take hold. Some social strata are much more resistant than others, however. See Dennis Pirages, *Modernization and Political Tension Management* (New York: Praeger, 1972), chap. 3.

7. See Leon Festinger, *A Theory of Cognitive Dissonance* (Evanston, Ill: Row-Peterson, 1957).

8. See Fred Hirsch, *Social Limits to Growth* (Cambridge, Mass: Harvard University Press, 1976), p. 12.

9. See Mihajlo Mesarovic and Eduard Pestel, *Mankind at the Turning Point* (New York: E. P. Dutton, 1974).

10. Garrett Hardin, "Living with the Faustian Bargain," *Bulletin of the Atomic Scientists* (November 1976).

11. See Garrett Hardin, "Lifeboat Ethics: The Case Against Helping the Poor," *Psychology Today* (September 1974), and Garrett Hardin, "Carrying Capacity as an Ethical Concept," in G. R. Lucas, Jr., and T. W. Ogletree, eds., *Lifeboat Ethics: The Moral Dilemmas of Hunger* (New York: Harper & Row, 1976).

12. See Jerome Frank, "Galloping Technology, A New Social Disease," *Journal of Social Issues* (Winter 1966.)

13. William Ophuls makes a distinction between planning and design. Planning refers to active management of a process, whereas design refers to establishing criteria to govern operations of a process so that the desired result will occur without further human intervention. See William Ophuls, *Ecology and the Politics of Scarcity* (San Francisco: W. H. Freeman, 1977), pp. 228–229, and Pirages, ed., *The Sustainable Society*, introduction.

14. Richard Sterling, *Macropolitics* (New York: Knopf, 1974), p. 6.

15. See Harland Cleveland, *The Planetary Bargain* (Aspen, Col.: Aspen Institute for Humanistic Studies, 1975).

16. See, among others, Saul Mendlovitz, ed., *On the Creation of a Just World Order* (New York: The Free Press, 1975), and Richard Falk, *A Study of Future Worlds* (New York: The Free Press, 1975).

17. These goals have evolved from the multinational World Order Models project, which has extended over the last decade and has represented an attempt by scholars from many cultures to formulate a common list of objectives.

18. See Davis B. Bobrow, "Transitions to Preferred Worlds: Some Design Considerations," and George Kent, "Political Design," in Louis Beres and Harry Targ, eds., *Planning Alternative World Futures* (New York: Praeger, 1975).

19. Harland Cleveland has called for a global fairness revolution based on a new world order. *The Planetary Bargain*, p. 3.

20. Mesarovic and Pestel, *Mankind at the Turning Point*, p. 7.

21. See Amilcar Herrera, et al., *Catastrophe or New Society? A Latin American World Model* (Ottawa: International Development Research Center, 1976).

22. See Paul Streeten, "Alternatives in Development," *World Development* (February 1974).

23. See Jan Tinbergen, *Reshaping the International Order* (New York: E. P. Dutton, 1976).

24. Organization for Economic Cooperation and Development, *Energy Conservation in Member States* (Paris, 1976), p. 14.

25. Ibid.

26. Lee Schipper and Allan Lichtenberg, "Efficient Energy Use and Well-Being: The Swedish Example," *Science* (December 3, 1976).

27. See Robert Williams, ed., *The Energy Conservation Papers* (Cambridge, Mass: Ballinger, 1975).

28. See the zero energy growth scenario sketched out in S. David Freeman, et al., *A Time to Choose* (Cambridge, Mass: Ballinger, 1974), chap. 4.

29. Bent Sorensen, "Energy and Resources," *Science* (July 25, 1975).

30. Amory Lovins and John Price, *Non-Nuclear Futures* (Cambridge, Mass.: Ballinger, 1975), introduction.

31. Amory Lovins, "Energy Strategy: The Road Not Taken?" *Foreign Affairs* (October 1976). See also Amory Lovins, *Soft Energy Paths: Toward a Durable Peace* (Cambridge, Mass.: Ballinger, 1977), and Denis Hayes, *Rays of Hope: The Transition to a Post-Petroleum World* (New York: W. W. Norton, 1977).

32. Herman Daly, *Steady-State Economics* (San Francisco: W. H. Freeman, 1977), p. 17.

33. See the essays in Pirages, ed., *The Sustainable Society*. See also Dennis Meadows, ed., *Alternatives to Growth I* (Cambridge, Mass.: Ballinger, 1977).

34. That these gaps will not be closed by current aid policies is documented by Wassily Leontief, et al., *The Future of the World Economy* (New York: Oxford University Press, 1977).

35. E. F. Schumacher, *Small Is Beautiful* (New York: Harper & Row, 1973), pp. 161–179.

36. See Pugwash Symposium, "The Role of Self-Reliance in Alternative Strategies for Development," *World Development* (March 1977). See also Samuel Parmar, "Self-Reliant Development in an 'Interdependent' World," in Guy Erb and Valeriana Kallab, eds., *Beyond Dependency* (Washington, D.C.: Overseas Development Council, 1975).

37. See H. Jon Rosenbaum and William Tyler, "South-South Relations: The Economic and Political Content of Interactions among Developing Countries," *International Organization* (Winter 1975).

38. Ricardo French-Davis, "The Andean Pact: A Model of Economic Integration for Developing Countries," *World Development* (January-February 1977).

39. Francisco Sagasti, "Technological Self-Reliance and Cooperation among Third World Countries," *World Development* (October-November 1976).

40. See Nicolas Jequier, ed., *Appropriate Technology: Problems and Promises* (Paris: Organization for Economic Cooperation and Development, 1976), p. 21. See also Langdon Winners, *Autonomous Technology* (Cambridge, Mass.: MIT Press, 1977), pp. 11–12.

41. This is the strategy suggested by John Mellor, *The New Economics of Growth* (Ithaca, N. Y.: Cornell University Press, 1976).

42. Johan Galtung and Fumiko Nishimura, "Can We Learn from the Chinese

People?" *World Development* (October-November 1976).

43. See Alan Strout, "Energy and the Less Developed Countries: Needs for Additional Research," in Ronald Ridker, ed., *Changing Resource Problems of the Fourth World* (Baltimore: Johns Hopkins University Press, 1976).
44. Arjun Makhijani, *Energy and Agriculture in the Third World,* (Cambridge, Mass.: Ballinger, 1975).
45. Robert Keohane and Joseph Nye, *Power and Interdependence* (Boston: Little, Brown, 1977), pp. 19–20.
46. See Brian Johnson, "Whose Power to Choose?" (Essex, England: The International Institute for Environment and Development, 1977).
47. Mark Sharefkin, "The Simple, Uncertain Economics of Multinational Reprocessing Centers," in Abram Chayes and W. Bennett Lewis, eds., *International Arrangements for Nuclear Fuel Reprocessing* (Cambridge, Mass.: Ballinger, 1977).
48. Constance Smith and Abram Chayes, "Institutional Arrangements for a Multinational Reprocessing Plant," in Chayes and Lewis, eds., *International Arrangements for Nuclear Fuel Reprocessing.*
49. See Stephen Schneider, *The Genesis Strategy* (New York: Plenum, 1976), chap. 3, and Reid Bryson and Thomas Murray, *Climates of Hunger* (Madison, Wisc.: University of Wisconsin Press, 1977), chap. 6.
50. Alexander Sarris and Lance Taylor, "Cereal Stocks, Food Aid and Food Security for the Poor," *World Development* (December 1976).
51. Philip Trezise, *Rebuilding Grain Reserves* (Washington, D. C., The Brookings Institution, 1976).

SUGGESTED READINGS

1. Louis Beres and Harry Targ, eds. *Planning Alternative World Futures.* New York: Praeger, 1975.
2. Lester Brown. *World without Borders.* New York: Random House, 1972.
3. Abram Chayes and W. Bennett Lewis. *International Arrangements for Nuclear Fuel Reprocessing.* Cambridge, Mass.: Ballinger, 1977.
4. Herman Daly. *Steady-State Economics.* San Francisco: W. H. Freeman, 1977.
5. Richard Eckaus. *Appropriate Technologies for Developing Countries.* Washington, D. C.: National Academy of Sciences, 1977.
6. Richard Falk. *A Study of Future Worlds.* New York: The Free Press, 1975.
7. Denis Hayes. *Rays of Hope: The Transition to a Post Petroleum World.* New York: W. W. Norton, 1977.
8. Amilcar Herrera, et al. *Catastrophe or New Society? A Latin American World Model.* Ottawa: International Development Research Center, 1976.
9. Nicolas Jéquier, ed. *Appropriate Technology: Problems and Promises.* Paris: OECD, 1976.
10. Amory Lovins. *Soft Energy Paths: Toward a Durable Peace.* Cambridge, Mass.: Ballinger, 1977.
11. Arjun Makhijani. *Energy and Agriculture in the Third World.* Cambridge, Mass.: Ballinger, 1975.
12. Saul Mendlovitz, ed. *On the Creation of a Just World Order.* New York: The Free Press, 1975.

13. Gerald Mische and Patricia Mische. *Toward a Human World Order: Beyond the National Security Straitjacket.* New York: Paulist Press, 1977.
14. Talbot Page. *Conservation and Economic Efficiency: An Approach to Materials Policy.* Baltimore: Johns Hopkins University Press, 1977.
15. Dennis Pirages, ed. *The Sustainable Society.* New York: Praeger, 1977.
16. E. F. Schumacher. *Small Is Beautiful.* New York: Harper & Row, 1973.
17. L. S. Stavrianos. *The Promise of the Coming Dark Age.* San Francisco: W. H. Freeman, 1976.
18. Richard Sterling. *Macropolitics.* New York: Knopf, 1974.
19. Frances Stewart. *Technology and Underdevelopment.* Denver: Westview Press, 1977.
20. Robert Stivers. *The Sustainable Society: Ethics and Economic Growth.* Philadelphia: The Westminster Press, 1976.
21. Jan Tinbergen. *Reshaping the International Order.* New York: E. P. Dutton, 1976.
22. Philip Trezise. *Rebuilding Grain Reserves: Toward an International System.* Washington, D.C.: The Brookings Institution, 1976.

INDEX

Ecopolitics: 32–40; definition of, 5, 30; and ecoconflicts, 68–69; foundations of, 29–32

Ecosphere: 31

Ehrlich, Paul and Anne: 14–15

Emmanuel, Arghiri: 240–241

Energy: 14; alternative sources of, 34–37, 133; conservation, 265–266, 268; and energy self-sufficient nations, 123, 124; and fertilizer, 95–96; and growth, 120–121, 187–188; politics, 110–141; and price rises, 11; renewable resources of, 270; shortages, 8–9

Engel's law: 232

Entropy law: 113–114

Ethical considerations: 261; and development planning, 227–228; and energy conservation, 265; and food production, 6; and industrialization, 249; and macropolitical perspective, 262–264; and technological imperialism, 185, 186–189

Etzioni, Amitai: 34

Eurodif: and nuclear power, 208

Expansionism: 12, 23–29, 184–185, 186

Famines: 14, 76, 78

Fertilizers: 188

Finland: population of, 20

Fishing: 84, 86–87, 88; by Japan, 190; regulation of, 200–201, 202; and technology, 188–189

Food production: 6, 15, 66–68, 272–273; and agricultural self-sufficiency, 85; and available land, 90–93; and climate changes, 75, 98–102; and consumption, 78–84; and energy crisis, 95–98; and environmental destruction, 188; and export crops, 77–78, 85, 88, 232–236; and ghost acreage, 84–88; politics of, 74–102; shortages, 94–98; technology of, 94–98; and ultimate constraints, 88–102; and water, 93–94; and world food market, 75–88

Ford, Gerald: 67

Foreign aid: 238, 239, 241–244, 267

Fossil fuels: 110, 111; basic constraints of, 113–141; consumption of, 25; and industrialization, 184; scarcity of, 112

Fourth World: 131, 173–174, 244, 247

France: agriculture in, 80; as colonizer, 26, 48; and nuclear power, 36

Future: strategy for, 262, 263–264, 264–268

Germany, East: population of, 20

Germany, West: agricultural imports of, 85

Gold production: 167–168

Goodin, Robert: 187

Gravitational energy sources: 110

Great Britain: as colonizer, 26, 48; as nuclear power, 36; and oil, 117; and trade, 85, 191, 195

Greenhouse effect: 100

Griffin, Keith: 238

Growth dilemma: 8; and limits to growth, 60–62, 63–64, 174

Hardin, Garrett: 186, 187, 200

Harman, Willis: 8, 11

Hoffman, Stanley: 33

Honduras: population of, 20

Hood, Robin: 131

Hubbert, M. King: 115

Hueckel, Glenn: 226

Human rights: 31, 65–68; and adequate food, 74; basic, 267; and industrialization, 249; and mineral scarcities, 177; and Rhodesia, 166

Icebergs: towing of, 94

Imperialism: and Agricultural Revolution, 5

India: agriculture in, 80, 81, 85; development in, 238; malnutrition in, 77; as nuclear power, 36, 211

Indonesia: oil in, 127, 139

Industrial expansionist paradigm: 261

Industrial Revolution: 4–5, 8; and energy, 110, 120; and expansionism, 11, 12, 24, 26, 29; and fossil fuels, 16; and population growth, 20; results of, 10, 12, 14, 39, 184–185

Industrialization: 222–251; and appropriate technologies, 267–268, 269–270; and ecopolitics, 185–215;

construction, 204–206; and reactor exports, 189, 206–207, 210–211; and reprocessing of fuel, 208–209, 271–272

Nuclear weapons: 33, 34, 36, 189; control of, 213–214, 271; production of, 203, 209, 211, 212–214

Nye, Joseph: 17, 30, 54, 271

Oceanic resources: 200–202

Oil. See Petroleum

Organization of Petroleum Exporting Countries (OPEC): 155; as cartel, 148, 149, 151; and food imports, 88; and foreign aid, 247; history of, 132–141, 152, 170; and Japan, 18; and new world economy, 55; and oil embargo, 111–112, 151; and price increases, 223, 226, 244, 245, 246–247; political power of, 31, 34, 123–125, 199; and refineries, 237; and Third World, 129–131

Ozone layer: 188

Pakistan: agriculture in, 81

Paradigms: 6–11; shifts in, 8, 10–11, 259–262

Pardo, Arvid: 202

Pestel, Edward: 264

Petroleum: 114, 115, 116–117; boycott, 33, 34, 111–112, 137, 151; and cartel formation, 155; exports, 122–123, 153, 157; off-shore, 200, 201–202; price increases, 124, 125, 131, 174, 240, 244–245, 246–247; transport of, 158; shortage, 8–9, 50; US imports of, 196, 197, 198–199

Philippines: population of; 20

Plagues: 14

Platinum production: 168

Platt, John: 187

Plutonium: 208, 209

Pollution: 9, 188; oceanic, 86; industrial, 38, 61, 63–65; in Japan, 190

Polyansky, Dmitri: 92

Population growth: 4, 5, 6, 19–23, 24–25, 48; control of, 60–61, 62; and definition of population, 13; and interaction, 12–14; and resources, 14–19

Portugal: as colonizer, 25, 26

Power configurations: international, 32–34

Ptolemaic paradigm: 6

Qatar: oil in, 138–139

Rawls, John: 228

Renshaw, Edward: The End of Progress, 9

Rhodesia: 20, 65; and chromium, 166

Rice production: 81, 232

Roman Empire fall: comparison with, 258–259, 261

Saudi Arabia: and foreign aid, 247; oil in, 116, 127; and OPEC, 136–138

Schumacher, E.F.: 268

Silver production: 167–168

Social paradigms: 260, 261; dominant, 7–8, 10, 187

Social traps: 187; and nuclear power, 204, 213

Sociocultural evolution; 259–262

Solar energy: 110, 114, 266

South Africa: 65; agriculture in, 81, 82; mineral resources of, 177; and nuclear power, 212

Soviet Union: agriculture in, 77, 78, 80–81, 82, 83, 85–86, 88, 92; fishing by, 86, 87, 201; mineral resources of, 172; natural gas in, 118; oil in, 117, 122–123, 126, 128, 129, 133, 139–140, 155

Soybean embargo: 84

Space colonization: 12

Spain: as colonizer, 26, 48

Spiegal, Steven: 35, 36

Starvation: 11, 66, 77

Stavrianos, L.S.: 258–259

Steinhart and Steinhart: 97

Sterling, Richard: 262

Suez Canal: closing of, 134

Sugar production: 83–84, 232, 236

Sukarno, President: 52

Technology: appropriate, 267–268, 269–270; and ecopolitics, 184–214; and oceanic resources, 200–202; and